"This is a landmark book! The first of its kind—
an engaging dialogue between scholars of two 'opposing' religious
communities presented in a context of civility and mutual
respect. It will have substantial significance both to Mormons and to
Evangelicals, and is sure to generate discussion."

RONALD ENROTH
Professor of Sociology
Westmont College

"No small step for the two writers, this book is a
giant step toward better understanding of some influential contemporary
Evangelicals and Mormons. All can learn from this model
of respectful dialogue, although readers from either side may differ at points
with their representative writer and wish some other
crucial issues could have been featured. The remaining deep differences
illustrate the urgent need for scholars and evangelists to transcend
their specialties and integrate Old Testament, New Testament, historical,
systematic, apologetic and practical concerns."

GORDON R. LEWIS
Professor Emeritus, Systematic Theology
Denver Theological Seminary

"In interfaith discussion, as in life, understanding begins
with listening, which at its best includes restating
what the other is saying to his complete satisfaction. It has happened too
rarely on either side of the separate Evangelical and Mormon
traditions. In this volume, Professors Blomberg and
Robinson demonstrate determined goodwill to listen and accurately restate
the insights and idioms of each tradition. Their characterizations
are careful and rigorous. Their comparisons and
contrasts are to the heart of issues and not glancing hit-and-run
stereotypes. The books stirs hope that both the
Evangelical and Mormon communities may together follow this example,
this first step t   illful
misunderstand   dition
advo

Professı   D1053421

HOW WIDE *the* DIVIDE?

A Mormon & an Evangelical in Conversation

Craig L. Blomberg & Stephen E. Robinson

InterVarsity Press
Downers Grove, Illinois

InterVarsity Press® is the book-publishing division of InterVarsity Christian Fellowship®, a student movement active on campus at hundreds of universities, colleges and schools of nursing in the United States of America, and a member movement of the International Fellowship of Evangelical Students. For information about local and regional activities, write Public Relations Dept., InterVarsity Christian Fellowship, 6400 Schroeder Rd., P.O. Box 7895, Madison, WI 53707-7895.

ISBN 0-8308-1991-6

Printed in the United States of America ♾

Library of Congress Cataloging-in-Publication Data

Blomberg, Craig.
    How wide the divide?: a Mormon & an Evangelical in conversation/
    Craig L. Blomberg, Stephen E. Robinson.
        p.   cm.
    Includes bibliographical references.
    ISBN 0-8308-1991-6 (alk. paper)
        1. Evangelicalism—Relations—Mormon Church.   2. Mormon Church—
    Relations—Evangelicalism.   3. Church of Jesus Christ of Latter-Day
    Saints—Doctrines.   I. Robinson, Stephen Edward.   II. Title.
    BR1641.M67B57   1997
    280'.042—dc21   96-51534
                                                                                  CIP

20   19   18   17   16   15   14   13   12   11   10   9   8   7   6   5   4   3

14   13   12   11   10   09   08   07   06   05   04   03   02   01   00   99   98

·

To Pastor Greg Vettel,
whose initial interest
led to the writing of this book.

Introduction

[R O B I N S O N]

I WAS A GRADUATE STUDENT at Duke University when our LDS bishop, along with other local ministers, received an invitation to attend a meeting of a citizens' committee combating the growth of adult bookstores and movie houses in our area. However, when LDS representatives actually showed up at the meeting, they were asked to leave because some of the Evangelical ministers threatened to walk out if Mormons were involved. So we withdrew, but the lesson was not lost on us—some Evangelicals oppose Mormons more vehemently than they oppose pornography.

More recently a friend of mine returned to Utah after her husband completed his twenty years in the military. As practicing Latter-day Saints, they do not smoke or drink, and they uphold certain nonnegotiable social and moral standards. They tell me that it was often difficult in the service to make friends who shared similar values. Early on they discovered that they generally felt comfortable in the company of Evangelical Christians and that Evangelicals tended to feel the same way about them—but only as long as the subject of religious affiliation was avoided. If they let their Evangelical friends know they were LDS, the Evangelicals frequently would not see them again.

I must confess my amazement that two communities with as much in common in so many areas as Latter-day Saints and Evangelicals are not on better terms, particularly since much of what separates us is in my opinion false impressions, which are generated by extremists on both sides or are caused by misunderstanding each other's theological terminology.

One of the great paradoxes in LDS-Evangelical relations is that we frequently gravitate toward each other, and then we are surprised that this is so.[1] In graduate school I found that my closest colleagues generally turned out to be the more conservative students. Evangelicals and Latter-day Saints share the same moral standards, the same family values, the same old-fashioned standards of personal conduct. We have the same reverence for the sacred. We both interpret the Scriptures literally and believe them to mean what they say. Latter-day Saints read C. S. Lewis with a sense of kinship; we read F. F. Bruce, Bruce Metzger and other Evangelical biblical scholars and seldom, if ever, find cause for disagreement. Most Evangelicals and Latter-day Saints alike would be surprised at the amount of theology we share. In any situation where denominational affiliations are not identified up front, Latter-day Saints and Evangelicals will sense shared values and a shared outlook and move toward each other—until individual affiliations are revealed. Then prejudice or proselytizing usually ends the fellowship.

Latter-day Saints and Evangelicals do not understand each other very well, and much of what we say about each other is untrue. There are many unintentional lies, since the most accessible sources of information on both sides are often untrustworthy or polemical. Thus we learn and pass on untruths. I believe both Prof. Blomberg and I were surprised to discover how little we really knew about each other when we first began corresponding. I have learned that what many Mormons believe about the theology of "born agains" or "saved-by-gracers" (as Evangelicals are sometimes labeled by LDS) is often a caricature of mainstream Evangelical beliefs, as distorted and unfair as the typical Evangelical view of Latter-day Saints.[2] Though unfortunate, it would be fair to say that the average Latter-day Saint honestly believes the average Evangelical to be mean-spirited and dishonest—mean-spirited because, as Prof. Blomberg has pointed out, we tend to identify *all* Evangelicals with the fundamentalist anti-Mormons who incessantly attack us, and dishonest because these so-called anticultists *always* insist the LDS believe things we do *not* in fact believe.[3] Since the Evangelicals of *our* experience—Professor Blomberg calls them fundamentalists—usually attack us and usually tell whoppers about us when they do[4] (i.e., are mean-spirited and dishonest), we naturally assume that all Evangelicals think and behave the same way.

In fact, most Evangelicals *do* at least passively accept and even actively disseminate the picture of Latter-day Saints created by rabid anti-Mormons, and so they share some responsibility for the continuation of these impressions. It was always a mystery to me as a Latter-day Saint how the Evangelicals who so consistently misrepresented my beliefs could be so right and so admirable in many other ways. Perhaps if mainstream Evangelicals could distance themselves a little from the repugnant literature of "extreme fundamentalists," as Prof. Blomberg calls them, Mormons could in turn do a better job of distinguishing between *mainstream* Evangelicals and fundamentalists.

Ironically, what I most appreciate about Prof. Blomberg is his fairness and honesty. If I say to him, "Look, I just don't believe that" (as I frequently do), he accepts it, whereas most Evangelicals of my acquaintance merely smile and think me a liar. A precedent of sorts is found in the orthodox Christian understanding of Judaism before events of the twentieth century forced a long-overdue correction. Until then, Jews had been vilified by Christians for doctrines and practices they *did not* really espouse, simply because Christians were unwilling to abandon their fantastic prejudices and accept what Jews actually said about themselves. In time the stereotypes (including the blood libel) became a part of orthodox belief (added precepts of the popular

Christian faith), just as a distorted stereotype of the LDS has become a *religious* conviction for some Evangelicals. It has become *their* orthodoxy that Mormons believe X, Y and Z, even though the Latter-day Saints emphatically deny it.

This is why the initial disagreements between us are always about *what* Mormons believe instead of about whether or not it is true. (This phenomenon alone should give thinking persons a sufficient clue to recognize the distortion.) I am very happy to discuss my beliefs with anyone, but it is absurd—and a sure and certain sign of bad faith—to argue with me that I do not really believe what I *think* I believe! Any religious group, whether Jewish, Mormon, Baptist or whatever, ought to be able to define itself rather than be defined by its antagonists.

Professor Blomberg is the first Evangelical scholar I have known of to examine the Latter-day Saints closely for any purpose other than where best to land a blow. Through my association with him I have come to accept that most Latter-day Saints have probably encountered only the more extreme factions of Evangelicalism and have mistakenly identified that part as the whole.

Quite frequently Prof. Blomberg and I have discovered that our initial ideas of each other have rested on totally erroneous information, and we continue to surprise each other in some degree every time we attempt to clarify our respective beliefs. There is still a long way to go. My point is this: if two individuals who hold doctorate degrees in religion and who are honestly attempting to get at the truth experience difficulty understanding each other, what chance do polemicists have of correctly understanding or representing the beliefs of the other side? It is our hope that with this book we will begin to tell and believe the truth about each other, the issue of who is ultimately right and wrong being set aside for the moment.

There are several other factors working against our understanding each other—we Latter-day Saints and Evangelicals. First, there is history. After all, Prof. Blomberg's great-great-grandfathers may very well have shot at my great-great-grandfathers as the Mormons were driven out of New York, Ohio, Missouri or Illinois and eventually out of the country altogether. For many Latter-day Saints such events as these are not yet ancient history. The murders, the rapes and the burnings are still a deeply felt part of our family heritage.[5] Many still cherish the memory of each nineteenth-century outrage committed against their forebears, and this frequently sours twentieth-century relationships. Perhaps if we start trying now, the twenty-first century may see the beginnings of better understanding between our two communities.

Besides history, another obstacle to mutual understanding is *terminology*—our respective theological vocabularies. Latter-day Saints and Evangelicals generally employ the same theological terms, but we usually define them differently, and this quite often makes communication more difficult than if we spoke different religious languages entirely. The similarity of terms makes us *think* we are communicating, but when all is said and done both sides go away with the feeling that nothing quite added up, and this raises suspicions of deception.[6] Evangelicals often forget that we Latter-day Saints are not Protestants, and that our theological language has not been shaped to the same extent as theirs by the theological and political concerns of the Reformation. Latter-day Saints are generally quite naive when it comes to the technical usage of theological language. Thus when Mormons speak on the subject of faith and works, for example, they usually do so in a way that seems from an Evangelical perspective to be inadequate or imprecise, though it makes perfectly good sense to us. This is not an issue of who is theologically right or wrong. New Testament Christians, were they suddenly transported to the twentieth century, would experience the same difficulty and for the same reasons—it is just a case of highly idiomatic terminology on the one hand and a lack of terminological sophistication on the other.

Unfortunately, Protestants and Catholics, when evaluating LDS statements, seldom bother to adjust their thinking to allow for LDS definitions and usage (if they even know them), usually assuming that we mean what they mean when they use the same terms. Often we do not. Unless Mormons and Evangelicals make greater efforts to investigate what the other *means,* rather than merely exploiting what the other *says,* we shall remain, to paraphrase Twain, two peoples divided by a common language. Presently, because Latter-day Saints do not say things the same way Evangelicals do, we are often made to be "offenders for a word" even in cases where we actually *mean* exactly the same thing as Evangelicals.[7]

Since very few Latter-day Saints or Evangelicals are theologically bilingual, the same misunderstandings tend to be compounded over and over, which is grist for the mills of prejudice on both sides. All this makes it difficult for Evangelicals to get completely and specifically correct explanations (as opposed to only general approximations) about what Mormons believe without themselves investing the time to study LDS Scripture with LDS mentors, which is the way the LDS do it.[8] I might add that the *worst* way for Evangelicals to learn about Latter-day Saints is to ask other non-Mormons or to read non-Mormon literature about the Saints. As Prof. Blomberg has discovered, it is a rare thing indeed for non-Mormons writing about the Saints to get it right even when they are trying to, and most contemporary non-LDS writing on the Mormons is frankly *not* trying to get it right.

Another frustration Evangelicals often experience in dealing with Latter-day Saints is the fact that we have no professional clergy, no creeds or catechisms, and no theologians in the strict sense.[9] Pure LDS orthodoxy can be a moving target, depending on which Mormon one talks to. Indeed, my part of this book represents only the views of one Latter-day Saint, though I hope a credible one. I do not speak in this volume for the LDS Church, only for myself, but I think I qualify as the world's authority on what I believe, and I consider myself a reasonably devout and well-informed Latter-day Saint.

On the other hand, those Mormons who most frequently talk to Evangelicals, the LDS missionaries, receive very little formal training before going out to proselytize. They are almost literally babes in the woods, and quite often, particularly where the Mormon Church is strong, the LDS missionaries might be among the least knowledgeable members in a congregation.[10] Yet when Evangelicals talk to LDS missionaries, they often assume, on the basis of a pattern that holds true for Protestants, that they are talking to trained professionals or at least to competent theological authorities. Actually such elementary understanding as most missionaries have, while it meets the needs of LDS proselytizing by bearing simple testimony, hardly constitutes a sophisticated guide to LDS doctrinal specifics. Missionaries frequently say more than they know. For these reasons, as Prof. Blomberg notes, LDS missionaries sometimes give incorrect or unintentionally misleading answers to specific doctrinal questions, most often because they do not know how their vocabulary is being understood by Evangelicals. This in turn contributes to suspicions of intentional deceit.

By and large the LDS do not worry as much about orthodoxy within their own community as do Evangelicals, though there *is* such a thing as LDS orthodoxy. In the short run, LDS orthodoxy is defined by the Standard Works of the Church (Bible, Book of Mormon, Doctrine and Covenants, and Pearl of Great Price) as interpreted by the General Authorities of the Church—the current apostles and prophets. In the long run the church depends on the cumulative study of Scripture by its individual members to ensure that doctrine is correctly understood and taught within the Church. Unfortunately, where the members disregard this responsibility, there is no systematic theology, no sophisticated and definitive creed, no lengthy catechism, no network of professional theologians to back them up. In these cases "speculative" or "popular" theology can overgrow scriptural orthodoxy. It is one drawback of having a nonprofessional clergy.

Unfortunately, up until now most of the dialogue between Mormons and Evangelicals has been dominated by those on both sides having the least training or the worst motives. Future discussion must move from this level to good-faith exchanges between informed parties.

So what are the major points of the "restored" gospel, the confession common to most informed Latter-day Saints? Partially paraphrasing Joseph Smith, I would summarize it this way:[11]

1. We believe in God, the Eternal Father, and in God's Son, Jesus Christ, and in the Holy Ghost. We accept the biblical doctrine that God is three and that God is also one, but we reject the post-New Testament attempts to explain how these two truths are to be reconciled.

2. We believe that humankind fell through the transgression of Adam and Eve and that humans in their present state are subject to sin, death and corruption. However, we believe that individuals are accountable for their own sins, not for guilt inherited from Adam and Eve. We accept both divine justice and human accountability, but we do not believe in original sin.

3. We believe that through the atonement of Christ, fallen humanity may be saved by accepting and obeying the gospel of Jesus Christ (cf. 2 Thess 1:8, 11; 1 Pet 4:17 for *obeying* the gospel). No one is predestined either to salvation or to damnation; anyone may be saved who responds appropriately to the good news of Christ.

4. We believe that we respond appropriately to Christ and we accept his gospel by having faith in and being faithful to Christ as Son of God and Savior, that is, by accepting him as Lord and Savior and making him Lord of and in our lives. We cannot merit salvation of ourselves (Alma 22:14), nor is it possible to "earn" the grace by which we are saved (Mosiah 2:21-25), but the obedience of faith (Rom 1:5; 16:26), a godly walk and conversation, is a necessary component of faith in Christ. Jesus will save us *from* our sins (Rev 1:5) but not *with* our sins (1 Cor 6:9-10). Beyond having faith in Christ, we must also repent of sin, consent to baptism by immersion for the remission of sins, and receive the regenerating and sanctifying gift of the Holy Ghost by the laying on of hands (cf. Acts 2:38; 8:14-18).

5. We believe that the Christianity of the first century, New Testa-

ment Christianity, is *true* Christianity. As such, it is the only standard by which to define Christianity, as opposed to defining it by post-New Testament councils and creeds. We believe that the priesthood authority, church organization, spiritual gifts, sacraments (i.e., ordinances) and doctrines of the modern church must be as they were in the New Testament church. This obviously includes the presence of apostles and prophets who receive direct, continuing revelation for the church in the world.

6. We accept the Bible (the LDS use the King James Version) as the inspired word of God—every book, every chapter, every verse of it—as revealed to the apostles and prophets who wrote it. We also hold the Book of Mormon, the Doctrine and Covenants, and the Pearl of Great Price to be the word of God.

7. We believe in the divine conception, substitutionary atonement, sacrificial death, bodily resurrection and present glory of Jesus Christ, and that he will return to this earth in judgment and in his glory to cleanse it from all wickedness and to establish his personal millennial reign. Both the saved and the lost will be resurrected, the former at Christ's coming or during his reign, the latter at the end of the millennium (1 Thess 4:14-17; Rev 20:7-15).

8. We believe that the church established by Christ in the New Testament was changed by later Christian intellectuals who believed the simple New Testament proclamation to be inadequate. Feeling the language of Scripture to be unsophisticated, incomplete, vague, ambiguous or imprecise, the second-, third- and fourth-century church sought to "improve" the New Testament gospel by the standards of Hellenistic philosophy, but compromised it instead.

9. We believe that the Lord in preparation for his imminent second coming has "restored" New Testament Christianity in the latter days through the prophet Joseph Smith. Nevertheless, all honest Christians of whatever denomination, not just LDS Christians, will be among the saved at the last day, and I am personally confident this will include Prof. Blomberg and my other Evangelical friends (see chapter four).

Perhaps an even more basic statement of the gospel is provided by
Jesus himself in the Book of Mormon:

Behold I have given unto you my gospel, and this is the gospel
which I have given unto you—that I came into the world to do the
will of my Father, because my Father sent me. And my Father sent
me that I might be lifted up upon the cross; and after that I had been
lifted up upon the cross, that I might draw all men unto me.... And
it shall come to pass, that whoso repenteth and is baptized in my
name shall be filled; and if he endureth to the end, behold, him will
I hold guiltless before my Father at that day when I shall stand to
judge the world. . . . And no unclean thing can enter into his
kingdom; therefore nothing entereth into his rest save it be those
who have washed their garments in my blood, because of their faith,
and the repentance of all their sins, and their faithfulness unto the
end. Now this is the commandment: Repent, all ye ends of the earth,
and come unto me and be baptized in my name, that ye may be
sanctified by the reception of the Holy Ghost, that ye may stand
spotless before me at the last day. Verily, verily, I say unto you, this
is my gospel. (3 Nephi 27:13-14, 16, 19-21)

The great irony of LDS-Evangelical relations is that not much of the
above, except point 9, would of itself cause serious contention, and,
in fact, most of it is accepted in one form or another in Arminian
churches or in nineteenth-century restorationist movements now considered to be Evangelical. The real sticking point is not what the LDS
think of Christ and his gospel, but rather the different ontological
frame or view of the nature of the universe into which Mormons fit
the gospel. For Latter-day Saints also believe in the *literal* fatherhood
of God and the brotherhood of humanity. We believe that God and
humans are the same species of being and that all men and women
were his spiritual offspring in a premortal existence. The main purpose
of the gospel of Christ is therefore not so much to get us to heaven as
it is to get us *home*.

We also believe that human families that come to Christ jointly can, through living and obeying Christ's gospel, be sealed together for-ever—hence the LDS emphasis on the importance of the traditional family, as well as the LDS slogan "Families are forever." Finally, the LDS believe that God intends, through the fullness of the gospel, to make us what Christ is and to share with the most faithful of his children the blessings, powers and glories of eternity.

It is this broader doctrinal framework into which the Latter-day Saints place the basic gospel of Christ, rather than the LDS under-standing of the gospel itself, that generates the most opposition from non-Mormons. In LDS orthodoxy, the ontological frame, while a vital part of our theology, is secondary to the truth of the basic gospel itself, yet Evangelicals and others (including many of our own people) often get this backwards. Thus the LDS tend to see agreement with Evan-gelicals in primary matters and disagreement in those of secondary importance, while Evangelicals tend to ignore our view of the gospel itself (the doctrines of Christ and salvation) and attack instead what is secondary (e.g., the literal or figurative fatherhood of God or the status and powers of the saved in eternity). This is perhaps one reason that Mormons, when comparing our relative views of salvation, see basic agreement with some disagreements, where Evangelicals tend to see basic disagreement with occasional agreement. Still, if it is true that LDS views of Christ and salvation are basically sound from an Evangelical perspective, then does not the insistence on agreement in _other_ areas constitute a "doctrinal test" for salvation, something I am told is abhorrent to Evangelicals?

The statement is sometimes made that Latter-day Saints now want to be known as Christians, whereas in the past we did not. This statement is both true and false. If we define "Christian" generically as someone who accepts the New Testament proclamation of Jesus as Son of God and Savior, then the first part of the statement is true: Mormons _do_ wish to be known as Christians. But the second half of the statement would then be false, since there has never been a time when we wished otherwise.[12] However, if we define "Christian" as meaning traditional, historical and creedal orthodoxy, then the first part of the statement would be false: Mormons do *not* now wish to be known as post-Nicene, "orthodox" Christians. But the second part of the statement would then be true, for Mormons have never wanted to be identified with post-New Testament Christianity. Latter-day Saints have always called themselves Christians in the sense that they worship Jesus Christ and attempt to live according to his teachings, but they have never wanted to be identified with the "Christians" who burned them from their homes and drove them into the wilderness.

Latter-day Saints do not, in fact, seek to be accepted as historically "orthodox" Christians or as Evangelicals. We are neither. Neither do we seek to have our beliefs approved or validated by Christian "orthodoxy." I do not expect we will ever accept one another's baptisms or stop proselytizing each other (and I don't think we should), but I would personally just like to find some Evangelicals willing to admit the truth—that Mormons accept the New Testament and worship the Christ who is described there. We seek to make him the Lord of our lives, whether or not we do this correctly by Evangelical standards. Perhaps more than anything else it is the Evangelical denial of these manifest truths that feeds the LDS stereotype of Evangelicals as people who lie about us.

Moreover, Evangelicals usually forget that the Bible is also Scripture for the Latter-day Saints, *and that there is not a single verse of the Bible that Latter-day Saints do not accept.* True, we do not interpret the Bible by the Hellenized philosophy of the early church councils (Nicaea, Chalcedon, etc.), but for us the Bible—*without* the councils and creeds—is the word of God (see chapter one).

Despite historical problems, terminology and the difficulty for Evangelicals of precisely pinning down LDS orthodoxy (and vice versa), it is past time for Latter-day Saints and Evangelicals to try to understand each other. Currently, Mormons and Evangelicals do *not* understand each other or even have a correct picture to work from, though generally they both think they do. It is this sad fact that motivates the authors of the present volume.

First contacts can be difficult. So it has been, at times, with this book, which would read much differently had it been written by either of its authors without the collaboration of the other. Since the volume is *jointly* authored, the reader should not assume that both authors would endorse every word, though this is often so. However, concessions have been made on both sides in matters as trivial as phrasing and terminology, and in matters as consequential as accommodating (or tolerating) each other's odd perspective. Nevertheless, as the reader will see, we pull no punches and make no concessions here in matters of truth or principle. The purpose of this book is neither to attack nor to defend—there will be no winner and no loser at the end of it. The purpose of this book is to explain and to educate—at last to hear and to tell the truth about each other.

[B L O M B E R G]

MY WIFE'S NIECE AND HER husband are Mormons. A few years ago we were playing a historical trivia game, and one of the questions on a game card was "What religious group in the United States still promotes polygamy?" When my nephew-in-law saw that the back of the card gave "Mormonism" as the answer, he stormed out of the room and refused to play any further. After all, he explained, his church had explicitly prohibited plural marriages as long ago as 1890.

On another occasion a Mormon friend and I were talking about each other's beliefs. At one point he commented, "I can't see how you Evangelicals can believe all the garbage that the televangelists spew forth." He was surprised when I replied that I *did not* believe a lot of what at least certain prominent TV preachers taught. He explained that he was used to reading in the newspapers about us "fundamentalists"—all lumped together as right-wing religious fanatics.

If an immensely successful game company cannot distinguish

between nineteenth- and twentieth-century Mormonism, and if many in the popular press cannot distinguish between Jim Bakker and Billy Graham, is it any wonder that grassroots Evangelicals and Mormons in churches around our country seem similarly confused? After all, few of us have extensive firsthand encounters with each other. Most Evangelicals gain their information about the Mormon Church, more properly known as The Church of Jesus Christ of Latter-day Saints (LDS), from three sources: (1) anticult literature, written by fellow Evangelicals in an often polemical spirit,[1] (2) doorstep conversations, as members of the two groups share their faith house to house using a standardized and extremely simplified presentation of their beliefs, and (3) information from ex-Mormons who have left the Church because they are bitter about how it treated them.

None of these sources provide thorough, balanced knowledge of the LDS. Yet every religion should be allowed to speak for itself. Evangelical writers, however well-intentioned, are not likely to know nearly as much about Mormonism as LDS writers, unless they have lived and ministered for years in predominantly Mormon parts of the country. Doorstep conversations seldom get beyond superficial treatment of issues. And individuals who have converted from one religion or denomination to another are usually the most likely to be antagonistic toward the group they have left and to describe only the worst aspects and most extreme manifestations of that organization or belief system.

In the case of relations between Evangelicals and Mormons, the situation is exacerbated by fringe elements of both groups engaging in genuinely hostile, sometimes violent and occasionally criminal behavior toward each other. When the fortieth LDS temple in the world opened in the Denver area in the late 1980s, only half a mile from my home, a handful of Evangelicals protested, picketed and taunted the first Mormon worshipers attending there. Stones flew through the air, and a firebombing scare was reported. More recently, a few Mormons slipped into the library at the seminary where I teach and stole or damaged numerous books they perceived to be anti-Mormon. Our librarian reported that at a regional conference of librarians in the mountain states region she learned that numerous area libraries had been similarly vandalized. Sadly, it is far too easy for the victims of such attacks, on either "side," to jump to the conclusion that the majority of the "other side" behaves the same way.

Even when things don't get nearly so out of hand, Mormons and Evangelicals do not have a very good track record of speaking to each other courteously. Undoubtedly the most famous Evangelical anticult writer, Walter Martin, had a penchant for phrasing his displeasure with groups he identified as non-Christian in fairly virulent language. Consider the following excerpts from his chapter on the LDS in his most widely read book, *The Kingdom of the Cults,* which has gone through dozens of printings:

> The author can quite candidly state that never in over a decade of research in the field of cults has he ever seen such misappropriation of terminology, disregard of context, and utter abandon of scholastic principles demonstrated on the part of non-Christian cultists than is evidenced in the attempts of Mormon theologians to appear orthodox and at the same time undermine the foundations of historic Christianity. . . . It is extremely difficult to write kindly of Mormon theology when they are so obviously deceptive in their presentation of data, so adamant in their condemnation of all religions in favor of the "restored gospel" allegedly vouchsafed to the prophet Joseph Smith.[2]

Despite much good work in Martin's overall ministry, this kind of "colorful" language consistently characterizes Martin's writing. Yet even if the claims behind such language were true, it is hard to imagine Mormons not being highly offended by Martin's inflammatory expressions, and harder still to imagine many Mormons being won over to his positions by this kind of rhetoric.

A high-ranking LDS contemporary of Martin, Elder Bruce McConkie, for thirteen years a member of the Quorum of the Twelve

Apostles, is probably the most widely cited and best known modern Mormon theologian in Evangelical circles. While not as consistently virulent as Martin, he too has his moments. Compare, for example, the following selections from the last work he wrote on Mormon doctrine, entitled *A New Witness for the Articles of Faith:*

Universal apostasy fell upon men between Jesus' day and our day. . . . Churches built on false gospels are false churches. They have no saving power. They may, as Jesus said, be "built upon the works of men, or upon the works of the devil" (3 Nephi 27:11). . . . The way to find the true religion and the pure gospel is to find what Jesus and the ancient apostles taught. It is, however, universally recognized by all professors of religion in all churches that such a system no longer exists either in any one sect or in all the sects of Christendom combined.[3]

With rhetoric like that of Martin and McConkie, is it any wonder that Mormons and Evangelicals barely talk to each other about their respective beliefs, except in overtly evangelistic confrontations?[4] And whatever happened to Ephesians 4:15 and "speaking the truth in love"?[5]

Can we move beyond this negative state of affairs? In the last few decades, leading Evangelical scholars have held numerous conferences and dialogues with their counterparts in Roman Catholicism, Judaism and even the Unification Church of Sun Myung Moon.[6] Within Protestantism alone there have been many multiauthor works reflecting evangelical-liberal dialogues.[7] A few Evangelicals have consistently participated in the international ecumenical body known as the World Council of Churches, so that the conservative Christian voice might not disappear from that forum altogether. The 1994 U.N. Cairo Conference on World Population and Development brought together representatives from all the major world religions, and Evangelicals found surprising allies there among conservative Catholics and Muslims. Recent years have seen Evangelical responses to issues of religious pluralism and to all the major world religions.[8] But where in this flurry of interdenominational and interreligious dialogue is a serious and courteous discussion between informed and scholarly representatives of Evangelical and Mormon traditions? Jerry Falwell and his Moral Majority took some small steps toward Evangelical-Mormon cooperation for a shared social, political and ethical agenda in the early 1980s, as the religious right emerged into the public arena. Why have these efforts given way to Evangelical snubbing of Mormon efforts to work together for common moral goals?

These are some of the questions that motivate my involvement in this book. Our aims in this slim volume are actually quite modest. Stephen Robinson and I both hold doctorate degrees in the field of New Testament studies. We each teach at church-related institutions (Brigham Young University and Denver Seminary, respectively). We each speak officially for no one other than ourselves, but unofficially we reflect a fair cross-section of the religious traditions we represent. Both of us stand in the progressive wing of our movements, and yet we clearly dissociate ourselves from the "dissidents" who flirt with the very boundaries and established parameters of our respective faiths.[9] We first met at an annual meeting of the huge international umbrella organization for biblical scholars of all religious perspectives (or none), the Society of Biblical Literature. Since then we have carried on extensive conversations by phone, by letter and in person. Those conversations have always been pleasant, courteous and informative, and yet neither of us has shrunk from frank discussion of our beliefs. We would like to reflect our discussions in this book in the hopes that they may advance Mormon-Evangelical dialogue beyond the relatively deplorable state in which it now languishes.

We have chosen four doctrinal issues that seem to us, and to most, to be the most central areas of division between us: *(1) Scripture, (2) the nature of God and the deification of believers, (3) the deity of Christ and the Trinity* and *(4) salvation and the eternal state.* Each of us has written a chapter on these four themes with the following three objectives in mind: first, to state succinctly what we understand a substantial number of people in our traditions to affirm on each doctrine; second, to dispel certain popular misconceptions held by the other group regarding our positions; and third, to discuss our misgivings about the other's perspectives. Each of us read the other's material after a first draft of the book was produced, and we then revised the chapters that we had written in that light. For balance, we alternate who leads off each chapter. But no matter who begins, we are writing in light of the content of the other's chapter on that subject and responding to what is said there. We have tried to write in an irenic spirit throughout, expressing gratitude for those areas on which we can agree, even while recognizing that important areas of disagreement remain.

Let us be equally clear on what we are not trying to do. *First, there are many interesting but less central areas of disagreement between Evangelicals and Mormons that we do not address.* We cannot hope to be comprehensive in a short book meant to be widely read by people in our churches. So we lay entirely to one side such issues as baptism for the dead (or the temple ritual more generally), the premortal existence of souls, forms of church government, the priesthood, the early history of the Americas, and so on.

Second, we do not go into detail on topics of substantial agreement, even though nuances of differences remain on several of them. It is important at least to note a number of these because readers may not generally be aware of them, for example, Christ's substitutionary, sacrificial atonement; his bodily resurrection; the personality of the Holy Spirit; the continued existence of all of the gifts of the Spirit; the literal, visible, premillennial return of Christ; freedom of worship and a general sociopolitical conservatism. Indeed, there are numerous parallels between the emergence of the Latter-day Saints and their tortuous pilgrimage westward in nineteenth-century America and the rise of other forms of "restorationist" Christianity—most notably the Disciples of Christ and the two splinter groups it spawned, the Christian Church and the Church of Christ.

All of these groups claimed to bypass the Protestant Reformation, going back to apostolic Christianity to restore, rather than merely reform, what was perceived as exceedingly corrupt forms of Protestantism and Roman Catholicism. With Methodism, Mormonism rejected most of the Calvinist distinctives, for example, predestination, total depravity and eternal security, and stressed the need for personal piety, holiness and a process of growth toward human perfection. With many Utopian communities of the day, the Latter-day Saints saw the wide expanse of unsettled America as an opportunity finally to create the ideal expression of Christianity on earth. To the extent that Evangelicals today are still heavily influenced by restorationist, holiness and utopian streams of influence, there are numerous points at which their convictions more closely resemble those of Mormonism than those of mainline Protestantism, Roman Catholicism or Eastern Orthodoxy.

Third, we recognize that crucial issues divide us and that both groups will continue their attempts at evangelizing each other. But for our conversations to be fruitful and honoring to God, we must stop misrepresenting or caricaturing each other, always speaking the truth to each other in love.

Fourth, we do not claim to speak for everyone in our traditions. Some will no doubt object, even strenuously, that their convictions are not represented by what we call Mormon or Evangelical, that we are either too entrenched in the conservatism inherent in our movements, or that we have transgressed more narrow conceptions of our traditions and have thus "gone liberal." The amount of diversity in both our movements means that anyone speaking for either tradition can almost expect to stimulate such a response. But we write because we believe that we do speak broadly, if not precisely, for many among our constituencies.

Because Evangelicals do not congregate exclusively in a single institutional church, some further definition of them is in order. We define Evangelicals as theologically conservative Protestants who make the truthfulness, authority and relevance of the Old and New Testaments central to their worldview, who have come to experience salvation from sin through a personal relationship with Jesus Christ and the forgiveness he offers on the basis of his death on the cross, and who believe in the importance of actively sharing that faith with others.[10] *Evangelical,* like *conservative,* is the opposite of *liberal,* but it refers only to *theological* conservatism. In other words, Evangelicals in the political arena may be either Republicans or Democrats. They may be conservatives or liberals on a variety of issues. But when it comes to religious issues, they believe in conserving the major *theological* truths of historic, orthodox Christianity.

Many Evangelicals trace their spiritual ancestry to the Reformation and to the churches and theological traditions derived from Luther, Calvin and Wesley. Others have more recent roots in the nineteenth-century restoration movement mentioned above. Many value the early creeds (i.e., the Apostles' and Nicene Creeds) and the Reformation-era confessions (especially the Augsburg and Westminster Confessions) as syntheses of biblical truth. Others reject all creeds in favor of maintaining the priority of Scripture. Yet almost all churches, even entirely independent ones, have some statement of doctrine that their members must affirm.

Virtually all who call themselves Evangelicals dissociate themselves from two other categories of professing Christians: (1) the theologically liberal members of virtually every major Protestant denomination and (2) the fundamentalists, more separatistic or sectarian conservatives who tend to reject interdenominational or interreligious cooperation and dialogue. These very conservative Protestants continue to apply the term *fundamentalist* to themselves despite its almost uniformly pejorative use by the media and despite its history of attachment to quasi-sectarian groups that have separated from other professing Christians in the aftermath of the "fundamentalist-modernist" controversy of the 1920s. Fundamentalists are particularly strong in America's so-called Bible Belt, especially in the Deep South and in various kinds of Baptist churches.[11]

A tiny handful of Roman Catholics and Eastern Orthodox and converts to those branches of Christendom employ the adjective *Evangelical* as well. But other Evangelicals are skeptical of the possibility of being both fully biblical in doctrine and members in good standing of Catholic or Orthodox communions. Thus the term *Evangelical* includes theologically conservative Lutherans (most notably the Missouri Synod), Presbyterians (especially the Presbyterian Church in America and the Evangelical Presbyterian Church) and many other Reformed Christians, Baptists (many Southern Baptists and almost all of the Conservative Baptists and Baptist General Conference), Free Methodist groups, the Disciples' Renewal Movement within the Disciples of Christ, most Pentecostals, a large number of African-American churches of all denominations, the Evangelical Free Church, the Bible-church movement, many Nazarenes, a fair number of Mennonites, the Christian and Missionary Alliance, some (primarily charismatic) Episcopalians, and a large number of independent churches, as well as other individuals and informal fellowships within otherwise more liberal churches and denominations.

What would an Evangelical confession from members of these diverse groups look like? The most widely affirmed North American document is the statement of faith of the National Association of Evangelicals. It reads as follows:

1. We believe the Bible to be the inspired, the only infallible, authoritative Word of God.

2. We believe that there is one God, eternally existent in three persons, Father, Son, and Holy Ghost.

3. We believe in the deity of our Lord Jesus Christ, in His virgin birth, in His sinless life, in His miracles, in His vicarious and atoning death through His shed blood, in His bodily resurrection, in His ascension to the right hand of the Father, and in His personal return in power and glory.

4. We believe that for the salvation of lost and sinful man regenera-

tion by the Holy Spirit is absolutely essential.

5. We believe in the present ministry of the Holy Spirit by whose indwelling the Christian is enabled to live a godly life.

6. We believe in the resurrection of both the saved and the lost; they that are saved unto the resurrection of life and they that are lost unto the resurrection of damnation.

7. We believe in the spiritual unity of believers in our Lord Jesus Christ.

Of course, the Bible itself has the form of a story. It does not present its doctrine in systematically arranged, itemized theological propositions. A brief synopsis of the theologically relevant highlights of that story might run something like this: The only true God, Creator of the universe, chose at some point to make creatures distinct from himself—human beings—with the capacity to have a personal relationship with him. But they rebelled against God's command and subsequently forfeited the relationship God had initially established with them. Thus all humans who have ever lived have been sinful and hence separated from God. The animal sacrifices prescribed throughout the Old Testament period, when offered with faith in God's promises, dealt provisionally with human sins and enabled Jewish people (and all others who accepted their God) to be brought into a right relationship with God. The Old Testament depicts successive phases of God's initiatives to win back the descendants of the first humans, particularly through the chosen nation of Israel. More often than not, however, the story is one of human disobedience and divine punishment.

Humanity's sin problem was finally solved in the New Testament era. In the person of the first-century Jew, Jesus of Nazareth, God assumed for the first time human form. Jesus, who was fully human and fully divine, was able, therefore, both to be an adequate substitute for sinful persons and to make an infinite atonement for the sins of those who by faith trusted in him. Since then, reconciliation between God and humanity continues to be possible only when we renounce any claims of being able to save ourselves or of meriting God's favor. Rather, we put our trust in Jesus, accepting the free gift of salvation made available wholly by God's grace. Those who accept this gift have the Holy Spirit come to live in them. To the extent that they yield the various dimensions of their lives to the Spirit's control, they are increasingly transformed into persons who follow God's moral standards and please him. The motivation for obedience is profound gratitude for God's having done for us what we could never do for ourselves. All true believers (and only true believers) can look forward, after death or at the end of human history as we know it, to God's newly re-created heaven and earth, enjoying God's presence forever in endless happiness and giving him all the glory.

Beyond their essential beliefs, Evangelicals disagree on all sorts of questions. Who should be baptized (and how)? What are appropriate forms of church government? How do divine sovereignty and human freedom interact in the process of salvation? What is the role of spiritual gifts in the present age? What will be the final events of human history? What happens to people after death and before the final resurrection? Disagreements over these issues have given rise historically to the various denominations. Increasingly, sparked by the "parachurch" movement (interdenominational Christian educational, missionary and service organizations), Evangelicals are agreeing to cooperate across denominational lines, playing down historic distinctives that have divided them. My own theology matches the doctrinal statements of the Conservative Baptist movement but is heavily indebted to the contributions of Luther and Calvin as well. It would be presumptuous to speak for the diverse collection of conservative Protestants listed above, but I will continue to do my best to reflect major areas of agreement among them and to note places where I perhaps differ from many.

While the subsequent four chapters, like this introduction, consist of two parts, one authored by each of us, we have agreed to write a joint conclusion that we can both affirm. We have also coauthored brief summaries at the end of each two-part discussion. That means that some things we each might want to say on our own will not appear there, but we think there is much to be said for reflecting on what we can agree about. We hope that we can spark many similar conversations between Mormons and Evangelicals and thus inaugurate a new era in which such conversations move us beyond the impasse of previous polemics, recognizing our areas of agreement and clarifying the nature of our disagreements.

But enough by way of introduction. Let the discussions begin!

1

Scripture
[BLOMBERG]

What Evangelicals Believe

Evangelicals value the Scriptures highly. That valuation is one of the defining characteristics that sets conservative Protestants apart from their more liberal counterparts. They believe that the Old and New Testaments were inspired by God and that they accurately convey God's revelation. They are held to be reliable and trustworthy, providing a normative guide for faith and practice. While there are conservative Catholics who would agree with these statements, Evangelicals stress that no ecclesiastical body or individual Christian can make proclamations that are on a par with the authority of Scripture. Most would agree that no church hierarchy, pope or anyone else has the right to add to, supersede or contradict the written Word of God as contained in these two testaments.

In twentieth-century America the term that Evangelical Christians heavily favor to describe their concept of the Bible is *inerrant*. They mean that Scripture, as God inspired its authors to write it, is without error. Other common terms include *infallibility* (the inability of Scripture to deceive anyone) and "verbal, plenary inspiration." *Verbal* means that the process of inspiration extends to the actual words of the Bible, not just the thoughts and concepts embraced in them. *Plenary* means that all sixty-six books in all their parts are inspired. It precludes an appeal to a "canon within the canon," that is, to treating only *parts* of Scripture as inspired, trustworthy or authoritative.

By far the most common text to which Evangelicals appeal for this doctrine is 2 Timothy 3:16: "All Scripture is God-breathed and is useful for teaching, rebuking, correcting and training in righteousness." The KJV reads "given by inspiration" for the Greek *theopneustos,* but the word is a compound adjective, literally meaning "God-breathed." In the context of his letter, Paul would have been speaking primarily if not exclusively of the Old Testament, but as apostolic Christianity began to treat the New Testament writings as "Scriptures" too (see, for example, 2 Pet 3:16), they would have considered these new books as equally inspired and relevant.

Other texts important to the Evangelical understanding of Scripture as inspired and inerrant include 2 Peter 1:19-21 (all prophecy of Scripture came from men who "spoke from God as they were carried along by the Holy Spirit," v. 21), John 10:35 ("the Scripture cannot be broken") and Matthew 5:17-20 (Jesus came not "to abolish the Law or the Prophets . . . but to fulfill them," and not the smallest part of what we call the Old Testament "will by any means disappear . . . until everything is accomplished" v. 18). Numerous other passages in both testaments disclose the supernatural claims their authors make for their writings.[1] Particularly significant is the high regard Christ had for the Old Testament and the prophecies he made about the coming work of the Spirit to inspire his followers to produce what became the New Testament (see especially Jn 14:26; 15:26; 16:13).[2]

Not all Evangelicals are comfortable with the term *inerrancy* because it can suggest a degree of precision that cannot be squared with various details in the Scriptures themselves. This discomfort led to a decade of intense study, as a large interdenominational body of Evangelical scholars and theologians met for a series of conferences from 1978 to 1988 and published numerous works under the auspices of an organization called the International Council on Biblical Inerrancy. Perhaps the most significant product of this council was the "Chicago Statement on Biblical Inerrancy," now widely used to articulate what a broad cross-section of Evangelicals can agree on when they use the term.[3]

An abbreviated version of that ten-page declaration by one of its shapers may form the foundation of our discussion here:

Inerrancy means that when all facts are known, the Scriptures in their original autographs and properly interpreted will be shown to be wholly true in everything that they affirm, whether that has to do with doctrine or morality or with the social, physical or life sciences.[4]

There are at least five important qualifications in this declaration of Scripture's truthfulness, the first one being "when all facts are known." Inerrancy is an affirmation of faith based on our conviction of the trustworthiness of God. Given our current state of knowledge, we cannot prove the Bible to be without error, and various critics are more or less inclined to speak of contradictions in a variety of places. Evangelical commentaries on the various books of the Bible have proposed solutions to every alleged contradiction,[5] but in a small number of cases, many of our scholars suspect that the best solutions await future discoveries.

The second qualification is "in their original autographs." We recognize that the Scriptures have not been preserved flawlessly as they were copied through the centuries, because the manuscripts that exist vary from each other in numerous (though mostly minute and theologically insignificant) ways. But the vast numbers of early manuscripts (over five thousand for parts of the Greek New Testament alone) that have been preserved enable scholars to reconstruct, with a very high degree of confidence, what the writers of the Old and New Testaments most likely wrote.[6] The majority of textual variants involve only matters of spelling and grammar; where they significantly affect the actual meaning of a given verse, modern English translations usually print alternate renderings in their footnotes so that readers are aware of the options. Even more important, no Evangelical (or for that matter no Protestant) doctrine depends on any textually disputed verse.

In contrast, distinctively Mormon doctrines regularly rely on the Book of Mormon's claims that "plain and precious truths" have been lost from the Bible. None of the ancient manuscripts support the contention that the type of "restorations" that the JST (Joseph Smith's translation) or the uniquely LDS Scriptures make were ever in the original biblical texts. Neither do any ancient manuscripts exist to support the claim that the early church left out entire books from the Bible that would have included distinctively LDS doctrine.

The third qualification is "properly interpreted." It is widely recognized that a legitimate understanding of Scripture requires adherence to the standard principles of "hermeneutics" or interpretation that would apply to any act of interpersonal communication. We must grasp the historical-cultural background, the literary context, the meaning of words at a given time and place, the rules of grammar and the "genre" or form of writing of each biblical author. We cannot treat parables like straightforward history, or prophecy like poetry, or proverbs as if they were absolute laws. We must recognize when a writer is speaking metaphorically, using figures of speech, free rather than exact quotation, and employing less than scientific standards of precision in describing an event.[7]

The fourth is "in everything that they affirm." Many features of the biblical cultures and worldviews are presupposed in passages of Scripture without forming part of what their authors were actually trying to teach. For example, even if the accounts of creation suggest that the author of Genesis believed in a "three-story universe" (a flat earth with heaven above held up by a solid "firmament"), we do not believe that idea to have been what the writer was trying to *affirm or teach.* Rather, the writer was stressing that *God* was the Creator of every part of the universe.

The fifth is "whether that has to do with doctrine or morality or with the social, physical or life sciences." This is the most controversial qualification of the five. Evangelicals who reject the term *inerrancy* usually do so because they are not prepared to extend Scripture's complete truthfulness to topics beyond matters of theology and ethics (or belief and behavior). More conservative Evangelicals reply that if

God cannot be trusted in the more peripheral areas, say, of historical dates, how can God be trusted on more central topics? Here Mormons usually agree with the more conservative Evangelicals. These Evangelical beliefs about Scripture are limited to the Old and New Testaments. We do not accept the claims of any other documents to be Scripture. What is more, we believe that these sixty-six books contain all the truths necessary to bring individuals to salvation and to enable them to live godly lives. A few Evangelicals would make even more ambitious claims and argue that only in Scripture can utterly reliable truth on *any* topic be found, but they are in the decided minority.[8] Most recognize truth in "natural" or "general" revelation (everything God has left in creation for humans to discover) as well as "special" revelation (God's direct communication to humanity through angels, prophets, Christ or Scripture).[9]

Avoiding Misconceptions

No reputable Evangelical scholar or theologian believes in divine dictation for more than a tiny fraction of Scripture (e.g., the Ten Commandments). In other words, despite periodic confusion among laypeople in our churches, we do not claim that the biblical authors typically heard voices, saw visions or were overtaken by some uncontrollable force as they wrote so that their normal human personalities and unique literary styles or historical circumstances were in any way circumvented. Luke 1:1-4 gives us the most extensive testimony of any biblical writer as to how he operated, and it is the account of a careful historian interviewing eyewitnesses of the events he narrates and utilizing previously written accounts of those same events.[10] We believe that God superintended this process so as to guarantee both the accuracy of the results and the specific nature of the content God wished the inspired text to include.

Neither do Evangelicals affirm that God providentially protected the entire process of copying and translating the biblical manuscripts over the centuries so that every copy after the original was inerrant.

In this respect we differ from Islam, which early in its history destroyed all variant manuscripts of the Qur'an and preserved one version that it declared to be the only true and reliable version—in Arabic.[11] We differ also from the LDS and the Book of Mormon in that we are able to consult very early copies in the original languages of the Old and New Testaments so that anyone who learns those ancient languages can check the accuracy of our translations. We marvel at the extent of the agreement among the thousands of manuscripts that have been preserved, particularly in the Greek, and we believe that we have, in the critical Greek editions of the New Testament and the Hebrew and Aramaic editions of the Old Testament, extremely close replicas of what the original authors actually wrote.[12] If particular scholars wish to defend a different reading of a particular verse, their choices are limited to the manuscript evidence available and any reasonable conjectures based on it.

Most Evangelicals are, therefore, suspicious of any church or even of the occasional members within our own churches who simply ignore all this evidence or, worse still, refuse to make it available to people. This is what can happen, for example, when only the KJV is used. Many in our churches, particularly among the older generation, still cherish the KJV, usually because they have grown up with its archaic English and have come to associate it with worship and with a sense of reverence. But many of the oldest and most reliable Greek and Hebrew manuscripts of the Bible were discovered after the KJV was published in 1611 so that at key points it does not represent what was originally written as accurately as more modern translations. Again we stress that no point of orthodox doctrine hinges on disputed texts, but we want to get as close as possible to God's inerrant Word, even in translation. Consequently, most of us prefer more up-to-date and accurate versions, such as the New International Version, the New American Standard Bible or the New Revised Standard Version.[13]

Obviously, one of the main issues separating Evangelicals and Mormons is whether or not the Old and New Testaments constitute the sum total of God's scriptural revelation to humanity. Most grassroots Evangelicals and not a few trained theologians would affirm a "closed canon" and insist that no further books could ever be added. They often cite the closing words of the book of Revelation, which threaten plagues and a loss of any "share in the tree of life and in the holy city" for those who would add or take away from the words of "this book of prophecy" (Rev 22:18-19).[14] Or they may appeal to the fourth-century ecumenical Councils of Hippo (A.D. 393) and Carthage (A.D. 397) in North Africa, which ratified the increasing agreement among Christians from the late second century onward that the twenty-seven books now included in the New Testament were the only books to be added to the Old Testament and thereby treated on a par with it as Scripture. Significantly, Protestantism, Roman Catholicism and Eastern Orthodoxy all agree on the same twenty-seven books for the canon of the *New* Testament.

But a number of Evangelical biblical scholars recognize that neither reason suffices to demonstrate a closed canon. John's words at the end of Revelation refer to that book only. And Protestants do not accept the various apocryphal books that Catholics and Orthodox include in their *Old* Testaments, even though the only churches that existed for over a thousand years, which include the previously mentioned councils, did treat these works as Scripture.[15] It is better to appeal to different arguments for limiting Scripture to the Old and New Testaments as we have them.

In principle, unless we want to fall back on the Catholic position that the church creates the canon and is ultimately responsible for giving its imprimatur to the books we will accept, we must allow for the possibility that if some other ancient book could meet all the qualifications that commended the other sixty-six books that all Christians agree belong in the canon, then it too might be added. This position has been well articulated by Bruce Metzger, the highly distinguished Evangelical representative on numerous ecumenical committees for editing the Greek New Testament and translating the

Revised Standard Version in English, and professor emeritus at Princeton Theological Seminary. He explains that Protestants understand the canon not as an "authoritative collection of books" but as a "collection of authoritative books."[16] It is the individual books of the Bible that are inspired, not an ecclesiastical pronouncement regarding the list of those books.

By what criteria then do we determine which documents are inspired? Conservative Protestants have always stressed the witness of the Spirit, but this is a highly subjective criterion and cannot by itself settle debates between Protestants and others, since different individuals may appeal to the same test with opposite conclusions. Indeed, almost all world religions refer to the results of private meditation, personal revelation or some internal, subjective testimony as a reason for believing in them. What makes traditional Christianity unique is the extent to which it depends on the truthfulness of objective, historical events, most notably those surrounding the life of Jesus.[17] Without some external checks and balances, it is simply too easy to misinterpret God's answer when we try to apply a test like that of Moroni 10:4-5 and ask him to reveal through his Spirit the truth or falsity of the Book of Mormon.

If we turn to the Bible itself, however, we get some help in our search for trustworthy criteria. The New Testament never once demonstrably refers to any of the Apocryphal Old Testament books that later Catholic and Orthodox communions canonized, but it does quote the substantial majority of "Protestant Old Testament" books.[18] There is reasonably strong evidence that the *Jewish* canon at the time of Christ and the apostles was identical to that of our current Protestant Old Testament,[19] and that New Testament writers or speakers who referred to "Scripture," "the Law" or "the Law and Prophets" meant these books.

It is harder to demonstrate the limits of the New Testament from Scripture itself, and indeed we would be open to a certain charge of circular reasoning if we tried too hard! But there are at least several reminders that we must "test the spirits" (1 Jn 4:1) and evaluate alleged prophecies (1 Cor 14:29) because not all that pretends to be from God really is. Almost certainly the standard by which the apostolic church carried out such evaluation was whether or not allegedly new revelation was consistent with what they already recognized as God's Word.[20] In other words, theological noncontradiction—consistency with previously revealed Scripture—was a foundational test for the canonization of new Scripture. Speaking of the Judaizers, 2 Corinthians 11:13-15 offers a sobering reminder that not all who called themselves apostles were genuine:

> For such men are false apostles, deceitful workmen, masquerading as apostles of Christ. And no wonder, for Satan himself masquerades as an angel of light. It is not surprising, then, if his servants masquerade as servants of righteousness. Their end will be what their actions deserve.

Verses like these explain why Evangelicals are very reluctant to accept claims for an apostolic or prophetic office that is equivalent in authority to New Testament offices, yet accompanied by significantly divergent doctrine.

Some Evangelicals have tried to go further and defend the uniqueness of the Bible's sixty-six books by attributing them all to the authorship of a prophet or an apostle (or their "secretaries").[21] But this goes well beyond what we can demonstrate. It is true that the earliest postapostolic church often spoke of "apostolicity" as a criterion of New Testament writings, but it meant that a book could be traced to the *era* of the apostles (the first century), not that every book was written by an apostle, because clearly Mark and Luke could not have qualified by that criterion. And the authorship of several of the Old Testament books remains entirely uncertain, so it would be impossible to prove that they were all written by prophets.

In fact, Prof. Robinson makes a claim that seems crucial for his case that the Book of Mormon and the other uniquely LDS Scriptures are truly from God: "prophets always add to the Scriptures."[22] This statement is demonstrably incorrect. In the Old Testament, entire guilds of prophets ministered for generations with little or nothing of their teaching preserved at all (see, for example, Num 11:25-30; 1 Kings 13:11-32; 2 Kings 2:7, 15-16; 4:38-41). Select words and events from the lives of numerous other well-known individuals called prophets—Aaron, Miriam, Deborah, Saul, Nathan, Gad, Shimei, Elijah, Elisha, Micaiah, Huldah and Zedekiah—are recorded in other Old Testament books (in the New Testament Simeon and Anna are also called prophets), but not because those persons themselves ever wrote any Scripture. It seems unlikely that even a majority of Old Testament prophetic activity resulted in the books that Mormons and Evangelicals agree belong in the Old Testament.

More important, there is a noticeable shift in the role of prophecy when we come to the New Testament. Some Evangelicals deny that the gift of prophecy persisted beyond the New Testament age, but this position seems to rely on spurious inferences from texts like 1 Corinthians 13:8, Ephesians 2:20 and Hebrews 2:4. These and other texts speak of the foundational role of prophecy in the establishment of the New Testament church, but none ever predicts its cessation with the close of the apostolic age. First Corinthians 13 declares that prophecies will cease "when perfection comes" (vv. 8-10), but this seems more likely to refer to the time of Christ's return.[23]

But even if prophecy persists throughout the entire period between Christ's first and second comings, its role is diminished from what it was in the Old Testament. In the days of Isaiah and Jeremiah, for example, no divinely accredited prophets were ever to be evaluated; their messages were simply to be believed and obeyed. In Paul's day, however, such evaluation becomes mandatory (1 Cor 14:29): one speaker may interrupt another (v. 30), the first must be quiet (v. 31), and no true prophet can ever claim to have been so overpowered by the Spirit that he or she was unable to stop speaking (v. 32).

What is more, genuine revelations from God could be misinterpreted by those who received them in ways that made the actual prophecy and its (mis-) interpretation difficult to distinguish. In Acts 21:4, believers in Tyre urged Paul "through the Spirit" not to go on to Jerusalem. (This is the identical Greek expression used in 11:28 for Agabus's *prophecy* of a famine in Judea.) Yet Paul does not heed this prophecy but continues on to Jerusalem. As he draws closer, Agabus reappears and declares, "The Holy Spirit says, 'In this way the Jews of Jerusalem will bind the owners of this belt and will hand him over to the Gentiles' " (21:11). Still Paul is undaunted. It seems that the Christians in Tyre received the identical prophecy but (falsely) concluded from it that Paul should not go to Jerusalem if he was going to be imprisoned there. But without Agabus's clarification we would not have realized that what these Christians put forward as a word from the Lord was a combination of genuine revelation and faulty human interpretation. So even if God does still grant prophecies today, *we must never treat them as if they were on a par with inerrant Scripture,* because they may not get to us in an inerrant form.[24]

It is perhaps not so surprising, then, that no New Testament author ever claims that his writing is the result of prophecy, except for John in the book of Revelation (Rev 22:18-19). The writers believed they were guided or inspired by the Spirit (as in 1 Cor 7:40), but that does not constitute a claim that they were writing as New Testament "prophets." We must revise Robinson's statement and insist that in the Old Testament age only *some* prophets added to Scripture, and that in the era beginning with the apostles, prophets *almost never* added to Scripture. So even if we could demonstrate that Joseph Smith were a prophet, we should not have any high degree of expectation that he would ever write Scripture.[25]

But then we must return to our original question. Why *should* we accept the twenty-seven books of the New Testament as uniquely canonical? We have already seen two hints from within the New Testament itself: (1) theological consistency with earlier revelation and (2) being produced during the apostolic era by someone closely associated with Jesus or the apostles.[26] These two criteria were explicitly adopted from the earliest days of the postapostolic church on. Whatever other corruption may have intruded into the church as Hellenization (the effect of the gospel's contextualization or acculturation into a Greek world) or early Catholicism began to affect it, there is no evidence for a shift in the church's understanding of why certain books belonged in the New Testament and others did not. Indeed, a prominent orthodox Christian writer as early as Ignatius, bishop of Smyrna at the very beginning of the second century, could declare that his letters did not carry the same authority as those of the first-century apostles (*Epistle to the Trallians* 3.3). The era of producing Scripture had passed, and soon Christian writers would be explicitly labeling New Testament documents (and no others) as Scripture.[27]

In addition to orthodoxy and apostolicity (defined as stemming from the apostolic era), the third major criterion employed by the earliest church was widespread usage as a divinely authoritative source of doctrine. Unless a book commended itself to the majority of churches scattered across the empire, it was deemed not to be significant enough for inclusion in the canon. That is presumably why Paul's "lost" letter to the Corinthians (see 1 Cor 5:9) was never preserved; its content was apparently so limited to specific circumstances that it was not perceived to have abiding value for the church at large. So even if it were to be discovered someday, it would not thereby qualify for Scripture.[28]

By this criterion, no work of any Jewish or Christian pedigree, however authentic, that was hidden from the world at large for centuries should ever qualify as Scripture. This is not narrow-minded prejudice against the LDS; all kinds of New Age movements, for example, claim to have uncovered hidden documents that rewrite the history of early Christianity. Some "unearth" alleged correspondence between Jewish and Roman officials about Jesus; some describe his travels as a young man to learn from Indian gurus or monastic Essenes; others revise New Testament documents to make them teach that Jesus was an alien from outer space who visited the planet via UFOs.[29] The origins of all these documents are always shrouded in enough mystery or secrecy that it becomes virtually impossible to disprove their claims conclusively. There is much wisdom, therefore, in the early church's refusal to treat as Scripture any book that God has not deemed worthy to preserve and to make accessible to people throughout the entire period from its composition onward. So even if Protestants can retain an open canon in principle, *in practice* our canon is closed, and it is difficult to see how any new book could ever successfully be added to it.

This is not a matter of limiting what God can do, but of appreciating the fullness of God's revelation in Christ. The book of Hebrews argues that revelation was progressive and partial, leading up to its consummation in the revelation of Jesus the Son. Once God revealed himself in Jesus, what need is there for further revelation? So even apart from the arguably spurious character of the specific documents that Mormons accept is the general Evangelical aversion to admitting *any* new revelation, because to do so is to diminish Christ.

Misgivings About the Uniquely Mormon Scriptures

A number of my misgivings about the uniquely Mormon Scriptures are by now obvious. The fact that the Book of Mormon, even if authentic, was hidden from the world for so many hundreds of years, and that the Pearl of Great Price and Doctrine and Covenants simply did not exist before the nineteenth century, makes me doubt that God could ever have intended for them to be Scripture.

I understand the argument that the church was allegedly apostate all those years, but I find that argument unpersuasive and untrue to history. To be sure, Protestants argue that in the heyday of medieval Catholicism many of the major truths of the gospel were significantly obscured, but we see this as having developed slowly, over a period of fifteen hundred years. We find no reason for wholesale rejection of the doctrinal consensus of the church, the councils and the creeds of the first five centuries. And we see pockets of Christendom that more closely resembled apostolic Christianity throughout the entire pre-Reformation period.[30] With the coming of the Reformation in the early 1500s, while not every detail of New Testament practice was reinstated, so many were restored that charges of continuing, widespread apostasy seem out of place. What is more, Christ promised to build his church so that the gates of hell would not prevail against it (Mt 16:19). It is hard to square this promise with a total and prolonged apostasy of the Christian church that LDS claims require.[31]

But I have other misgivings as well. Some issues, often stressed in Evangelical anti-Mormon literature, deserve brief mention, but I suspect they are not as crucial as some have alleged. For example, it is often customary to point out so-called contradictions between the Book of Mormon and the Old or New Testament. A famous example calls attention to Alma 7:10, which prophesies that the Son of God would be "born of Mary, at Jerusalem which is the land of our forefathers."[32] Yet I have little doubt that Joseph Smith, as well as he knew his King James Bible, was fully aware that Jesus was born in Bethlehem, a small town about five miles south of Jerusalem (Mic 5:2; Mt 2:5-8). I have no idea why he allowed this discrepancy to stand; one Mormon apologist points out that in the ancient world a small town could naturally be described as in the land of a major city nearby.[33] Interestingly, that is almost exactly the type of harmonization I employ to account for the seeming discrepancy between Mark 5:1 and Matthew 8:28—did Jesus exorcise the demoniac in the region of the Gerasenes or of the Gadarenes? Probably it was near Khersa, a town that in Greek transliteration could easily turn into Gerasa, in the larger territory of Gadara named after the more prominent city by that name within the region.[34]

Most other "contradictions" between the Book of Mormon and the Bible are likewise similar enough to the alleged contradictions within the Old and New Testaments themselves that I am not sure how fruitful it is to pursue them.[35] An irrefutable contradiction—two affirmations that cannot possibly both be true at the same time—is difficult to demonstrate in many ancient texts. The same must be said with arguments from archaeology. There is much in the Book of Mormon about ancient societies that remains without corroboration. But the same is true of at least smaller parts of the Protestant Bible, particularly in the earliest portions of the Old Testament. In fact every religious believer has to accept much on faith, in the face of ridicule from liberal or unbelieving skeptics, trusting that one day the evidence will be greater than it currently is.

Now that I understand Robinson's views on the inspiration of Scripture, I see little need for pursuing the arguments from changes and corrections in successive editions of the Book of Mormon. Evangelicals believe that ancient scribes did similar things to their texts, although we argue that we must go back as close as possible to the original for the authoritative version and that in many cases scribal activity was not restoring the original but actually changing it. Mormons, with their doctrine of ongoing revelation, reverse this, so that the latest authorized revision becomes the authoritative one. For example, 1 Nephi 11:18, 21 and 13:40 all have statements in which Jesus was called "God" or the "eternal Father" in the first edition of the Book of Mormon, but in the second edition the words "son of" were inserted before "God" or "eternal Father." It seems an unlikely coincidence that three such identical discrepancies would all reflect merely "typographical errors," as the preface to the current edition suggests, or that they were merely "accidental omissions" (despite the occurrence of the word *son* in an early edition owned by the Reorganized LDS),[36] when so much doctrine hangs on the difference.

Be that as it may, the LDS base their official beliefs only on the current state of revelation within the church, and in many instances they have reversed earlier practices (most notably in outlawing polygamy and admitting blacks to the priesthood). So we should be grateful for what Evangelicals perceive as overall progress, and we should interact with the *current* state of that "revelation," not earlier expressions of it.

What concerns me most is a cluster of phenomena in the Book of Mormon to which Evangelical apologists have not always drawn sufficient attention. All of them have to do with a substantial percentage of the book that simply seems out of place in the historical context to which it is attributed but fits perfectly the religious climate and theological concerns of the early nineteenth century. Let's consider five such phenomena briefly.

First, the Book of Mormon is full of the widespread use in Old Testament times of New Testament doctrines, language, concepts and even specific verses. One needs only to open the book almost at random to find examples. The cross-references in the footnotes make many of these clear. I am not thinking here of isolated expressions like the terms *gospel, Christian* or *church,* but passages that reflect a combination of all sorts of New Testament texts. For example, 2 Nephi 31:13 reads,

Wherefore, my beloved brethren, I know that if ye shall follow the Son, with full purpose of heart, acting no hypocrisy and no deception before God, but with real intent, repenting of your sins, witnessing unto the Father that ye are willing to take upon you the name of Christ, by baptism—yea, by following your Lord and your Savior down into the water, according to his word, behold, then shall ye receive the Holy Ghost; yea, then cometh the baptism of fire and of the Holy Ghost; and then can ye speak with the tongue of angels, and shout praises unto the Holy One of Israel.

Here is almost the whole plan of salvation, as distinctively revealed in New Testament times (e.g., the threefold combination of repentance, water baptism and reception of the Holy Spirit in Peter's Pentecostal sermon in Acts 2:38), combined with echoes of John the Baptist's teaching (baptism with the fire and the Spirit—Mt 3:11) and Paul's later reference to tongues of angels (1 Cor 13:2). Other more subordinate parts in the passage also echo exclusively New Testament language—"beloved brethren" and Christ as "Savior."

In 2 Nephi 31:21 appears a clear reference to Acts 4:12 combined with Jesus' characteristic topic of "the kingdom of God" ("there is none other way nor name given under heaven whereby man can be saved in the kingdom of God"). And all this in 555-549 B.C.! Indeed, the entire Book of Mormon abounds with explicit references to Christ, to his life and ministry and to the three persons of the Godhead long before New Testament times (see chapters two and three), even though none of these concepts or terms ever appear in these forms in our Old Testament or any other ancient Jewish literature (exclusive of the portions of the Old Testament found only in the JST).

I understand that the Book of Mormon also claims that "the great and abominable church" has "taken away from the gospel of the Lamb many parts which are plain and most precious; and also many covenants of the Lord have they taken away" (1 Nephi 13:26), so that all these Christian concepts included in the pre-Christian stories of the Book of Mormon were supposedly known in earlier times. The trouble is that there is not a shred of historical evidence from the ancient world that the suppression of such literature ever took place. It defies imagination how every hint of the vast panorama of New Testament texts and concepts could have disappeared from both the Old Testament and other pre-Christian Jewish documents, even had a censor deliberately tried to destroy it all.[37]

It is extremely easy, on the other hand, to imagine a nineteenth-century writer, well versed in the KJV, composing such a collage of concepts. The New Testament itself insists that the distinctive truths of the gospel were not as clearly known in Old Testament times as the Book of Mormon or the JST would make them (Eph 2:2-6). But Christians have always puzzled over what "Old Testament saints" knew and how they were saved, and it is understandable that Joseph Smith should have wanted them to know the entire plan of salvation. After all, this feature of the Book of Mormon actually makes it *more* doctrinally consistent with the New Testament in this respect than the Old Testament is when taken by itself!

Second, although it is understandable that Joseph Smith should translate texts that resembled passages from the KJV into KJV language—the only standard English language translation of his day—the fact that the Book of Mormon frequently reproduces KJV language even where textual criticism has demonstrated the KJV to have followed an inferior and inauthentic text betrays its merely human origin. Consider, for example, three of the most famous passages in the KJV New Testament that were almost certainly absent from the original biblical manuscripts: part of Matthew 5:13 ("for thine is the kingdom, and the power, and the glory, forever. Amen"); Mark 16:9-20, which includes the potentially fatal verse "They shall take up serpents; and if they drink any deadly thing, it shall not hurt them" (v. 18); and 1 John 5:7 ("For there are three that bear record in heaven, the Father, the Word, and the Holy Ghost; and these three are one"). The first and third of these are theologically orthodox but missing from the earliest and most reliable Greek manuscripts. They make good sense as pious additions by later Christian scribes.[38] The second is highly aberrant and dangerous. Yet all three are quoted and alluded to in the Book of Mormon (3 Nephi 13:13; Mormon 9:24; 3 Nephi 11:27, 36 respectively).

If this book really were some pristine, long-lost word from God, correcting the errors and restoring the deficiencies of the corrupted Scriptures, then it would not parallel the corruptions that early orthodox Christianity itself introduced. But if it were the invention, however well motivated, of Joseph Smith, then all this makes sense, since no one in his day yet knew of the KJV deficiencies in these areas. Indeed, that seems to me to be the most reasonable explanation of the widespread similarity of the Book of Mormon to KJV texts, including whole multichapter sections that reproduce parts of Isaiah, the Sermon on the Mount, 1 Corinthians and so on. That Joseph often altered the wording of the KJV does not rule out his widespread dependence on it; if two of my students turn in term papers in which even 10 percent of the wording is identical, I immediately suspect collusion, however different the rest may be!

Third, while I recognize that the JST is not treated as canonical Scripture by Mormon authorities, its very existence makes me uneasy. Why would Joseph Smith produce what he called an "inspired revision" of the Old and New Testaments, complete with entire verses and chapters that correspond to nothing in any ancient manuscript, but that dovetail perfectly with numerous distinctive Mormon doctrines, unless he was trying to bolster support for his other claims of being able to translate and prophesy? The first time I ever saw a copy of this version of the Bible, I experimented by looking up John 1:1 ("the Word was God"), John 4:24 ("God is Spirit") and 1 Corinthians 15:40 (on different kinds of heavenly bodies), knowing these to be important in Protestant-Mormon debates. In every one of these passages, the JST significantly differed from the unanimous witness of the ancient manuscript evidence in favor of a version more in line with Mormon doctrine than historic Christianity. I want to be as charitable as I can, but it is hard for me to read these unsupported revisions of God's Word and still give Joseph the benefit of the doubt when it comes to his other, more official "revelations."[39]

Fourth, the same must be said about the Book of Abraham in the Pearl of Great Price. I am glad that many Mormons are no longer claiming that this is a literal translation of the papyri Joseph used, since Joseph Smith's translation of the Book of Abraham facsimiles has been challenged by Egyptologists.[40] But until this was challenged, the LDS consistently defended a more literal translation procedure. Should not Joseph's track record where he can be tested influence our assessment of his work where he cannot be tested?

Fifth, the whole range of issues that the uniquely LDS Scriptures seek to answer fits perfectly the spirit of the early nineteenth century. It is not difficult to imagine a creative, biblically literate individual, frustrated with the moral corruption of many of the established churches of his day, composing what Joseph Smith claims to have had revealed to him. Once people became aware of the American Indians, surely they would have been curious about their opportunities for salvation prior to the arrival of the Europeans with the gospel. Others were speculating about the same questions.[41] And what about babies who died, and the people in Old Testament times who seemed to know so little of the gospel? Joseph confessed a greater affinity for Methodism than Presbyterian or Baptist thought *prior* to his supposed encounter with God (Joseph Smith History 2:5-11). Is it a coincidence that Mormonism subsequently turned out to be closer to Methodism than to its Protestant competitors on a whole host of doctrines, from denying the major tenets of Calvinism (predestination, original sin, eternal security) to affirming the strong call for holiness and moral perfection? Even the testimony of Methodism's founder, John Wesley, that he found his heart "strangely warmed" at his conversion is reminiscent of Mormonism's "burning in the bosom." None of these were issues that concerned the ancient Jews or Central Americans who populate the pages of the Book of Mormon, but they all fit the religious climate of nineteenth-century North America very readily.

In trying to date documents in historical research more generally, there is a well-established principle that later writers regularly try to simplify what is complicated or to solve problems that were previously unsolved in earlier works. In textual criticism in particular, the principle is that the "harder reading" is more likely to be the original one. In other words, copyists are less likely to alter manuscripts to introduce new difficulties than to attempt to resolve difficulties they perceive in them. Religious movements, too, are likely to develop to try to satisfy perceived inadequacies in existing options. And it is clear to an outsider, at any rate, that Mormonism seems to have done just that. It tries to resolve all the thorny theological problems that Jews and Christians before them never could. For that very reason it seems highly unlikely that the Book of Mormon or the JST distinctives predate Joseph Smith's lifetime. If anybody in antiquity ever really knew all this, surely it would not have disappeared without a trace.

A More Positive Conclusion

The very feature of the Mormon doctrine of Scripture that Evangelicals find most objectionable holds the key, paradoxically, to improved Evangelical-Mormon relations. Evangelicals reject the idea of continuing revelation beyond the Old and New Testaments *on the same level with* the Bible. Mormons accept the idea and apply it not only to the three additional nineteenth-century books they deem Scripture but also to authoritative decisions of official church leaders in every era. This enables them to revise interpretations of earlier doctrines or dramatically alter church policy.

I find Robinson's views of inspiration considerably less objectionable than most Mormon explanations of that doctrine. The history of Mormon-Evangelical debate on this topic has centered on such issues as how exactly or literally the characters on the golden plates or in the book of Abraham scroll corresponded to what Joseph Smith wrote, whether or not there truly was such a language as "Reformed Egyptian," whether or not the Book of Mormon's narrative of the early history of the Americas is credible, and whether or not the minor changes in its successive editions invalidate its claims. If, on the other hand, "translation" includes interpretation, adaptation and application, if the media of plates and scrolls were merely a means to an end—proclaiming the gospel irrespective of the literal significance of the written characters—then these debates diminish somewhat in importance.[42] If the heart of the LDS claim is that God gave Joseph Smith inspired messages for humanity (theoretically even irrespective of the existence of any golden plates at all), then the nature of the debate with Evangelicals shifts considerably—to whether or not Joseph exhibited prophetic credentials and to whether the additional LDS Scriptures merely supplement or actually contradict biblical theology.

To me, Robinson's explanation seems to be quite a stretch in understanding the meaning of Joseph's claims to be "translating," and they differ remarkably from what Mormons have traditionally seemed to hold. But I welcome them as a substantial improvement over what

I previously understood (rightly or wrongly) Mormons to believe. His views do not require me to accept what seem to be historically unsubstantiated (if not blatantly contradicted) claims about the nature and composition of the LDS Scriptures. I am grateful for Robinson's rejection of the widely touted Mormon claim that I am part of a willfully apostate church in denying these additional Scriptures. It leaves the door open for further clarifications in LDS doctrine, even at the level of official church teaching, and for new revelations.

One thinks, by way of comparison, of the substantial improvements in Roman Catholic and Evangelical relationships after Vatican II (in the late 1960s), which were based largely on papal and conciliar pronouncements that granted greater legitimacy to Protestants and toned down some of the more inflated rhetoric of previous generations about the extent of the authority of the Catholic hierarchy.[43] Interestingly, that is the advantage of a magisterium—Catholics and Mormons both have official mechanisms for modifying past pronouncements, whereas Protestants have to rely solely on an appeal to Scripture and on influence by consensus and persuasion across a wide spectrum of denominations and congregations to effect any lasting change on matters of belief or practice.

Evangelicals would be even more grateful if Robinson's more relaxed understanding of how Joseph Smith "translated" led to more modest claims for Joseph's writings, which did not commend them as of equal or greater authority than the Old and New Testaments. Then we might think of them as constituting for the LDS what Luther's collected works do for Lutherans or what Calvin's *Institutes* do for Presbyterian and Reformed thought—important, foundational theological works that nevertheless do not supplant the unique role of the Old and New Testament Scriptures. The Reorganized LDS Church has already adopted this position, but Robinson himself doubts that he or most Mormons could ever go so far.

Since I do not believe that the gift of prophecy has ceased or that God cannot continue to reveal truth to his people at this lesser nonscriptural level, I cannot in principle reject Mormonism lock, stock and barrel just because it claims to have received additional prophecy. Even though I cannot accept claims that put this "prophecy" on a par with Scripture, it is surely the case that the LDS provide some important reminders for Evangelicals of wholesome morality and fervent belief through their supposed revelations in areas that agree with the Old and New Testaments as well.[44] In other words, we must move on from discussing the doctrine of Scripture to looking at the actual content of the uniquely LDS Scriptures and see what similarities or differences emerge between those writings and the biblical books. This we will proceed to do in the remaining chapters in the three areas of doctrine that in the past have seemed most to divide Evangelicals and Mormons.

Scripture

[R O B I N S O N]

What Latter-day Saints Believe

Latter-day Saints accept the Bible (without the Apocrypha),[1] the Book of Mormon, the Doctrine and Covenants, and the Pearl of Great Price as canonized Scripture and as the word of God to the church and to the world.[2] As Prof. Blomberg points out, the LDS view of the *nature* of Scripture is actually closer to the Evangelical view than is the view held by liberal Protestants or Catholics. We take the Scriptures to be literally true, and we hold symbolic, figurative or allegorical interpretation to a minimum, accepting the miraculous events as historical and the moral and ethical teaching as binding and valid. What separates Latter-day Saints from Evangelicals is less our view of the nature of Scripture and more our view of *canon,* to which subject I will return below.

The eighth article of faith, written by Joseph Smith in 1842, states that "we believe the Bible to be the word of God, as far as it is translated correctly; we also believe the Book of Mormon to be the word of God." Evangelicals sometimes take offense at the phrase "as far as it is translated correctly," but this should not be so. The wording is intended to communicate *exactly* the same caution to Latter-day Saints that the phrases "when all facts are known," "in their original autographs," and "properly interpreted" from the Chicago Statement on Biblical Inerrancy are intended to convey to Evangelicals (see pp. 35-36). By setting these very similar parameters, both Latter-day Saints and Evangelicals stipulate that the present text of Scripture may contain errors,[3] and neither Mormons nor (most) Evangelicals would insist that any modern version can claim absolute verbal inerrancy.

On the other hand, the wording of the eighth article of faith, which leaves out "as far as translated correctly" after the Book of Mormon, should *not* be construed to mean that the modern text of the Book of Mormon is absolutely inerrant, even though many LDS do make this assumption. Current editions of the Book of Mormon contain the following information at the end of the introduction: "Some minor errors in the text have been perpetuated in past editions of the Book of Mormon. This edition contains corrections that seem appropriate to bring the material into conformity with prepublication manuscripts and early editions edited by the Prophet Joseph Smith." In other words, the same type of text-critical concerns exist with the various Book of Mormon manuscripts as with the Bible—but to a lesser degree since there are vastly fewer Book of Mormon manuscripts, a shorter period of transmission, and far fewer variants to the Book of Mormon text.[4] So while it would be fair to say that most Mormons think the Book of Mormon much less textually uncertain than the Bible by virtue of a shorter and simpler transmission history, we attribute verbal inerrancy in the strict sense to neither the Bible nor the Book of Mormon in their present forms. The original revelation understood in its original context might have been "inerrant" as given to the original apostles or prophets, but the point is moot since the autographs themselves, their exact historical and cultural contexts, and the precise linguistic understanding of their authors are not available to us. Therefore, Latter-day Saints would agree with the five qualifications of the "Chicago Statement on Biblical Inerrancy," although, as usual, we would probably use different terms to express the same ideas.[5]

The initial revelation may be divine, but human languages and cultures are not. For Latter-day Saints, as for Evangelicals, what gives Scripture its normative power is its origin in God—its *inspired* character. However, the specifics of language, style and vocabulary are conditioned by the capacities, education, cultural context, time and place of the inspired writer to whom God speaks.[6] Scripture, including the Book of Mormon, is in our view recorded by men who can and do make mistakes, and it is possible to mistranslate or to misinterpret the Hebrew and Greek (or Nephite) texts.[7]

Moreover, written Scripture is mediated revelation, derivative revelation. The direct revelation to a prophet or an apostle is immediate and primary, and this is the word of God in the purest sense—as *word* and *hearing* rather than as *text*. However, the recording, transmission and interpretation of the word depends on fallible human beings, using the fallible human tools of reason and language. Thus, Scripture is the word of God for Latter-day Saints, "as far as it is translated correctly."[8]

For Latter-day Saints, the church's guarantee of doctrinal correctness lies primarily in the living prophet, and only secondarily in the preservation of the written text. This is, after all, the New Testament model. The ancient apostles and prophets themselves were the *primary* oracles. What makes Scripture normative is not anything that may have happened to the text as a text, but rather that it records what "holy men of God spake as they were moved by the Holy Ghost" (2 Pet 1:20-21). In other words, what makes Scripture *theopneustos* ("inspired," or "God-breathed") is not its *written* character but its *revealed* character. Writing it down preserves the inspired revelation and makes it accessible to the wider church, but that is secondary to the original revelation itself. The *record* of revelation cannot logically be more authoritative than the *experience* of revelation.

There would have been no Scripture in the first place had not God revealed his word, person-to-person, to a living, breathing human being. And it is the continued presence of the one who received the revelation in the first place, or his inspired successors (prophets in the Old Testament, apostles in the New), that ensures the written word will be interpreted and applied correctly to new contexts.[9] This is the biblical pattern. Latter-day Saints find it inconsistent that Evangelicals who often voice a desire to return to New Testament Christianity usually do so with a distinct aversion to the presence in it of *living* apostles and prophets. It often seems to Mormons that Evangelicals are embarrassed by the nontextual nature of direct revelation and are anxious, once the apostles and prophets have written down their message, to gag them and hustle them offstage before they can add any information that might increase our understanding—clearly preferring written texts to living oracles.

The apostles and the prophets were not merely secretaries who took down divine messages; they were leaders of the community of believers, and they interpreted and applied the meaning of the revelations to their communities within their own lifetimes. Just as the apostle or prophet is necessary to receive what becomes the written word of God in the first place, he is necessary to authoritatively interpret it in the second.[10] Again, this is not because the gospel changes, but because human language, culture, perception, and the needs of the people do; God is constant—we are not. As long as "holy men of God" (apostles and prophets) remain in the church to interpret and apply the written revelations that they and their predecessors have received to changing times and new cultures, there is a presumption of doctrinal continuity and correctness.

And here is the rub, for if inspired prophets are around to interpret the revelation authoritatively, there is always the chance that God might reveal some new wrinkle as well or might give added insight to subjects already recorded in Scripture, as Chronicles does with Kings, or adapt previous revelations to a new historical or cultural context, as Peter's revelation in Acts 10:10-15 does with Jesus' instructions in Matthew 10:5, and as Paul's teaching on circumcision for the adopted children of Abraham does with Genesis 17:10-14.

Professor Blomberg concedes that the canon must be considered open *at least in principle,* but adds that it is closed in practice. This sounds to me suspiciously like declaring the canon closed while admitting there is technically no biblical warrant for doing so. To this I would add that no one since the New Testament period has had the authority to declare the canon closed either in principle or in practice, and that such a declaration—even in practice—is an addition to what the Bible actually says.

Finally, what God has said to apostles and prophets in the past is always secondary to what God is saying directly to his apostles and prophets now. I know this makes Evangelicals wince, but the spiritual hazards of this position are logically no greater than they were in the earliest church when Peter or Paul were still alive and interpreting previously received Scripture for the church, sometimes contrary to tradition, even while they continued to receive and record more.

Avoiding Misconceptions
First of all, it would be nice for Evangelicals to bear in mind that the King James Bible *is* the LDS Bible. No other version, not even the JST, supplants the KJV. Leaders of the LDS Church from Joseph Smith to the present have tended to use the Bible even more than the Book of Mormon in their teaching and preaching. Often Evangelicals assume that we LDS accept the Book of Mormon *in place of the Bible,* and this is incorrect. There isn't a single verse of the Bible that I do not personally accept and believe, although I do reject the interpretive straitjacket imposed on the Bible by the Hellenized church after the apostles passed from the scene.

Perhaps it should also be noted that Evangelicals who take the time to read the Book of Mormon generally do not find much in it to object to. It is the claim of scriptural authority that offends more often than the actual content of the book. And while one (or both) of us will surely be wrong about the scriptural nature of the book, this disagreement does not seem to me to justify the animus that it generates on both sides, especially since Prof. Blomberg has agreed that the canon of Scripture remains open in theory. Yes, Latter-day Saints believe things that Evangelicals do not, but the huge amount of doctrinal and scriptural overlap and agreement between us is much greater than the disagreement.

Further, there is a difference between "adding to" and "contradicting." Mormons surely "add to" the canon, but Evangelicals are often too hasty in assuming that this automatically means "contradicting" the Bible. If this were true, since the Bible is also *my* Scripture, the many contradictions created would trouble *me,* but I do not find such contradictions—at least not until I encounter the theology of the postbiblical councils and creeds. I would point out, however, that disagreeing with the Councils of Nicaea and Chalcedon is not the same as disagreeing with the New Testament.

In my experience, it is typical of Evangelicals (and understandable) that they cast Mormons as intentional innovators replacing the pure New Testament gospel with a modern substitute or at least festooning it with modern additions. But such a characterization does violence to Mormon self-understanding. We would not do that because we are as devoted in principle to the pure New Testament gospel as Evangelicals are. But Evangelicals start with the assumption that modern Christianity has preserved that gospel intact over the centuries, while Mormons start with the assumption that some of it was lost in the Hellenization of Christianity and the corruptions of the great church and must now be restored in the latter days. Common ground here to both Evangelicals and Mormons is found in an attempt to be loyal to the New Testament gospel, though we certainly understand it differently.

Latter-day Saints, on the other hand, are frequently guilty of doing the same kind of violence to Evangelical self-understanding by referring to them, as well as other orthodox Christians, as "apostates," charging that they have somehow willfully removed "plain and precious" truths from the Christian gospel. But genuine apostasy requires informed rejection of the gospel. Since Mormons do not believe that the fullness of the gospel has been available to orthodox Christians since the second or the third century, it is not internally consistent with the Saints' own theology to refer to modern Christians as "apostates"—though many still do it. This is rhetoric left over from the nineteenth century. Informed Latter-day Saints do not argue that historic Christianity lost *all* truth or became *completely* corrupt. The orthodox churches may have lost the "fullness" of the gospel, but they did not lose all of it nor even most of it. Many Evangelicals caricature or overstate the actual LDS view, which is that the orthodox churches are incomplete rather than corrupt. It is their postbiblical creeds that are identified in Joseph Smith's first vision as an "abomination," but certainly not their individual members or their members' *biblical* beliefs.[11]

On the finality of God's revelation in Christ, Evangelicals and Mormons are in total agreement. Where we disagree is in our assessment of how well that revelation was preserved down through the centuries in Christian "orthodoxy." If the gospel record were always what it was in the first century, and if the church were always what it was in the first century, then there would have been no need for a restoration in the latter days. But there is no guarantee recorded in the Bible that the perfect revelation in Christ would always and forever remain perfectly recorded in Scripture and unaltered by human agency. After all, I assume both of us would agree that the Roman Church of the sixteenth century was no longer the pure bride of Jesus Christ. Then why is the idea of a *restoration* so repugnant to Evangelicals who already fervently insist on the need for *reformation?* The Puritan Seekers had also claimed the true church was lost and that it could not be reestablished until God sent new apostles and prophets to restore it.[12] Is it so vile for the LDS to hold the same view?

Both caricatures, Mormons as willful innovators and orthodox Christians as willful apostates, disregard the actual motives common to both parties—loyalty to the pure gospel of Christ as each understands it. It is not necessary that Latter-day Saints and Evangelicals agree entirely on what the Christian gospel is (Lk 9:49-50), but it is time that we admit, each to the other, the sincerity and the rightness of our common intent. It is a lie—and one told too often on both sides—that the mainstream of either party *intentionally* perverts or departs from that gospel.

Professor Blomberg has objected to my claim that prophets always write, and on this I readily concede.[13] It was an incautious and sweeping generalization. However, my original point was that if Joseph Smith were a true prophet, we might expect him to write new Scripture, and that point is just as well served if I more precisely state that ancient prophets *very often* wrote Scripture and added to the canon. From the LDS perspective the question is not so much, Is this document Scripture? The question is rather, Was this person divinely inspired when he wrote it? If the answer is yes, then what a prophet writes under inspiration is Scripture, as 2 Peter 1:20-21 indicates.

I fear that Prof. Blomberg and I have talked past each other with the word *prophet*. Latter-day Saints use this term in two ways: to distinguish between (1) prophets who hold the apostolic keys of the kingdom and preside over the whole church (like Peter anciently or Gordon B. Hinckley today) and (2) local individuals who exercise the gift of prophecy in a more limited stewardship (like Agabus). The first sense is more usual among the Mormons, the latter among Evangelicals. Also, the LDS believe that *all* apostles are prophets in the former sense, and therefore we often do not distinguish between apostles and prophets, but customarily use the term *prophet* for both.[14] I certainly did not intend to make a distinction between apostolic office and prophetic calling. Latter-day Saints normally assume that one implies the other.

An area in which Evangelicals almost always misunderstand LDS theology (and in which the average Mormon often does, too) is the relationship between the Joseph Smith Translation (hereafter JST) and the biblical text.[15] The Book of Mormon teaches that "plain and precious" things have been taken out of the Bible (1 Nephi 13:24-29). Both Latter-day Saints and Evangelicals often assume this means that the present biblical books went through a cut-and-paste editing process to remove these things, and that the JST restores the edited texts back to their original forms. However, I see no reason to understand things this way, and in fact I think it is largely erroneous. The pertinent passages from the Book of Mormon give no reason to assume that the process of removing plain and precious things from Scripture was one exclusively or even primarily of editing the books of the present canon.[16] The bulk of the text-critical evidence is against a process of wholesale cutting and pasting,[17] and the JST—despite assumptions to the contrary—does not make very many or very major doctrinal changes in the received text.[18] In fact, combining the JST and the KJV does not restore most of the information that Latter-day Saints would call "the plain and precious truths" removed from the originals.[19]

It is clear to me, therefore, that "the plain and precious truths" were not necessarily in the originals of the *present* biblical books, and I suspect that the editing process that excised them did not consist solely or even primarily of cutting and pasting the present books, but rather largely in keeping *other* apostolic or prophetic writings from being included in the canon.[20] In other words, "the plain and precious truths" were primarily excised not by means of controlling the *text,* but by means of controlling the *canon.*[21] I think that informed Latter-day Saints will affirm with me that the present books of the Bible are the Word of God (within the common parameters of the eighth article of faith and the Chicago Statement on Biblical Inerrancy) and that the texts are essentially correct in their present form—but that there once were *other* "God-breathed" writings that are now missing.[22]

Then what of the JST? First of all, the JST is not canonized Scripture even for the Latter-day Saints, JST Genesis 1—6 and Matthew 24, which are both found in the Pearl of Great Price, excepted. The JST is not the LDS version of the Bible—the KJV is and always has been. Of course we believe the JST is "inspired," but that is not the same thing as saying it always restores the original texts of the biblical books. In 1828 the word *translation* was broader in its meaning than it is now, and the Joseph Smith *translation* (JST) should be understood to contain additional revelation, alternate readings, prophetic commentary or midrash, harmonization, clarification and corrections *of* the original as well as corrections *to* the original.[23] It is not my understanding that Evangelicals would argue that every passage of Scripture has only one correct meaning. Joseph Smith often saw more than one meaning in a passage and brought many of these explicitly to our attention by means of the JST. Certainly the existence of a JST variant reading for a passage ought *not* to imply that the KJV is *incorrect,* since the Book of Mormon and Doctrine and Covenants sometimes agree with the KJV rather than the JST.[24]

Most of the objections I hear concerning the JST result from assuming we know what Joseph was doing and how he was doing it, and from assuming a view of the texts and a translational philosophy on the part of Joseph Smith that cannot be established from the documents. For example, Evangelicals might assume that a "prophetic" translation would be one that restored the *original* text, word for word and without any additions and subtractions, but this is not an LDS assumption. Joseph Smith did not explain his "translation" process. He did not describe the parameters of his work or explain either the procedures or the principles he employed, but it seems to me that his main concern was not merely to reproduce God's word to ancient prophets but also to produce a correct text for the use of Latter-day Saints in the latter days. Since Evangelicals place the highest authority in the biblical text itself and make the prophetic calling secondary, they would naturally see the task of a modern prophet (if there is such a thing) as rendering a perfect copy of a perfect original. But Latter-day Saints place the highest authority in living, prophetic/apostolic guidance, and therefore see the rightful task of a modern prophet as revealing what the church needs in the latter days. If the original wording is misleading, rewrite it; if the original reading is ambiguous, clarify it.

I happen to believe Joseph did frequently restore ancient information in the JST and that the JST is "correct" in all its doctrinal particulars, but this does not necessarily mean that the received text is corrupt or that the JST always represents the original, unexpurgated text of Matthew, Mark, Luke or John. I do not personally assume this. I affirm only that the JST is "inspired" and that the LDS should consult it as a supplement to their canonical Scriptures. In this I may be wrong, but I would argue that believing it does not nullify my belief in the KJV New Testament or its power in my life.

Similarly, Joseph Smith never explained how he was "translating" the Book of Abraham in the Pearl of Great Price, and I do not claim to know the relationship between Joseph's Egyptian papyri and the finished text. I do believe that the finished text is true, is the inspired word of God, and is historically correct and authentic, but I do not know how Joseph arrived at it other than that it was "by the gift and power of God." Many critics claim that if they can demonstrate that Joseph was not translating directly from the papyrus in the same way and getting the same English product that an Egyptologist would, then the finished Book of Abraham is discredited. But the church has never been bound to defend the proposition that Joseph did what an Egyptologist does to get his finished text—only that the finished text is true.

Professor Blomberg, along with many others, feels that the Book of Mormon "seems" to be a product of the nineteenth century. To me it "seems" otherwise. To the scholars of the Jesus Seminar, it "seems" that Jesus could not have taught the Lord's Prayer or the Sermon on the Mount.[25] I assume it "seems" to most Evangelicals, as it does to most Latter-day Saints, that he did. It "seems" to most biblical scholars that the book of Daniel was not written by Daniel and that it wasn't written until after the so-called prophecies it contains had already come to pass.[26] It "seems" to most scholars that Moses did not write the five books of Moses in the Old Testament, that Paul did not write Colossians, Ephesians or the Pastoral Epistles in the New Testament, and that Peter could not have written both 1 and 2 Peter.

I understand that in most of these cases it "seems" otherwise to many Evangelicals, as it does to the Latter-day Saints. When so many Evangelicals reject what "seems" to the scholars to be wrong with the Bible, I do not think they can at the same time fault the LDS too severely for resisting what "seems" to some to be wrong with the Book of Mormon. "Seems" cuts both ways, and proof is more difficult than "seems." On the other hand, if the more critical biblical scholars are right and Evangelicals are willing to grant that genuinely inspired Scripture can be written pseudepigraphically and ex post facto, as is claimed for "deutero"-Isaiah, Daniel, the four Gospels, the Pastoral epistles, Ephesians, Colossians, one of the Thessalonian letters and one of the Petrine letters, then I do not know what fault can be found with Joseph Smith—even if he *did* write the Book of Mormon pseudonymously and ex post facto in the nineteenth century (though I personally do not believe he did).

However, it appears that what Prof. Blomberg means, based on the examples he has cited, is not just that the Book of Mormon is specifically a nineteenth-century work as that it is distinctly post-Christian, even in its "B.C." sections, since it obviously uses Christian terms and concepts. Latter-day Saints believe that the fullness of the gospel was revealed to Adam, Enoch, Noah, Abraham and many other of the ancient prophets whose blessed assurance came on the strength of the Lord's promises of future events. It was also revealed to Moses, but the children of Israel proved unready for the revelation and, when they sinned, they were given a lesser law to be their schoolmaster until the fullness would be revealed to them again in the future.[27]

In my view the absence of specifically Christian language in the Old Testament from Sinai on is not primarily due to "editing out," as

Prof. Blomberg assumes. Rather it is due to the Old Testament's being part of the "lesser" law of Moses. The language of the gospel was never in most of the Old Testament, since the Old Testament postdates Moses and is adapted to the understanding of those who were under the law of Moses. It is a text for those under the Old Covenant, not those under the New.

However, the fullness of the Christian gospel was revealed to the Book of Mormon peoples in the New World before the birth of Christ just as it had been revealed to Adam, Noah and Abraham. In describing their Christian beliefs in the Book of Mormon, Joseph Smith did not hesitate to use the KJV idiom wherever he could. This was not "plagiarism" but a conscious decision to use the sacred language he knew to render similar ideas from the ancient record. It may "seem" anachronistic to some, but regardless of what may have been on the plates, why should Joseph be required to invent new terminology when both he and his audience already knew intimately the KJV idiom? It seems to me that this boils down to whether Latter-day Saints (or Evangelicals) are wrong about pre-Christian prophets possibly knowing the Christian gospel.

Further, I do think that Prof. Blomberg and other Evangelicals have misjudged what is happening in the contemporary LDS Church when they refer to the LDS "modifying" their doctrines and making other "changes." During the past decade our former president, Ezra Taft Benson, and other leaders have emphasized the importance of per-sonal study of the Book of Mormon and other Scriptures for the Latter-day Saints.[28] He also reminded us that the Lord has not been pleased with the gap between scripturally revealed beliefs and the level of "popular" LDS understanding.[29]

As the Saints have returned to careful study of the Scriptures, we have been reminded of the importance of what we share with mainline Christians: Christ-centered living, the doctrine of the atonement, grace, justification by faith, and sanctification by the Spirit. These are all LDS doctrines; they are all Book of Mormon doctrines; they have always been part of our Scriptures and of our theology. However, in an understandable backlash against mainline churches who drove them from their homes and from the United States, many nineteenth-century Saints chose to distance themselves from traditional Christians and to exaggerate any differences that did exist. In this distancing, "orthodox" anti-Mormons have been only too happy to assist. Thus, much of the sermons and other homiletic material from the late nineteenth century recorded in the *Journal of Discourses* (which is *not* part of the LDS canon) has a distinctly different historical context and therefore a distinctly different flavor than the LDS Scriptures themselves or similar homiletic material from the late twentieth century.

President Benson, in returning us from a sometimes "popular" theology and homiletic to our scriptural roots, has at the same time returned the theological emphasis of the church to many things we *share* with other Christians. During my lifetime, and especially during the last decade, the instructions to members have consistently run along these lines: Never mind the *Journal of Discourses;* return to the Scriptures; stick to the Standard Works.

From our perspective this is not a change, any more than Protestants would see the Reformation as a change in the nature of Christianity. Rather it is a return to our scriptural base largely in response to Doctrine and Covenants 84:57 as interpreted by President Benson, "And they shall remain under this condemnation until they repent and remember the new covenant, even the Book of Mormon and the former commandments [the Bible] which I have given them." The only change precipitated by President Benson is that Mormonism now seeks to define itself in terms of its own canonized Scriptures rather than the sometimes polemical or speculative sermons of the nineteenth century or the popular theology of the twentieth century. I would argue that this is not an innovation but a course correction, a return to original headings. Inevitably, non-LDS will see it as a change in doctrine, but viewed from within the church it is merely a reemphasis on the basics—*our* basics.

Either way, it is true that the LDS Church is somewhat different today than it was a decade ago, largely as a result of President Benson's emphasis on the Book of Mormon. I find it highly revealing that as LDS theology has moved away from late nineteenth-century rhetoric to the specific doctrines of the Book of Mormon, it has also been perceived as moving *closer* to Evangelicals. Of course, as Prof. Blomberg has noted, this is because the Book of Mormon itself is fairly "orthodox" in its theology. Again, it is not usually the *doctrine* of the Book of Mormon that Evangelicals find offensive (if they have read it), but rather the book's claim to scriptural authority.

Finally, Prof. Blomberg goes on to fault the uniquely LDS Scriptures for failing the three criteria for Christian canonicity: apostolicity, agreement with previous Scripture, and widespread use and relevance in the churches. But once again, I must point out that these criteria are nonbiblical and therefore without much force in the LDS view. They are arbitrary post hoc explanations of what the "orthodox" churches in fact *do* to define the canon, not an authoritative formula—and certainly not a *biblical* formula—for what they *should* do. Indeed, as stated, criterion number three (widespread use) would by itself logically preclude any new document from ever being considered Scripture (as Blomberg himself points out). And any criterion that could under any circumstances and for any document produce only a negative judgment is not a criterion of judgment at all. These three criteria are nonbiblical, arbitrary, self-validating and therefore irrelevant. Give me some *biblical* criteria of canonicity that exclude the LDS Scriptures, and you create a problem for me. But these objections are based on extrabiblical assumptions, and there is no reason to believe the New Testament church would have agreed with them.

Moreover, Mormons would argue very strongly for the "apostolic" nature of their Scriptures. They would also insist that the "new" revelation of the Book of Mormon, etc., *does* agree with that found in the Bible—it just doesn't agree with the Hellenized theology of the church fathers. The perception that new Scripture agrees with old is itself a conclusion of faith rather than a conclusion from data. For example, I have many good Jewish friends who will resist most vigorously the proposition that the New Testament does not contradict the Old. For Evangelicals (and for Latter-day Saints) it does not, but that is because our common theology requires that it be so. Those without our common theology come, objectively and in good faith, to different conclusions. Unbiased (non-Christian) observers usually conclude that the Bible contains many contradictions. Christians have ways of explaining why apparent contradictions are not *really* contradictions, but these usually depend on a prior faith conviction that there can be no contradictions. Yet, I repeat, Mormons would agree with Evangelicals that new Scriptures must and do agree with older Scripture. As Latter-day Saints interpret the Old and New Testaments, there are no contradictions with the Book of Mormon.

From the LDS perspective, the LDS Scriptures are apostolic, they do agree with former Scriptures, and they are widely used and relevant among the congregations of The Church of Jesus Christ (of Latter-day Saints). I hope it can be seen that validation by the criteria proposed by Prof. Blomberg is a subjective matter, dependent on the faith orientation and assumptions of those who apply the criteria.

Misgivings About the Evangelical Position

What bothers me the most about the Evangelical doctrine of Scripture is that Evangelicals claim divine authority for statements *about* the Bible, which are not found *in* the Bible. Three claims about Scripture that Evangelicals often make to Latter-day Saints that we do not find sufficiently corroborated in the Bible are (1) the canon of Scripture is closed, (2) the present Christian canon is sufficient to answer all religious questions and (3) the Bible in and of itself conveys to those who read it the authority to act for God.

Professor Blomberg assures me that statement one is not a claim made by all knowledgeable Evangelicals and that on the basis of the biblical evidence the canon must be considered at least *in principle* to be still open (pp. 39-40). Well and good—but not many of the Evangelicals whom Latter-day Saints encounter seem to have gotten this message. I would be delighted if Evangelicals would say, "Well, I think it highly unlikely that the Book of Mormon could be inspired by God, and I don't personally believe it is, but there's always the faintest possibility, at least in principle, that it *could* be."

However, on the basis of the practice of the church (rather than any biblical warrant), Prof. Blomberg insists that the canon is functionally closed. This merely illustrates my earlier point: On the subject of canon the "orthodox" position is derived not from any biblical information but from tradition. While the strictly *biblical* data have left the canon open, the tradition of later "orthodoxy" has closed it—that is, they say things *about* the Bible that are not found *in* the Bible.

According to Prof. Blomberg, it makes Evangelicals nervous that Mormons add books to the canon. Well, it makes Mormons equally nervous that if God *did* choose to reveal or to restore something to the world, Evangelicals would be prevented from accepting it by their unbiblical conviction of sufficiency and their biblically unwarranted closing of the canon. If God did have something more to say, there is no way God could reach them with the information, and this because of a *traditional* belief not explicitly stated in Scripture. If the Bible only *said* that the Bible provides sufficient information and authority for salvation in the kingdom of God, the LDS would find that a more convincing case.

While *informed* Evangelicals would not declare the canon in principle to be closed or prophecy to be ended, on the popular level many other Evangelicals do make these claims. I will not press this, however, for in the pages that follow the shoe will often be on the other foot, and I will ask the reader and Prof. Blomberg to understand that scripturally informed Latter-day Saints hold a position on some things that is at odds with the "popular" understanding of many uninformed members.

Second, I find it troubling for Evangelicals to argue on the one hand that the Bible is the *sole* authoritative source of inspired information, and then to insist on the other hand that the Bible can only be interpreted within limits set by later councils and creeds. When they accuse Mormons of not believing the Bible, they usually mean that we do not believe interpretations formulated by postbiblical councils. If Evangelicals are going to insist on the doctrine of *sola scriptura* or *ad fontes*,[30] then they ought to stop ascribing scriptural authority to postbiblical traditions. *There is not a single verse of the Bible that I do not believe.* It is the postbiblical interpretation that I reject.

In my judgment Evangelicals, like all other Christians, accept much that has been added to the Bible—they just do not like to admit that they do. The "orthodox" distinctions, definitions and interpretations of the councils and creeds are specific additions to and intrusions on the biblical text. This is revealed by the demand not only that we Mormons believe the Bible but that we accept the councils and creeds as well. But Evangelicals can't have it both ways. If they are going to insist that there be no additions to the Bible at all (like the Book of Mormon, for example), then they cannot demand in the very next breath that Latter-day Saints accept the added doctrines of the councils and creeds in order to be Christians.[31] On the other hand, if they are going to invest the councils and creeds with the authority of God's word, then they probably ought to stop getting after us for adding the Book of Mormon to our canon.

Another area where Evangelical assumptions and definitions interfere with understanding LDS doctrine is in our doctrine of a universal apostasy of the true church. For Evangelicals, such an event would imply that after the apostasy and until the Restoration (1830) there were no true Christians or "sons of the kingdom" (see pp. 45-46, esp. n. 31). But the LDS do not believe this at all. While the "fullness" of the gospel was not available during that time, there was a knowledge of Christ, there was some light left in the world, and the "sons of the kingdom" were those who moved toward the light rather than away from it (like Luther, Calvin or Wesley), and who would have accepted more light if it had been available (see p. 153). In the LDS view the fullness of the gospel is ultimately necessary to salvation, but not necessarily in this life. I personally have many, many non-LDS friends, some of whom dislike my faith very much, with whom I fully expect to sit down along with Abraham, Isaac and Jacob in the kingdom of heaven (Mt 8:11). From the Evangelical point of view, the loss of the full gospel might necessarily mean the loss of all souls—but not in the LDS view.

On another issue, Latter-day Saints do not understand why Evangelicals seem to mistrust the direct guidance of the Holy Spirit in interpreting Scripture. I would judge it perilous to dismiss the direct answers of the Spirit to individual prayer, a course of action that was endorsed to me by several Evangelical friends in the past and that seems to be suggested above (p. 40). After all, it is the teaching of Scripture that God hears and answers prayers (Mt 21:22; Jn 11:22), even prayers for information and guidance (Jas 1:5). The individual believer is both instructed to ask (Mt 7:7-8; Lk 11:9; Jas 1:5) and promised an answer (Mt 21:22; Lk 11:10, 13; Jn 14:13-17; Jas 1:5). To suggest that such answers are untrustworthy or should be ignored when they conflict with *nonscriptural* traditions seems to me to be on perilously thin scriptural and spiritual ice.

Finally, it irritates the LDS that some Evangelicals keep trying to add the *Journal of Discourses* or other examples of LDS homiletics to the canon of LDS Scripture. The *Journal of Discourses* is not part of the LDS canon; it is a collection of nineteenth-century talks and sermons. It is often a valuable resource, but it does not have normative force in declaring LDS doctrine. Most of the anti-Mormon rhetoric coming from Evangelical circles focuses on the *Journal of Discourses* rather on our *Scriptures*—on what one or another nineteenth-century Mormon *may* have believed instead of on what all twentieth-century Mormons *must* believe. However, some of our own members make this same mistake, so I think the Evangelical confusion is understandable. Nevertheless, the parameters of LDS doctrine are clear—Scripture is normative; sermons are not. Almost anything outside the Standard Works is also outside those parameters.[32]

A More Positive Conclusion

If we can agree, and apparently we have, that (1) the canon of Scripture is, at least in principle, open and that (2) acceptance of the councils and their creeds *in addition to* the Bible is not a sine qua non for being authentically Christian, then the two major thorns will have been pulled from the collective LDS paw, so to speak, in their discussions with Evangelicals on the nature of Scripture. Latter-day Saints do not necessarily expect objective and sincere Evangelicals to be immediately persuaded of the truth of LDS Scriptures. People of good faith may in good faith not be so persuaded. But to insist in principle on the impossibility of the LDS Scriptures (other than the Bible) being authentic and to claim this on *biblical* grounds is a misrepresentation of what the Bible actually does and does not say. I personally would be happy to agree to disagree on this and many other subjects—just as I disagree with many Evangelical beliefs while granting that one might in good faith believe them without thereby rejecting God or the Bible as God's divine word.

It seems that Prof. Blomberg may be ready to make that same concession to the LDS, though he obviously thinks us wrong on many points, being willing to grant that the biblical language might consistently and in good faith be understood as the LDS understand it without thereby rejecting God or the Bible as God's word. This changes the discussion from "I am right, and no one who believes otherwise can do so without rejecting the Bible," which both sides find insulting, to "I grant that things *could* in good faith be interpreted your way, but I do not believe it is the *correct* interpretation." It would be agreeing to disagree, without attributing evil motives to each other for the disagreement. It would also be a step forward in LDS-Evangelical relations.

Joint Conclusion

[BLOMBERG & ROBINSON]

WE FIND ON THE TOPIC OF Scripture more agreement between us than we had expected to find. Both Blomberg and Robinson agree that all Scripture is "inspired" *(theopneustos)* of God. Moreover, we are closer to each other in our views of the nature of Scripture than either is to liberal Protestantism, maintaining alike that Scripture is literally true in its teachings, both historically and morally. We hold the same understanding of "inerrancy," though the LDS would use different terms to say the same things. We agree that the present biblical text is the word of God within the common parameters of the Chicago Statement and the eighth Article of Faith. At least some Evangelicals believe the canon of Scripture is open in principle, though virtually all believe it is closed in practice, while Mormons believe the canon to be open in both principle and practice.

We further agree that JST variants do not necessarily imply that the KJV text is corrupt. The present text-critical evidence does not support the claim of massive doctrinal revisions of the present biblical text. Since the available evidence establishes the text back only to the late second or early third century, such "revisions" either were made before that time or did not actually occur. We judge that changes or corrections in successive copies and editions of the LDS Scriptures are not a sufficient reason to judge those Scriptures inauthentic, since the biblical texts themselves were subjected to a similar process. We agree that assertions that are unbiblical are not necessarily contrabiblical, and we agree that if Joseph Smith and the LDS use the term *translate* to include interpretation, adaptation and application (as they do), then the issue in question becomes less one of text and becomes more one of Joseph's prophetic credentials.

Both Evangelicals and the LDS accept the beliefs and practices of the New Testament saints as normative for the modern church, and both are trying to replicate them, but we differ in our assessment of what those beliefs and practices may have been.

Finally, in principle both Evangelicalism and Mormonism ought to be defined by their canonical Scriptures, the Bible and the Standard Works (which includes the Bible), respectively. Supplemental material from either tradition ought not to be presented as the normative word of God or as authoritative beliefs.[1]

The major differences between the two of us on the doctrine of Scripture thus boil down to (1) the extent of the canon, (2) the authenticity of revelation received by Joseph Smith and his LDS successors and (3) whether or not any of that revelation actually contradicts previously revealed Scripture. We agree that appropriately modest and nuanced claims of modern revelation need not jeopardize the authority of the Bible, since prophecy is a gift of the Spirit and is consistent with a testimony of Jesus, and that authentic contemporary prophecy will be consistent with the doctrines of the Old and New Testaments. This chapter has not raised, for the most part, issues about the most distinctive *content* of the uniquely LDS Scriptures. For this we must proceed to our next three chapters.

2

God & Deification

[R O B I N S O N]

What Latter-day Saints Believe

In the LDS view God is omniscient, omnipotent, omnipresent, infinite, eternal and unchangeable. Besides all the biblical passages attributing these qualities to God (passages that the LDS accept as God's word), the Book of Mormon adds concerning God's omniscience, "O how great the holiness of our God! For he knoweth all things, and there is not anything save he knows it" (2 Nephi 9:20). Of God's omnipotence, Mosiah 3:5, also in the Book of Mormon, testifies, "For behold, the time cometh, and is not far distant, that with power, the Lord Omnipotent who reigneth, who was, and is from all eternity to all eternity, shall come down from heaven among the children of men." While God in the LDS view is not *physically* present in all things but rather spiritually present, I don't think this really differs very much from the Evangelical view in which God's omnipresence is likewise not a *physical* or *material* presence, but a *spiritual* presence.

In the LDS view, the "light" or spiritual power of Christ the creator fills the immensity of space and permeates all things (Doctrine and Covenants 88:11-14). It is his power and influence, which has its origin in the Father, that holds all creation in place atom by atom and moment to moment. The Doctrine and Covenants further states, "He comprehendeth all things, and all things are before him, and all things are round about him; and he is above all things, and in all things, and is through all things, and is round about all things; and all things are by him, and of him, even God, forever and ever" (Doctrine and

Covenants 88:41). The LDS Scriptures also assert, "By these things we know that there is a God in heaven, who is infinite and eternal, from everlasting to everlasting the same unchangeable God, the framer of heaven and earth, and all things which are in them" (Doctrine and Covenants 20:17). This is followed closely by the statement that "[the] Father, Son, and Holy Ghost are one God, infinite and eternal, without end" (Doctrine and Covenants 20:28).

My point in citing these few sources of the many that might be appealed to from LDS Scripture is that it just won't do to claim Mormons believe in a limited God, a finite God, a changeable God, a God who is not from everlasting to everlasting, or who is not omniscient, omnipotent and omnipresent. Such beliefs would violate the expressly stated official doctrines found in our own Scriptures.

Latter-day Saints also affirm that "the Father has a body of flesh and bones as tangible as man's; the Son also; but the Holy Ghost has not a body of flesh and bones, but is a personage of Spirit. Were it not so, the Holy Ghost could not dwell in us" (Doctrine and Covenants 130:22). We believe this not because it is the clear teaching of the Bible but because it was the personal experience of the prophet Joseph Smith in his first vision and because the information is further clarified for us in modern revelation. It is understandable that some Latter-day Saints would want to find this view of God the Father explicitly taught in the Bible, but I think Prof. Blomberg is correct in pointing out that it is not there (pp. 104-5). However, this is not because the Father is immaterial but because he has been represented in most things by his Son, the Word of God, acting as his agent or mediator in creation, in revealing his will to humans and in the work of redemption.

Latter-day Saints believe that *before* the incarnation of Jesus—during the Old Testament period—the God described in Scripture as Jehovah or Yahweh was God the Son (Jesus Christ), at that time still a spirit who had not yet entered into the flesh. In my view, it is unlikely that very many Israelites or Jews before Christ understood the true nature of the Godhead as Father, Son and Holy Spirit. For reasons I have explained above (pp. 66-67), I do not expect to find the true nature of the Godhead or the corporeality of God described clearly in the Old Testament, nor do I argue that it was once there and has been removed. I do maintain that the Bible makes no unambiguous statement about the materiality or immateriality of the Father, and that we may therefore think of him either as having a body or as not having a body without "contradicting" the Bible. Of course, the former does contradict Plato.

I also heartily affirm that God is *aoratos* (1 Tim 1:17) and that "no mere human being has ever seen or can see him" (see p. 97). However, the Greek word *horatos* means "seen." Its negation, *aoratos,* as at 1 Timothy 1:17, means "unseen" or "not seen." It means "invisible" in the sense of "unseeable" only by inference. Howard Hughes was "unseen" for many years without, I think, having become personally invisible. In regard to whether it is *possible* to see God under any circumstances, the term *aoratos* is ambiguous, since the most literal translation is "unseen" rather than "unseeable."[1]

In addition, no Mormon would propose that any "mere human being has ever seen or can see" God. To see God would incinerate mere mortals. But certain Scriptures, which the LDS take *literally,* but Evangelicals do not, confirm that "mere" human beings can be lifted by God above their "merely" human condition and then see God spiritually, as did Jacob (Gen 32:30), Moses (Deut 5:4; 34:10), Nadab, Abihu, the elders of Israel (Ex 24:9-11) and Isaiah (Is 6:1, 5). Jesus promises that humans who are not "merely human" but "pure in heart" *will* see God (Mt 5:8), as does Paul (1 Cor 13:12), so it can hardly be credible to deny the explicit promise of Christ and say that no human ever *can* see God. Of course one might insist that the limitations implied by the term *human* apply only in this life, not in eternity, so that Jesus' promise means that those who are "merely human" now will be something more in eternity and thus able to see God—but then one makes my case that the distinction between human and divine applies only in mortality (see p. 82).

Latter-day Saints believe that humankind is created in the image of God (Gen 1:26-28). We take this quite literally to mean that God has a physical image and that humanity is created *in* it. By definition, an image is the representation of physical qualities. As Adam is created in the likeness and image of God, so after the Fall Adam begets Seth in *his* own likeness and image (Gen 5:3). The language of orthodox Christians in making the "image" in which Adam was created a nonphysical image, a spiritual image, necessitates taking the word *image* figuratively. This is fine with me—the passage can be coherently interpreted that way—but it is another instance of the LDS's taking Scripture *literally* where the "orthodox" make it merely figurative and then charge *us* with being unbiblical!

In the matter of deification, Latter-day Saints believe that God intends through the gospel of Jesus Christ to transform those who are saved by Christ to be like Christ. Moreover, we believe that God will succeed in what God intends.[2] Since Latter-day Saints take seriously and literally the scriptural language about becoming the children of God (Rom 8:16), it makes sense to us that the children will grow up to be like their Father. According to Scripture, God is the Father of spirits (Heb 12:9). We are his offspring (Acts 17:29), and offspring grow up to be what their parents are.[3] Certainly through the atonement of Christ we have been begotten sons and daughters of God (1 Pet 1:13), we partake of his divine nature (2 Peter 1:4), and we have been designated heirs to all he has (Rom 8:15-17; Rev 21:7), which is all that the Father has (Jn 3:35). Latter-day Saints might again be charged here with taking the language of Scripture too literally, but the doctrine is scriptural, and the same passages of Scripture have led many others in the history of the Christian tradition to conclusions similar to those of the Latter-day Saints.

For example, long before Joseph Smith, Clement of Alexandria (c. 150-c. 215) could state that those who are perfected through the gospel of Christ "are called by the appellation of 'gods,' being destined to sit on thrones with the other gods that have been first installed in their places by the Savior."[4] It could of course be argued that Latter-day Saints have misinterpreted the evidence from the New Testament and the early Christian church in this case, but that is merely to stipulate that we disagree over how to interpret what is *in fact* New Testament and early Christian evidence. And in that case deification ought not to be considered some pagan idea that the Latter-day Saints have invented and imposed on the text, but as a biblical doctrine that may be, and has been, understood variously by different groups.[5]

After all, when Christ appears, the sons and daughters of God will be like him (1 Jn 3:2), changed into the same image from glory to glory (2 Cor 3:18). We receive his glory (Jn 17:22-23) and sit on his throne (Rev 3:21). We become joint heirs with Christ to all that the Father has (Rom 8:15-17; Rev 21:7; 1 Cor 3:22), and we partake of his divine nature (2 Pet 1:4). What could it possibly mean to "partake of the divine nature" if the divine nature is not extended to us and does not become part of us? To Latter-day Saints the glorified and resurrected Christ illustrates in his person what the saved can become through his grace. For us the logic of the Scriptures is inescapable: (1) Jesus Christ is divine, and (2) through the atonement and the grace of Christ the saved become one with Christ, become like him (1 Jn 3:2) and receive his image and glory (Jn 17:21-23; 2 Cor 3:18). Therefore, (3) through the atonement of Christ the saved become in some sense divine. If A equals B, and B equals C, how shall one resist concluding that A equals C?

Prof. Blomberg asserts that a key concern for Evangelicals is to preserve the distinction between the Creator and the creatures. This may be the heart of the disagreement between us, for Latter-day Saints maintain that God's work is to *remove* the distinctions and barriers between us and to make us what God is. We do not deduce this by philosophical argument; it is flatly stated in the New Testament:

> That they all may be one; as thou Father, art in me, and I in thee, that they also may be one in us: that the world may believe that thou hast sent me. And the glory which thou gavest me I have given

them; that they may be one even as we are one: I in them and thou in me, that they may be made perfect in one. (Jn 17:21-23)
We become one in them as they are one in each other. Whatever the relationship is between them, we can share it. Assuredly not as fallen mortals, but as saved, resurrected and glorified sons and daughters of God, we can participate in the life of God through God's grace and the atonement of Christ. If the redeemed really do become one with the Father and the Son, in the same way that they are one with each other (and the Scripture cannot be broken), then how can anyone deny that the redeemed share their divine attributes—even the so-called incommunicable attributes (p. 96)?[6] If God the Father communicates the attributes of God to the Son, and I am one with the Father and the Son in the same way they are one with each other, then their attributes—by the grace of God—become mine, that I may be *made perfect* and one with them. Once again, Latter-day Saints may be accused of taking the Scripture more literally than Evangelicals in this case, but we can hardly be called unbiblical.

The soil from which the LDS doctrine of deification grows is the belief that humans are of the divine species and that the scriptural language of divine paternity is not merely figurative. Is God our Father or not? Will we receive God's glory and sit on God's throne or not? Will we become one with God or not? Granted there is a gulf between fallen humanity and exalted divinity, but Mormons believe this gulf is bridged in Christ Jesus. In our fallen condition, we are utterly different, but in our saved and glorified state we will be what God is through God's grace, even in God's so-called incommunicable attributes.

The strict wall of separation between the human and the divine ("we aren't *really* his children; we can't *really* be like him") in my view is not *really* biblical but, once again, philosophical. It rests on the same objection to the clear sense of Scripture that led to the equally unbiblical doctrine of the two natures in Christ, which was added to historic Christianity by the Council of Chalcedon in A.D. 451. Scripture says that God in Christ became man, that "the Word was made flesh" (Jn 1:14), that "in all things it behoved him to be made like unto his brethren" (Heb 2:17). Nevertheless, Greek philosophy, the intellectual fashion of the day, demanded that the divine could not become truly human, and vice versa, since Plato had decreed that the human and the divine were mutually exclusive.[7] So the Council of Chalcedon *invented* a second nature for Christ, something never stated in the Bible, to satisfy the philosophers by keeping the human and the divine separate in Christ as Plato insisted they must be. According to Chalcedon, Christ's divine nature never became human, never suffered, never died—the claims of Scripture notwithstanding.[8]

Latter-day Saints reject all that. The Word was made flesh. In Christ, God became man. And if the divine can become fully human and then as human be raised up again to be fully God (Phil 2:6-11), then it is established that what is fully human may also be divine— Q.E.D. And by the grace of God we humans can also be raised up to be joint heirs of God with Christ (Rom 8:16-17). Christ is the example of what God finally desires of us and for us. It is God's intention, through the atonement and the gospel, to make us what Christ is and share with us what Christ has.

Most Evangelicals assume that the LDS belief in human deification is totally foreign to both biblical tradition and Christian history. But many in the history of the Christian church have seen that if the saved look like God, inherit all things from God, partake of the divine nature, sit on the throne of God, receive the image and glory of God, and rule and reign with God, such beings can rightly be referred to in some sense as gods.[9] On the other hand, it is important to understand that what defines the doctrine of deification for Latter-day Saints is a much smaller body of normative sources than most Evangelicals would think. Anticultists uniformly cite nonauthoritative LDS sources to define LDS doctrine, but apart from the Bible there are only three passages in LDS Scripture that deal directly with deification.

1. Doctrine and Covenants 76:58 describes those who are saved in

the celestial kingdom with these words: "Wherefore as it is written, they are gods, even the sons of God—Wherefore, all things are theirs, whether life or death, or things present, or things to come, all are theirs and they are Christ's, and Christ is God's." This is essentially a restatement of Psalm 82:6, John 10:34-36, Romans 8:38 and 1 Corinthians 3:22-23, so it should not be objectionable to Evangelicals.

2. According to Doctrine and Covenants 121:28, 32, in the last times, "A time [shall] come in the which nothing shall be withheld, whether there be one God or many gods, they shall be manifest . . . according to that which was ordained in the midst of the Council of the Eternal God of all other gods before this world was." But note that this is not a doctrine at all, strictly speaking. No proposition is asserted here about deification. Rather, it is merely a promise of an explanation of all things, including even the most speculative topics, at some future time which, I might add, has not yet arrived. The reference to "the Eternal God of all other gods" is not substantially different here, and therefore should be no more offensive to Evangelicals than the same construction in the Bible (e.g., Deut 10:17 or Ps 136:2).

3. This means that the main scriptural authority for the LDS doctrine of deification is to be found in section 132 of the Doctrine and Covenants. I know that other sources are often cited by both LDS and non-LDS writers, but most of these are noncanonical homiletic sources and have no binding force on the present LDS Church—the insistence of both conservative Mormons and rabid anti-Mormons notwithstanding. As a believing Latter-day Saint, I am not trying to minimize the importance of this doctrine to Mormons, but rather to correctly delineate the official sources for it.

The pertinent passage of section 132 (vv. 19-20) describes married couples who have entered into the covenant of the gospel and have been sealed to one another as eternal partners. The Scripture promises them that

they shall pass by the angels, and the gods, which are set there, to their exaltation and glory in all things, as hath been sealed upon their heads, which glory shall be a fulness and a continuation of the seeds forever and ever. Then shall they be gods, because they have no end; therefore shall they be from everlasting to everlasting because they continue; then shall they be above all, because all things are subject unto them. Then shall they be gods, because they have all power, and the angels are subject unto them.

From this one canonical source (Doctrine and Covenants 132:19-20) flow most of the commentary, sermons, expansions and speculations on this subject—all of them, I might add, without canonical standing. Surely Protestants understand the difference between the excellent interpretive writings of Luther, Calvin or Wesley on the one hand and the authority of the Bible itself on the other. The same difference exists between the homiletical statements and writings of Brigham Young or Orson Pratt on the one hand and the canonical Standard Works on the other. On this subject, speculative statements of Brigham Young, Orson Pratt, etc., that have not been canonized are not the official doctrine of the church.[10]

The official doctrine of the Church on deification does not extend in essentials beyond what is said in the Bible, with its Doctrines and Covenants parallels, and in Doctrine and Covenants 132:19-20.[11] Again, don't misunderstand me; there can be no doubt that the doctrine of deification is firmly and officially asserted by the LDS Church. I am only trying to sort out what is canonical from what is homiletical for the benefit of non-LDS readers, and also to show that most of the bizarre claims made on this topic by anticultists misrepresent speculation and homily as official pronouncements.

To the scriptural passages above I would add Lorenzo Snow's epigram[12] and Joseph Smith's statement in the funeral address for King Follett that God is an exalted man.[13] Neither statement is scriptural or canonized in the technical sense, and neither has been explained or elucidated to the church in any official manner, but they are so widely accepted by Latter-day Saints that this technical point has become moot. Each of these two quasi-official statements asserts flatly that there was once a time before the beginning of our creation when God was human, just as there will be a time after the final resurrection and judgment when exalted humans will be gods. One element in Jesus' ambiguous title "Son of Man" is his role as Son of the archetypical, heavenly Man in whose image all other men are created.[14]

What do Latter-day Saints mean by "gods"? Latter-day Saints do not, or at least should not, believe that they will ever be independent in all eternity from their Father in heaven or from their Savior Jesus Christ or from the Holy Spirit. Those who are exalted by his grace will always be "gods" (always with a small *g,* even in the Doctrine and Covenants) by grace, by an extension of *his* power, and will always be subordinate to the Godhead. In the Greek philosophical sense—and in the "orthodox" theological sense—such contingent beings would not even rightly be called "gods," since they never become "the ground of all being" and are forever subordinate to their Father.[15] Any teaching beyond this involves speculation without support from either the Bible or the other LDS Scriptures, and these are waters I refuse to swim in. I grant that some LDS do indulge in speculation on this point (it is a favorite jumping-off place for LDS fundamentalists)—but they go beyond the teaching of the LDS Church and the advice of LDS leaders when they do.

In truth, what God did before the beginning and what humans may do after the end are unfortunately not the subjects of biblical information. As Prof. Blomberg points out (p. 108), Joseph Smith is here not contradicting the Bible but rather filling in its theological gaps. Joseph may be right or wrong in doing this, but he cannot be accused of contradicting the Bible where the Bible is silent. There *are* gaps. I would be quite happy to have Evangelicals say to me, "You Latter-day Saints have beliefs and doctrines on subjects about which the Bible is silent or ambiguous." That is a fair statement. However, I believe it is unfair to say, "Since you hold opinions where the Bible is silent, you contradict the Bible," or, "Because you contradict Nicaea and Chalcedon, you contradict the Bible."

I suspect most Evangelicals would probably agree with Doctrine and Covenants 132:20 that those who inherit the kingdom of God have no end (Lk 1:33) and that they are above all things and have all things subject to them (1 Cor 3:21-22). The only real disagreement seems to be over whether such beings can be called "divine" in any sense. But if we are in agreement that through the atonement of Christ the saved can be conformed to his image, can be raised up and glorified with him, can sit on his throne and reign with him, then I would argue that the question of whether such beings should be called "divine" or not is merely a semantic quibble.[16] Besides, the Bible itself sets the precedent of calling those who exercise divine powers "gods" (e.g., Ex 7:1; Ps 82:1-6; Jn 10:34-36).[17]

If I believed that the saved carry harps and walk up and down streets of gold singing hymns all day (I don't), and if you believed they went fishing in the morning and played golf in the afternoon (you probably don't), one of us is surely wrong—but is either of us necessarily non-Christian as a consequence? Does being Christian require agreement, in the absence of specific biblical data, on what happened before the beginning or on what happens after the end? Latter-day Saints and Evangelicals may disagree about whether the saved in heaven live in family groups or not, or about whether they spend their time playing harps or building new worlds—but it ought to be our view of how the saved *become* saved, our Christology and soteriology, that determines whether we are Christians or not, rather than our views on what the saved do to "pass the time" in eternity.

To sum up, it is the official teaching of the LDS Church that God the Father has a physical body (Doctrine and Covenants 130:22). The belief that God the Father was once a human being rests mainly on two technically uncanonized sources (sermons of Joseph Smith and Lorenzo Snow) which have, however, in effect become normative. The church does teach officially that through the grace of God exalted humans, husbands and wives sealed to one another forever, will participate in the divine nature and exercise divine powers, including the power of creation—though remaining subordinate always to God. We choose to call such beings "gods" (with a small *g*), though Evangelicals find that term incorrect by Evangelical definitions and would prefer we use a different term.

Avoiding Misconceptions

Many Evangelicals are convinced, wrongly, that Latter-day Saints believe in a finite, limited or changeable God, even though that notion is repugnant to us. The explanation for this is that Evangelicals make certain *philosophical* assumptions about the nature of the universe and about what is possible and what is not possible that Latter-day Saints do not share. Much traditional Christian theology has been wedded to Greek philosophical categories and assumptions. Latter-day Saints just do not make the same assumptions.

For example, one such assumption I hear a lot is that if God were to possess a physical body, this would make divine omnipresence impossible; such a God would be "limited" or rendered "finite" by that body. Therefore, the argument continues, God as perceived by the LDS could not be omnipresent. But Latter-day Saints affirm only that the Father has a body, not that his body has him. The Father is corporeal and infinitely more, and if a spirit can be omnipresent without being *physically* present, then so can a God who possesses a body and a spirit.

The only real question is whether God can be present without being *materially* present, and both Evangelicals and Latter-day Saints say yes. If an immaterial God can be immaterially omnipresent, then a material God can also be immaterially omnipresent (even where his body is not), in the same way. Similarly, I would agree with 1 Kings 8:27 that God cannot be contained by an earthly temple or by heaven and earth themselves.[18] This is because God, with or without a physical body, is also *spiritually* omnipresent. God is Creator of heaven and earth, and God's power and influence permeate all things. Of course God cannot be contained by them! Again, God has a body, but God's body does not have him.

Evangelicals often point out biblical passages on these topics to me in a way that implies I might not know them or might not agree with them, but this is not the case. For me the Bible is the word of God. For example, Prof. Blomberg cites Numbers 23:19 against the LDS concept of God. But I do not believe God is a (mortal) man—or the son of one, or that God ever changes his mind—any more than Prof. Blomberg does. Yet neither do I think the author of Numbers intended here to provide information about what God may have been *before* the beginning of time, and therefore that is not really "what the Scripture affirms."

The insistence that the presence of a deity who possesses a physical body must somehow be limited to his material body is not biblical, and it is certainly not LDS. This is another assumption that comes from Greek philosophy. It has been my experience that when theologians want precise definitions for biblical terms and concepts, they go not to the Bible but to philosophy. When Latter-day Saints refuse to do this, we are not accused of being "unphilosophical," which is probably true, but of being "unbiblical," which is not true. Either way, I would argue that if the full divinity of Christ was not impaired or limited by his incarnation, then the assertion above is disproved—God *can* have a physical body and still be God, infinite and eternal. The incarnation of the Son proves this.

Please note that I am not arguing against the Evangelical doctrine of God. I am only insisting that the Evangelical view is influenced by certain logical assumptions that are not themselves found in the Bible. Absent those assumptions, the Bible is silent on the subject of the Father's materiality and therefore accommodates equally either the Evangelical or the LDS point of view.

In regard to the possibility that God was once a man in some prior eternity before the beginning of this one, let me point out that the Chicago Statement on Biblical Inerrancy stipulates that Scripture is only inerrant "in what it affirms." Though Scripture may use the phrase "four corners of the earth" (Is 11:12; Rev 7:1), it is apparently not the intent of the authors in these passages to affirm the squareness of the earth. Therefore, these passages cannot be used to argue that the earth is square. In the same vein, I suggest that no biblical passage intends to inform us about the condition or career of God before the beginning or after the end of eternity. The Bible neither affirms nor denies what God may or may not have done or have been in any theoretical prior eternity.

The biblical concept of "eternity" is problematic, and most constructions translated "forever" or "eternal" actually read "to the end of the age" or just "to the age." Indeed, the words usually rendered "forever" or "eternal" are the Greek and Hebrew words for "age" (*aiōn* and *'ôlām* respectively). First-century Jews understood eternity to consist of successive ages or eons—all within the parameters of the beginning and the end.

God is the *First* and the *Last,* the only being who exists from the beginning to the end (Is 44:6; Rev 1:8), that is, from the first moment of creation to the last. This is clearly a temporal frame. The phrase "before all ages" (Jude 25) simply means "from the beginning," from before the succession of ages began—before the clock started ticking. I firmly believe God did exist as God "before all ages" (from the beginning), but that still does not say anything about *before* the beginning. Certainly my understanding of "eternity" is different from that of the average Evangelical, but it is not without ancient precedent, nor is it internally inconsistent. So despite Prof. Blomberg's assertions (pp. 96-97), I still do not see that expressions like "the First and the Last" or "before all ages" affirm anything about conditions before the beginning or after the end of this creation.

I would agree completely with Evangelicals about the eternality of God—defining eternity as encompassing every *'ôlām* or *aiōn* from the beginning to the end. We apparently disagree on the immateriality of God, but I cannot find *immaterial* (another philosophical word) or its cognates in the Bible, and I do not think that the Bible states a clear opinion on this subject either. Prof. Blomberg essentially grants this point when he says, "God's immateriality and invisibility *we deduce* from numerous texts" (p. 97). Latter-day Saints might try (ill-advisedly) to deduce the Father's materiality from yet other texts, but the fact remains that the Bible does not make a clear statement one way or the other about the corporeality of the Father.

Nothing I say here should be interpreted as denying the importance for Mormonism of God's corporeality and God's nature as an exalted man. Neither am I denying the importance of LDS belief that we humans are literally God's children and can become what God is. These are linchpins in LDS theology. However, more important, more in evidence, more often preached, more often studied, explained and pondered by the Latter-day Saints are the more central doctrines of the gospel of Christ.

In summary, I believe the dispute here boils down to a disagreement over topics on which the Bible is silent. The LDS believe something about what God may have been before the beginning. Evangelicals do not believe it because it is not stated in the Bible. Such a belief as the LDS hold implies to Evangelicals that God cannot be infinite now; to Mormons it implies no such thing—certainly we believe no such thing. Latter-day Saints believe that the scriptural promises about the state of the exalted after their resurrection justify the label "gods." Evangelicals do not deny the biblical promises, but they do not like the label "gods" being applied to such beings. Latter-day Saints believe that after the end these "gods" will, by God's grace, be engaged in the sorts of activities that God engages in now. Evangelicals do not believe this because the Bible does not say it. This is not strictly speaking a doctrinal "conflict," though it is distinctly a doctrinal "difference."

To those who are offended by Joseph Smith's suggestion that God the Father was once, before the beginning, a man, I point out that God the Son was undoubtedly once a man, and that did not compromise his divinity. The incarnation proves, in the person of the Son at least, that God is, indeed, a corporeal being. It also proves that humanity and divinity are not incompatible categories,[19] nor should it offend us that God can cross over the line to our side, or that God by his grace can take us across the line to God's side as well. Surely the finite cannot of itself become infinite, but does the infinite not bestow infinity upon the finite with which it is joined together in one?

Misgivings About Evangelical Beliefs

Evangelicals often accuse Latter-day Saints of believing in a limited, finite or changeable God, but there is absolutely nothing in LDS Scriptures or LDS beliefs to justify such a charge. I have never heard any such propositions stated in my church—*never!* Evangelicals come to these conclusions only when they attempt to impose their Platonic assumptions and categories on LDS theology. For example, it may seem incorrect by Platonic philosophical standards to believe both in the materiality of God and in the omnipresence of God. Nevertheless, that is what Mormons believe. We simply reject the philosophical assumptions adopted by Evangelicals about the nature of reality— about what God can and cannot do or be. The LDS are troubled by the fact that the God of Christian "orthodoxy" is virtually indistinguishable from the God of the Hellenistic philosophers.[20]

If I understand Prof. Blomberg one of his major objections to the LDS view seems to be that finite beings cannot become infinite, and that infinite beings cannot ever have been finite—good Platonic thinking. I simply point out that this objection is philosophical rather than biblical. *Why* can't the finite become infinite, or vice versa, other than that the idea contradicts Plato's assumptions about the nature of things?

Other Evangelicals have charged, on the basis of statements made by Joseph Smith and Lorenzo Snow to the effect that God was once a man, that the Mormon God is *"merely* a man." But again, I have never heard God referred to in all my days as "just a man" or "merely a man." No Mormon would say such a thing. God is *God,* and Mormons attribute to God every honor, power, glory and perfection that Evangelicals do.

Evangelicals, however (the precedent of Jesus' incarnation not-withstanding), assume that no being that has ever been finite could ever become infinite—again, a nonbiblical, philosophical assertion. But let us take a nice finite quantity like the number 10, for example, and pose a simple problem in math. What is the sum of 10 plus infinity? The mathematically correct answer is *infinity*. So what do I amount to, finite though I am now, if I genuinely become one with the infinite Father and Son (Jn 17:21-23)? Christ can make the finite infinite.

Once again, if Latter-day Saints and Evangelicals will confine themselves to what the Bible actually says, *in the language in which the Bible actually says it,* we will find we have surprisingly little on which to disagree, and most of the disagreement will be on topics where Mormons have added information to fill a biblical void. Well I know that Evangelicals are troubled by such "prophetic" additions, but Latter-day Saints are just as troubled by the philosophical extrapolations that Evangelicals add to the Bible from councils and creeds. I must insist that if the Bible really *meant* what the Nicene Creed means concerning the nature of God, then the Bible would have *said* what the Nicene Creed says—but of course it does not.[21] For the LDS it is highly problematic that the Evangelical doctrine of God cannot be expressed in its fullest form without abandoning biblical terminology and adopting instead the language of philosophy. Latter-day Saints see this as an unequal yoking of the biblical word with the "wisdom of this world" (1 Cor 3:19).

Another source of LDS negativism toward Evangelicals is their apparent unwillingness to distinguish official, canonical, mainstream Mormonism in its actual twentieth-century persona—how the LDS do *now* actually define themselves to themselves—from the caricature constructed by anticultists, which is based on unofficial, noncanonical or speculative sources (mostly from the nineteenth century). It would be helpful if Evangelical criticisms of current LDS beliefs and practices would use currently accepted LDS language and sources.

A More Positive Conclusion

The LDS will be pleased to learn, as I have been, that in theory at least,

Christian orthodoxy should be defined by the Bible alone, rather than by the Bible and the creeds in conjunction, and that believing the creeds should not be considered a prerequisite for salvation. If Evangelicals generally will grant this, then our faiths become in large part two different ways of interpreting common Scriptures, and we can then, perhaps even as friends, agree to disagree with each other.

Also, if Evangelicals generally will recognize the LDS right to declare and define our own faith, as Prof. Blomberg seems willing to do, instead of dictating to us what it is (and getting it wrong), perhaps we can move past the absurd deadlock of "what Mormonism is" to the real issues of how we agree, how we differ, and where we stand in relationship to each other.

Finally, the LDS need to do a better job of identifying correctly which of their beliefs originate in the Bible and which originate from modern revelation. We need to stop imposing concepts from the Restoration on biblical passages that do not really accommodate them very well (e.g., Gen 18:33 as hard evidence for the corporeal nature of God).[22] After all, if we insist on the one hand that "plain and precious things" were taken out of the Bible, we probably should not also insist, on the other hand, that they are all clearly still there!

God & Deification

[BLOMBERG]

What Evangelicals Believe

"As man now is, God once was; as God now is, man may be." Quoting this famous couplet by Lorenzo Snow, fifth president of the LDS church, Stephen Robinson writes, "It is indisputable that Latter-day Saints believe that God was once a human being and that human beings can become gods."[1] These statements bring us to the two doctrines that we are examining in this chapter: the past and present nature of God and the future nature of redeemed humanity.

Evangelicals often speak of the God of Israel who revealed himself throughout the period of Old Testament history as "the Father." But this term for God rarely appears in the Old Testament. When it does, it usually refers to God's relationship with Israel *as a nation* (as in Deut 32:6; Is 64:8; Mal 2:10). But Jesus, particularly in John's Gospel, repeatedly distinguished himself as the Son of his heavenly Father (for example, Jn 5:19-48; 6:29-59; 8:18-58). Mark 14:36 preserves the Aramaic term *abba* as Jesus' characteristic form of address to God. This was a strikingly intimate term for a Jew to use, almost equivalent to our "Daddy," and it has been the Christian claim ever since that Jesus made possible a new and uniquely intimate access to the Father through his atoning death (see esp. Heb 4:16). In this chapter we focus on the first person of the Godhead, God the Father. In chapter three we will take up questions of who Christ was as well as the trinitarian debates more generally.

Evangelicals and the LDS hold many beliefs in common that are worth noting. God is Creator, Revealer, Sustainer of the universe. God is active in initiating the plan of salvation for humanity and ultimately, through the Holy Spirit, is the power and person behind the redemption, sanctification and glorification of all human beings who trust in Christ. The key area of debate, however, has to do with what God is like. Classically, this question has been unpacked by means of a discussion of the "attributes" of God.

A representative list of God's attributes as enumerated in a recent major work of evangelical theology includes "spirituality, personality, life, infinity, constancy, holiness, righteousness, justice, genuineness, veracity, faithfulness, benevolence, grace, mercy and persistence."[2] Another pair of writers organizes God's attributes under six headings:

Metaphysically, God is self-existent, eternal, unchanging [and omnipresent].

Intellectually, God is omniscient, faithful and wise.

Ethically, God is holy, just, merciful and loving.

Emotionally, God detests evil, and is long-suffering and compassionate.

Volitionally, God is free, authentic, and omnipotent.

Relationally, the transcendent divine being is immanent universally in providential activity and immanent with his people in redemptive activity.[3]

The best-known categorization of God's characteristics stems from the distinction that Protestant Reformers made between "communicable" and "incommunicable" attributes. The former include attributes that Scripture teaches humans can share, to a partial extent in this life and then fully in the life to come, such as holiness, love, justice, mercy and so on. The latter refer to attributes that Scripture teaches are unique to God, particularly the three "omnis": omnipotence, omniscience and omnipresence.

Historic Christianity—Protestant, Catholic and Eastern Orthodox branches alike—has always included two other features of God's nature under the incommunicable attributes: eternality and immateriality. Here we come to the heart of traditional Christianity's disagreement with Mormonism on the doctrine of God. We believe the Scriptures to teach that there is only one being in the universe who has always existed, and who existed in eternity past in immaterial form. Ephesians 3:21 ascribes glory to God "throughout all generations,[4] for ever and ever," while Isaiah and Revelation both refer to God as the First and the Last, the Being who existed when there were no others and "apart from whom there is no God" (Is 44:6; cf. Rev 1:8). This God does not change—at least not to the extent of ever having once been finite or human (Num 23:19—"God is not a man that he should lie, nor a son of man, that he should change his mind"). We read texts like Psalm 90:2 ("from everlasting to everlasting you are God") or Jude 25 ("to the only God our Savior be glory, majesty, power and authority, through Jesus Christ our Lord, *before all ages,* now and forevermore"[5]) and see no evidence for interpreting them to mean anything other than that God has always existed as the one supreme, uncaused Being who alone is worthy of worship. An expression like "before all ages" does seem to contradict Mormon theology; it is not merely the case that the LDS fill in the gaps where Scripture is silent (though this is *often* the case).

God's immateriality and invisibility we deduce from numerous texts. John 4:24 declares "God is spirit,"[6] which by itself does not prove that God might not have a "spiritual body." But *in context* Jesus is pointing out the irrelevance of the debate that existed between Jews and Samaritans over where to worship God—in Jerusalem or on Mount Gerizim. Jesus' point is that God is everywhere, and so it does not matter where we worship him. But the omnipresence of the Father (see esp. Ps 139) is hard to square with having a body; how can God be everywhere present, not just by the Spirit, but in a body, at one and the same time? Similarly, we read that no human building can contain God, *not even the totality of earth and heaven* (1 Kings 8:27), that God is invisible[7] (1 Tim 1:17), and that no mere human being can see or ever has seen God (1 Jn 4:12[8]; Jn 1:18[9]).

Evangelicals are determined to preserve the distinction between the Creator and the creation, particularly in light of Paul's teaching in Romans 1:18-32 that the heart of idolatry and rebellion against God is to worship the creature rather than the Creator. We are mindful, too, of the second of the Ten Commandments (Ex 20:4), which forbade the Israelites to make any graven image of their God, in sharp differentiation from the pagan, polytheistic cultures surrounding them. If God were an exalted man, why should this matter? One might argue that physical images *could* become objects of worship in and of themselves, but surely they *need* not. After all, Catholics retain their crucifixes of Christ and the Orthodox their icons of biblical scenes *without necessarily* abusing them. But if God is essentially immaterial, then the commandment makes sense: no material representation of the Father can adequately reflect God's glory and any attempt to make one, however well-intentioned, is inherently idolatrous.

How then can an immaterial God reveal himself? As one who is all-powerful, God can make himself heard through audible voices and can make himself seen through temporary visions, as occurs periodically throughout the Scriptures, without demonstrating that *by nature* God has a body.[10] To be sure, the Hebrew writers used what are called anthropomorphisms—language about God's hand, finger, face or back—to describe God's activity, but Hebrew scholars are virtually unanimous in recognizing these as vivid figures of speech, never intended to be taken literally.[11] That is why, for example, Matthew 12:28 can reword and yet faithfully interpret Jesus' teaching in Luke 11:20—"if I drive out demons by the finger of God"—as "if I drive out demons by the *Spirit* of God." Even Mormons presumably recognize this when it comes to descriptions of God as being like a mother hen and as having wings and feathers (e.g., Ps 17:8; 36:7; 57:1; 61:4; 68:13; 91:4).

With the incarnation of Christ, however, historic Christianity affirms that something new took place within the Godhead. *God himself,* not merely some sort of preexistent spirit being waiting for a body, took upon himself human flesh. That is why John 1:1 reads, "In the beginning was the Word, and the Word was with God, and the Word was God,"[12] while verse 14 goes on to add, "the Word became flesh and made his dwelling among us." Throughout the New Testament, Jesus is God's Word and therefore God's way of revealing his very self to humanity (e.g., Jn 14:9-10, in which Jesus and the Father are said to be "in" each other; see also Mt 11:27-28). *"God was in Christ reconciling the world to himself"* (2 Cor 5:19 KJV). After citing similar passages in John 17, Evangelical theologian Millard Erickson comments, "There is apparently an interpenetration and closeness in the relationship of Father and Son like that of Christ to the believer and of believer to believer, except taken to the infinite degree." It is this interpenetration and closeness, he goes on to note, that guards against tritheism—the idea that Father, Son and Holy Spirit are entirely distinct or separate individuals.[13]

Prior to the conception and birth of Jesus, then, the Godhead had never previously contained a person with a permanently human nature; from now on it would (see also Col 1:19; 2:9). We do *not* argue that Jesus was simultaneously incarnate and omnipresent. Instead, we claim that there was more to God than Jesus, lest there be no spiritually omnipresent Being left to rule the universe. Jesus had a fully divine nature, inseparable from the Father's divine and essentially immaterial nature. But Jesus was also aware of a center of personal, divine consciousness outside himself, so that, for example, when he prayed, he was conscious of praying to the Father as distinct from merely praying to himself.

The early Christian church wrestled with how to preserve the unity of Father and Son without overly confusing or overly separating them. Their discussion employed terminology that is not found in the Bible, but the *concepts* expressed by their language were firmly grounded in the New Testament, especially the Gospel of John. We will come back to this topic in chapter three, but for now we may simply summarize by saying Evangelicals believe Mormons have overly separated the Father and the Son. Without wrenching Father and Son asunder, it is impossible to assert that God had a human body before the incarnation.[14] And may the reader please note that none of this discussion has appealed to the statements of the early creeds or councils or to any concepts of Plato or other Greek philosophers. We Evangelicals may be wrong in what we "deduce" from Scripture, but it *is Scripture* that we believe we are exegeting.

Turning to the issue of deification, a key question concerns what the Bible means when it asserts that humans were created "in the image of God." Although the three main branches of Christendom continue to discuss this issue, they can be said to agree that God's image does *not* refer to a physical or bodily form. No text of Scripture ever asserts this. Scripture does link humans as bearers of the divine image with their task in exercising dominion over creation (Gen 1:26,

28), with their ability to form relationships in community (1:27), and above all with their capacity for receiving divinely revealed truth, leading to righteous and moral living in relationship with their Creator (Col 3:10; Eph 4:24).[15] Even more specifically, 2 Corinthians 3:18 speaks of Christians being re-created in God's image as successively approximating God's "glory." In that identical context, Paul alludes to Exodus 33—34, in which God reveals his glory to Moses in terms of God's communicable attributes: "The LORD, the compassionate and gracious God, slow to anger, abounding in faithfulness, maintaining love to thousands, and forgiving wickedness, rebellion and sin. Yet he does not leave the guilty unpunished" (Ex 34:6-7). So it seems clear that humans' unique capacity, among the entire animal kingdom, for moral, interpersonal relationships with one another and with God constitutes the heart of what it means to be created in God's image.[16]

This line of reasoning is confirmed by one additional observation. The image of God carried by human beings was seriously marred as a result of the Fall. It is still present in them, after both the Fall and the flood (Gen 5:3; 9:6; Jas 3:9), but it has been so corrupted that when a person becomes a Christian, the image must be progressively re-created, beginning in this life (Col 3:10; Eph 4:24). But our physical bodies are hardly reenergized as we grow older. They deteriorate. It is our inward spiritual lives that are renewed daily (2 Cor 4:16). So the image of God in humanity can have nothing to do with our bodies or our physical form. Therefore, the creation of humans with bodies proves nothing about God the Father's having a body.

On the other hand, we certainly do look forward to perfected, re-created, resurrected, glorified and exalted bodies that Christ will give us when he returns (1 Cor 15). Does this mean that we become gods or that we become like God? The early church, like Eastern Orthodoxy throughout its history, felt much freer than Protestantism or Catholicism has felt to speak of believers' deification, divinization, or even of their becoming gods or godlike.[17] To be sure, 2 Peter 1:4 speaks of believers receiving God's "very great and precious promises, so that through them you may participate in the divine nature and escape the corruption in the world caused by evil desires." And of course there are the texts that both Mormons and Eastern Orthodox like to cite: John 10:34 and the passage that it quotes, Psalm 82:6, "I have said you are gods."

But in context 2 Peter 1:4 is clearly talking about becoming like God *morally,* not metaphysically. The previous verse declares that God's divine power has given us everything we need for life *and godliness.* Verse 4 itself links participating in the divine nature with escaping the corruption of the evil world. And verse 5 continues with the encouragement to add to one's faith goodness, knowledge, self-control, perseverance, godliness, brotherly kindness and love.[18] The context never blurs the ontological distinction between Creator and creature.

The passages in John and Psalms are even more limited in their application. In Psalm 82:1 "God presides in the great assembly; he gives judgment among the gods." This most likely refers either to God's council among angelic creatures or to God's declaration to a gathering of mighty men and judges on earth—two well-attested Old Testament uses for the term "gods."[19] In view of the conclusion of the Psalm (esp. v. 7, "You will die like mere men"), the latter seems more probable. But in any case, the context of the psalm refers not to anyone's *exaltation* but to the *judgment and downfall* of those who defend the unjust and show partiality to the wicked (v. 3). Jesus' point, then, in quoting this text in John's Gospel is that if the Jews acknowledge in their Scripture that certain kinds of men, even wicked ones, can be called gods, they should not object, simply on the basis of the word itself, if he also claims to be God or God's Son. In other words, the term by itself need not designate anything more than a mighty person (cf. Ex 7:1[20]). We would not dispute, of course, that Christ goes on to apply the concept of deity to himself in a stronger sense, but that is not his point *in this passage.*

For the most part, historic Christianity, when it has spoken of believers becoming gods or becoming godlike, has preserved the necessary distinction between Creator and creature. We can come to share perfectly in God's communicable attributes, but we can never usurp God's unique role by becoming all-powerful, all-knowing or all-present. To be "like God" is different from "becoming" or "being" God (or being identical in kind to God). We will never be objects of worship in our own right. We are never told in Scripture that we will be able to create worlds; only God is said to do that. So we have no problem with Prof. Robinson's list of New Testament passages that show how we will become like God or Christ (pp. 80-81), as long as no one is tempted to predicate anything of believers that would infringe on God's unique omnipotence.[21] What we are concerned most to preserve is God's distinctive as the only Being in the universe—Father, Son and Holy Spirit—worthy of eternal adoration. This is the glorious picture we see in the book of Revelation—heavenly beings falling down before God's throne, with Christ standing in its center, acknowledging God in Christ alone as worthy to receive all glory, honor, power, wisdom, strength and blessing (Rev 4:11; 5:4, 9-10, 12-13).

Avoiding Misconceptions

Evangelical theologians and philosophers continue to debate precise definitions of many terms that we use to describe God, and they try not to define one so that it jeopardizes the existence of another.[22] For example, divine omnipotence does not mean that God can create a stone so big God can't lift it or that God can sin. Omnipotence means that "God can do anything that is an absolute possibility (i.e., is logically possible) and not inconsistent with any of his basic attributes"[23] (e.g., holiness). Divine immutability (unchangeableness) does not mean that God cannot be affected by our prayers or that the nature of events in this world cannot genuinely change as a result of those prayers. Rather, immutability stresses God's faithfulness in keeping his word (Ps 89:34-35; 2 Tim 2:13).

Most Evangelicals agree that the old Greek and Latin emphases on "impassibility" led to misconceptions about God's not having emotions. Historically the term *impassibility* referred to God's inability ever to be merely a *passive* rather than an active agent. But that definition has often been lost sight of. Nor do we claim to have solved God's relation to time; does God exist eternally separate from it, eternally acting within it, or somewhere in between? The very fact that we are finite creatures operating within the world of time makes it impossible even to conceptualize or to speak of "before" or "after" time without using temporal terminology, so it is not likely that we will solve these issues on this side of eternity!

Further, we acknowledge that Jesus genuinely "grew in wisdom and stature, and in favor with God and men" (Lk 2:52) and that "he learned obedience from what he suffered" in order to be made perfect (Heb 5:8-9). There is a kind of perfection that comes only through experience. Prior to the incarnation, no member of the Godhead had ever experienced the limitations of a bodily nature; therefore, Jesus truly had to grow and had to learn what it was like to be human.[24] We acknowledge that the early church, with its infusion of Greek and Roman ideas, at times lost sight of the more "dynamic" concept of God that the Hebrews had bequeathed to Christianity, and we roundly reject all Hellenistic attempts to deprecate either the body or the material world as inherently evil. Donald Bloesch offers a good summary of the balances we seek to preserve:

An authentically evangelical theology will uphold the supremely personal God of biblical religion over the suprapersonal God of speculative philosophy on the one hand and the crudely personal God of culture-religion on the other. It will side with the transcendent God of the prophets over the immanent God of the mystics. It will proclaim the infinite God of the historic catholic faith over the finite God of modernistic theology. . . . The true God is the holy, majestic Lord who gives himself in love but who demands our faith and love in return.[25]

Despite the insistent media portrayal of the Christian hope in the life to come as some boring, ethereal existence, usually replete with clouds and harps, we look forward to nothing less than the re-creation of the entire heavens and earth (Rev 21—22). The ultimate destiny of redeemed humanity is life in community, with all believers sharing a kind of intimacy that is even better than what spouses experience with each other in the marriage relationship. We believe, following Jesus' teaching, that in the life to come we, like angels, will not be sexually active beings (Mt 22:30). We do not hold this belief because we consider sex evil (as certain forms of traditional Catholicism often did), but because we assume that the relationships all Christians will have with each other will make the excitement of sex pale in comparison! We imagine that the new heavens and new earth will contain opportunities for productive work, learning and the cultivation of myriads of new friendships. Above all, it will afford opportunities for pure, unbroken, exhilarating worship of the one and only true Creator God.[26]

Misgivings About Mormon Doctrines of God and Deification

Clearly, our major concern over the LDS beliefs about God the Father is the claim that God was once a man and that God now has a body. It is reassuring that Prof. Robinson notes how slender is the scriptural thread on which these doctrines hang, even including the LDS Scriptures, but this cautionary note does not seem to be widely echoed. Consider, for example, the well-known reference work *A Topical Guide to the Scriptures of the Church of Jesus Christ of Latter-day Saints.* Under the heading "God, Body of (Corporeal Nature)" appear no fewer than forty-three entries![27] Upon closer inspection, however, sixteen of these passages refer to humans or to Christ's being created in God's image, which as I have already noted has no demonstrable connection to physicality. Eleven involve anthropomorphisms, and twelve refer to the incarnate or exalted Christ, which is irrelevant to the question at hand. Two merely speak of God as "living," and one passage simply says "the Lord went his way." As Robinson notes, that leaves only Doctrine and

Covenants 130:22 of the strictly canonical sources.[28]

Given the conviction held by both Prof. Robinson and the Evangelicals—that Jesus is both fully God and fully man—it is not theologically objectionable to speak of humanity in the Godhead per se. Belief in the humanity of God the Father could then be viewed merely as a curiosity, if it were not for the additional claim that God was once a *finite* human.[29] This is what seems to compromise God's sovereignty and metaphysical uniqueness, characterized by God's omnipotence, omniscience and omnipresence. There seems to be no way for finite beings *by themselves* ever to become infinite.[30] It is one thing for an infinite God to voluntarily restrict himself to certain limitations of finitude. It is quite another for a finite being to become infinite unless by means of some more powerful agent.[31] That realization appears to me to be the reason unofficial Mormonism developed its notion of the Creator God as merely one among other gods, who was created by them. But then we find ourselves in the logical quagmire of asking who created those gods, and so on, ad infinitum.[32] At this point we find ourselves face to face with polytheism, which the Bible defines as idolatry. Robinson helpfully repudiates this popular misconception, but it is not clear how he can do so and *consistently* still believe in a finite man on his own becoming God. Please note that none of this argument depends on distinctively Hellenistic philosophy; it is a matter of universal logic of the kind to which Robinson himself appeals (pp. 81, 83).

We also see striking parallels between Joseph Smith's thought and developments in nineteenth-century liberal theology that eventuated in this century in what is known as process theology—God evolving as God oscillates between finite and infinite poles of existence.[33] Ironically, this line of theologizing is more akin to the Greek or Hellenistic thought that Mormons like to accuse the early church of emulating than to anything that can be demonstrated from the Old or New Testament.[34] What is more, it is hard not to suspect an evolution of Joseph Smith's own beliefs, since the Book of Mormon contains no clear affirmation of the humanity or the finitude of God the Father. The Doctrine and Covenants introduces the former, and Joseph's 1844 funeral sermon for Elder King Follett the latter.[35] Nevertheless, Robinson again proves encouraging by noting that no text of the LDS Scriptures or any other revelation *officially and canonically* teaches this doctrine of a once-mortal god (other than, of course, the human Jesus).

The same is true of Brigham Young's "Adam-God" theory. Evangelicals usually fear the worst when they hear popular-level Mormon conversation or read high-level, albeit unofficial, pronouncements about Adam as becoming the god of this world or as being identical with God the Father.[36] Again we are grateful for Robinson's complete dissociation of himself and official Mormonism from these interpretations of Brigham Young's statements.[37] Still, it remains a little disconcerting to read him quote all of the early church fathers who made pronouncements similar to the couplet of Lorenzo Snow (see pp. 80-81 and 209 n. 9), without noting that every one of them was referring to the *incarnation* when they said "as man now is God once was," not to a prehistoric period in which God the Father was a mere mortal, as popular Mormonism has often professed.[38]

At some point along the way, too, Evangelicals must raise serious questions about the story of Joseph Smith's walk in the woods. He saw what he believed to be both Father and Son appearing to him in bodily form (Joseph Smith—History 1:17) and condemning the creeds of Christendom without remainder (v. 19). In this situation it would have been absolutely crucial for Joseph to "test the spirits" (1 Jn 4:1). And how better to do this than to compare this revelation with all previous known revelations from God? If nowhere in the Old or New Testament or in the history of Christian experience had God the Father ever appeared to anyone together with Christ *in two separate bodies,* why was Joseph not immediately skeptical of what he saw? Where, for that matter, is there any evidence that he *ever* tried to apply any objective criteria to assess the source of the vision he had seen? Even Peter needed a threefold repetition of a vision from God and a supernaturally timed encounter with Cornelius to be convinced that God was actually rescinding the Old Testament dietary laws (Acts 10:13-17)!

Regarding the issue of human deification, if all Mormons mean by it is that we are re-created in God's image, perfect in holiness and immortal in nature, with physically resurrected and glorified bodies, then we join hands with them in looking forward to such a wonderful day. If, however, they mean that humans can take on God's being and God's incommunicable attributes (or the ability to create or to redeem), then we demur, claiming that they have not adequately preserved the distinction in essence between the creature and the Creator.[39] Robinson's own language seems appropriately nuanced when he insists that "the Latter-day Saints do not believe that human beings will ever become the equals of God, or be independent of God, or that they will ever cease to be subordinate to God." But in the same context he writes about the promise in 1 Corinthians 3:21 (we shall inherit all things) that this includes "the power to create and to beget."[40] The phrase "all things" in Paul's context, however, refers to spiritual blessings, not godlike powers.[41]

The common Evangelical *perception,* and we hope we are mistaken, is that Mormons talk a whole lot more about the process of human exaltation than about the eternal worship of a one-of-a-kind God. Their focus seems to be human-centered rather than God-centered, as men and women are strongly encouraged to marry and have large families, either so that their eternal families will be off to a good start in populating planets and ruling worlds (a more aberrant LDS perspective) or so that they may provide more bodies for spirits waiting to be born (a more mainstream belief). Granted that these views of what humans do in their exalted state do not necessarily contradict any really crucial or foundational truths of the Bible, neither does any of it appear in the Bible, and it seems to the outsider at least to diminish the central focus of biblical revelation. As the Westminster Confession so aptly captured it, "The chief end of man is to glorify *God* and to enjoy him forever."

Above all, as with the doctrine of Scripture, it is difficult for Evangelicals to imagine the doctrines of God and deification that the LDS promote as God's true revelation on the topic. It seems more plausible to suggest that Joseph Smith was understandably frustrated with the gaps in God's revelation, the enigmas surrounding God's nature and attributes, the theological impasses at which historic Christianity had arrived, and the inanity of popular Christian conception of the afterlife. Mormonism tidily "solves" each of these problems, and for that very reason should be suspect. Why would anyone in antiquity ever have exchanged such a neat and orderly system for one that leaves the unanswered questions that remain in the Bible and early Christianity? How could all traces of those original answers have disappeared? The principle of the "harder reading" (see pp. 52-53) again makes it far more likely that the LDS doctrines reflect a human unwillingness to accept the number of "loose ends" contained in God's Word and a desire to tie them all down with subsequent "revelation." Ought we not expect that a God capable of creating the universe, a God who declares that his ways and thoughts are as high above fallen humanity's musings as the heavens are above the earth (Is 55:7-9), would be beyond our full comprehension at more than one key point?[42]

A More Positive Conclusion

Despite all my misgivings with popular, unofficial LDS emphases, Prof. Robinson has successfully distinguished his type of Mormon orthodoxy from the stereotypes that concern Evangelicals the most. Where some cite Scripture irresponsibly to make it appear that dozens of texts, even in the Bible, support the corporeality of God the Father, Robinson recognizes that the doctrine is explicit only in the account of Joseph Smith's first vision and in one other passage in the canonical LDS Scriptures, Doctrine and Covenants 130:22. Similarly, the unique slant of the LDS on deification, he insists, boils down, canonically at least, to Doctrine and Covenants 132:19-20. The assertion that the Father was once human or was once a mortal man, though he affirms it as mainstream LDS orthodoxy, Robinson recognizes as stemming from noncanonical declarations of Joseph Smith and Lorenzo Snow (one each). Robinson insists that the Adam-God theory, as proposed by the various interpreters of Brigham Young, makes no sense and was never officially endorsed. These clarifications would seem to hold the door open for significant rapprochement between Evangelicals and Mormons on these doctrines, especially if the LDS can continue to avoid using unofficial statements from their past to define present official LDS doctrine.

Evangelicals, at the same time, are increasingly expressing dissatisfaction with their classical formulations of doctrines such as the immutability, impassibility and simplicity of God. Spurred on in part by parallel developments in other modern theologies, various Evangelical theologians are now speaking of God's openness, God's suffering, God's ability to change his mind, God's choice to remain ignorant of certain future events so as to allow his creatures genuine freedom, the growth in God's Being that inevitably comes by interaction with those creatures, and the like.[43] Some Evangelicals, of course, object for various reasons to all such suggestions, and, as in Mormonism, stereotypes held at the grassroots level are the last to be changed. In what ways both groups will continue to develop remains to be seen. Meanwhile, we must proceed to additional controversies surrounding the Godhead, specifically the ones that led to the early creedal confessions about the Trinity.

Joint Conclusion

[B L O M B E R G & R O B I N S O N]

THIS CHAPTER MAY REFLECT where Evangelicals and Latter-day Saints are farthest apart, though both Evangelicals and Latter-day Saints believe in an omniscient, omnipotent, omnipresent, infinite, eternal and unchangeable God. Latter-day Saints take the anthropomorphisms of the Bible literally and believe that God the Father and Jesus Christ both have physical bodies, while the Holy Spirit does not. Evangelicals, following the traditional interpretations common to most of the history of Orthodox, Catholic and Protestant churches, focus on biblical passages that stress the unseen and bodiless nature of God. They dispute that a material God can be infinite, though this *is* the LDS assertion.

Based on the strength of two statements by LDS prophets, Latter-day Saints believe that before the beginning of this universe, time and existence, God experienced mortal life in a prior existence. They further insist that this does not violate any of the biblical information about the nature of God but is a supplemental revelation that "fills in the gaps" where the Bible is silent. While at times agreeing that this doctrine is not explicitly denied in the Bible, Evangelicals maintain that it certainly does go beyond the information found therein and believe at the very least that the doctrine is *implicitly*—or *logically*—excluded.

Technically, both Evangelicals and Mormons affirm the biblical doctrine that human beings can participate in the divine nature through the atonement of Jesus Christ (2 Pet 1:4). However, Mormons take this to be literally true of every aspect of the divine nature, asserting that God and humanity are of one species, that the children can and will grow up to be like their parents, and that through the grace and atonement of Christ the "saved" can eventually become "gods," though in a subordinate sense. Evangelicals, on the other hand, focusing on the immediate context of this verse, stress that Peter is speaking only of the moral attributes of God. They typically deny that humans can ever possess what have been called God's incommunicable attributes—omnipotence, omniscience, omnipresence and the like. Further discussion about the nature of God leads to topics like the nature of Christ and the nature of the Trinity, to which we now turn.

3

Christ & the Trinity

[BLOMBERG]

What Evangelicals Believe

Mormon-Evangelical debates about the divine go beyond the nature
of God the Father and the godlike potential of the exalted believer.
Protestants, Catholics and Orthodox alike have affirmed belief in a
triune God—Father, Son and Holy Spirit—as a central tenet of the
Christian faith. There are some issues that may or may not divide
Mormons and Evangelicals with respect to the Holy Spirit,[1] but these
differences are less significant than differences Evangelicals have on
the issue with Jehovah's Witnesses, who view the Spirit as an imper-
sonal force. Far more crucial for a mutual understanding of what we
believe is a focus on our doctrines of Christ. In this chapter we will
address the key issues of Christology as well as our understanding
more generally of God as a trinity.

In agreement with all branches of historic Christianity, Evangelicals believe in one God eternally existing in three persons.[2] The Greek
and Latin wings of the church of the first five centuries increasingly
elaborated this biblical formula, particularly in a series of creeds that
have been enormously influential in the history of Christendom. The
oldest of these, the Apostles' Creed, though not demonstrably predat-
ing the third century, is short enough to be reproduced in full:

> I believe in God the Father Almighty, Maker of heaven and earth;
> And in Jesus Christ his only Son our Lord; who was conceived
> by the Holy Ghost, born of the Virgin Mary, suffered under Pontius
> Pilate, was crucified, dead, and buried; He descended into hell; the

third day He rose again from the dead; He ascended into heaven, and sitteth on the right hand of God the Father Almighty; from thence He shall come to judge the quick and the dead.

I believe in the Holy Ghost; the holy catholic Church; the communion of saints; the forgiveness of sins; the resurrection of the body; and the life everlasting.[3]

The Nicene Creed was developed by the early fourth century because various interpretations that existed at the time were deemed by the majority in the church to be sub-Christian. It too contained three paragraphs, one per person of the Godhead, but elaborated on the deity of Christ in its second paragraph by affirming, "[We believe] . . . in one Lord, Jesus Christ, the only begotten Son of God, begotten of the Father before all worlds, [God of God], Light of Light, very God of very God, begotten, not made, being of one substance [essence] with the Father; by whom all things were made."[4]

A little over a hundred years later, debates had shifted to the issue of how to explain Christ as simultaneously God and man. The Council of Chalcedon (451) defined what would remain the standard of orthodoxy:

> One and the same Christ, Son, Lord, Only-begotten, to be acknowledged in two natures, *inconfusedly, unchangeably, indivisibly, inseparably;* the distinction of natures being by no means taken away by the union, but rather the property of each nature being preserved, and concurring in one Person and one Subsistence, not parted or divided into two persons, but one and the same Son, and only begotten, God the Word, the Lord Jesus Christ; as the prophets from the beginning [have declared] concerning him, and the Lord Jesus Christ himself has taught us, and the Creed of the holy Fathers has handed down to us.[5]

Some branches of Christianity have given great weight to these creedal statements, but Protestantism's doctrine of *sola scriptura* (Scripture alone) by definition means that to be consistent we support nothing but what can legitimately be derived from the Old and New Testaments. On the other hand, the early creeds and councils are much closer in time and culture to the apostolic age than we are; surely their formulations should at least be taken seriously as well-intentioned attempts to make sense of the biblical data in ways that frequently turn out to be right.

Some Christians have made extravagant claims regarding the extent to which they can find the Trinity in the Bible, particularly in the Old Testament.[6] Responsible scholarship requires greater modesty. In fact, the most crucial observation about God to be gleaned from the Old Testament is its unrelenting monotheism. Every day the faithful Jew recited from Deuteronomy 6:4, "Hear, O Israel: The LORD our God, the LORD is one." There was no more central theological affirmation in the whole of Judaism. Jesus would later endorse this affirmation as his introduction to answering the scribe who asked him about the greatest commandment in the law: it is that *one* God whom we are to worship with all our heart, soul, mind and strength (Mk 12:29-30). The first of the Ten Commandments declared, "I am the Lord your God. . . . You shall have no other gods before[7] me" (Ex 20:2-3). Israel's prophets repeatedly inveighed against polytheism that the Israelites borrowed from the pagan religions of neighboring peoples (for example, Isaiah's classic ridicule of idolatry in Is 44:6-20).

Still, there are hints in the Old Testament of a plurality within the one God. The plural pronouns of Genesis 1 could point in this direction (as in "let us make man in our image," v. 26). However, it is more likely they are either what grammarians call a plural of majesty (as when a king says, "We declare that . . .") or of deliberation (as when someone says, "What shall we do?") or God speaking to the angels making up his heavenly "council."[8] The most common word for "God" in the Hebrew Bible is *'ĕlōhîm*, a plural form. Apparently this term was borrowed from the word *'ēl*, which was used by the polytheistic religions of the day, *but was redefined* so as to refer to the one God, inasmuch as it is consistently used with singular pronouns, adjectives and verb forms throughout the entire Old Testament.[9] The particular word for "one" in Deuteronomy 6:4, however, is not the Hebrew

yāḥîd, meaning "one and only," but *'eḥād,* which leaves room for the
idea of some form of plurality within an otherwise single entity.[10] In
addition, a handful of messianic prophecies use language that seems
to equate the coming deliverer with God, even though that Messiah is
distinct from God the Father (Ps 2:7-12; 110:1-4; Is 9:6). Compare
also the threeness in oneness of Isaiah 48:16 and 61:1.

The issue becomes clarified through God's progressive revelation
in the New Testament. As Jesus gives his disciples "the Great Commission," he commands them to baptize new followers "in *the* name
of the Father and of the Son and of the Holy Spirit" (Mt 28:19). The
Greek is even plainer than the English: Father, Son and Holy Spirit
constitute one name, yet that name encompasses three persons. John
14—17 expounds at length on the respective roles of these three
members of the triune God, from which chapters also derives (in part)
the doctrine of the "eternal generation" of Son and Spirit: the Father
sends the Son, who in turn goes away (to return to the Father) so that
the Spirit may come.[11]

In the Epistles we find a variety of explicitly trinitarian references.
First Corinthians 12:4-6 speaks of spiritual gifts coming from Spirit,
Lord and God interchangeably. Second Corinthians 13:14 offers the
famous benediction "May the grace of the Lord Jesus Christ, and the
love of God, and the fellowship of the Holy Spirit be with you all." In
Ephesians 1:3-14 Paul praises the one God who has chosen us in the
person of the Father, redeemed us through the Son and sealed us by
means of the Spirit. First Peter 1:2 describes God's elect as those "who
have been chosen according to the foreknowledge of God the Father,
through the sanctifying work of the Spirit, for obedience to Jesus Christ
and sprinkling by his blood." And Jude 20-21 parallels prayer in the
Holy Spirit with God's love and the mercy of our Lord Jesus Christ.

These explicit references, however, are relatively rare and do not
disclose the historical development of the doctrine. The key issue is
how the seeds of trinitarian faith ever began to grow *within Judaism.*[12]
The basic answer is that the earliest church was forced into it, against

all its contrary inclinations, by the undeniable facts of history and by public experience. To be specific, the Jewish disciples' direct encounter first with the man Jesus of Nazareth and then with God's personal, invisible presence revealed to them at Pentecost convinced them that the only way to account for their experience was to make room for both Jesus and the Spirit in their understanding of the one God of the universe.[13]

Trinitarian thought initially had nothing whatever to do with the philosophical arguments of the later church. Undoubtedly the first Christians were quite sure that they could not exhaustively explain, by means of Aristotelian logic, their affirmations of Jesus and the Spirit as being part of the same God they had worshiped as Jews. But the stubborn reality of historical experience—not a private, unverified vision nor an alleged revelation in documents subsequently hidden from the rest of the world—over time, from many different angles, convinced hundreds and thousands of monotheistic Jews (Acts 21:20) that their God included Jesus and the Spirit. They did not postulate more than one physical personage; rather, they became persuaded that the historical Jesus so shattered conventional categories of what humans could do or could be that he had to be the Spirit-filled incarnation of God (Yahweh) himself.

For the most part Mormonism seems to agree with all the evidence Evangelicals conventionally cite for the deity of Christ (and of the Spirit). Thus B. H. Roberts could compile the following "evidence of Christ's divinity from the Scriptures":

Jesus Christ is called God in the Scriptures (Isa. 7:14; Matt. 1:23; Isa. 9:6).

Jesus declares himself to be God—the Son of God (John 5:18, 10:33; Matt. 27:63-64 [*sic* for chap. 26], 28:18-19; Heb. 1:8).

Jesus Christ [is] to be worshiped, hence God (Rev. 19:10; Heb. 1:5-6; Phil. 2:9-10).

Jesus Christ is the Creator, hence God (John 1:1-4; Col. 1:12-17; Rev. 14:7)

Jesus Christ is equal with God the Father, hence God (Matt. 28:18-19; Phil. 2:6; Heb. 3:3; 2 Cor. 4:4; Col. 1:5 [*sic* for v. 15], 19, 2:9).[14]

Two questions remain to be answered: (1) How separate are the three persons of the Trinity, especially the Father and the Son? and (2) Have they always been essentially and entirely deity?

Regarding the first question, it is important to observe that within the first five centuries of intense Christian discussion about the nature of God, tritheism was never nearly the temptation that unitarianism was. In other words, as Christians wrestled with how to keep the three persons of the Trinity both separate and unified, they far more commonly erred on the side of *not* adequately distinguishing the three.[15] No early Christian theologian ever identified Jesus as a completely separate God from Yahweh, Lord of Israel. "Son of God" in its Jewish context was a messianic title (see Ps 2; 89; 2 Sam 7:14) and was never taken to suggest that Jesus was the literal, biological offspring of his heavenly Father.[16] That would have surely violated monotheism, much as Islam today often charges Evangelical Christians with doing (by believing that we allege that God and Mary biologically united to produce Jesus).

The New Testament adequately safeguards against overly separating God the Father and Jesus in at least two ways. First, the apostolic writers, with "20/20 hindsight," often replace the name of God with a reference to Jesus when they quote the Old Testament. Now that they understand that God created and redeemed the world by means of the Son, they can attribute the Father's action to Christ. So, for example, Hebrews 1:8-9 claims that Psalm 45:6-7 ("Your throne, O God, will last for ever and ever") is actually about the Son, and verses 10-12 go on to quote Psalm 102:25-27, which speaks of "the Lord" laying "the foundations of the earth." But whereas the Old Testament clearly refers to God the Father, the author of Hebrews believes that the Son too was present in this activity.[17]

Second, the New Testament not only speaks of Jesus and the Father as "one"—language that Prof. Robinson rightly points out need not mean anything more than "oneness of mind, purpose, power and intent,"[18] but it also employs language of "coinherence": the Father is *in* the Son and vice versa. For example, in John 14:10-11 Christ claims, "Don't you believe that I am in the Father, and that the Father is in me? The words I say to you are not just my own. Rather, it is the Father, living in me, who is doing his work. Believe me when I say that I am in the Father and the Father is in me." That is why he is able to say that "anyone who has seen me has seen the Father" (v. 9)—not merely the image of God, though Christ is that too, but God himself. If Jesus is the incarnation of the otherwise immaterial Father, then it is one and the same God that is revealing himself in Jesus Christ.[19]

The second question is whether Jesus and the Father have always been fully God. Evangelicals do not deny a "subordinationist" strand of teaching in the Scriptures. John 14:28 gives the clearest example of this: "the Father is greater than I." Jesus is explaining that his "state of humiliation" is soon to end, and he will then return to the Father. Clearly Christ gave up the independent exercise of his divine attributes in the incarnation, voluntarily accepting a "lower" position than God the Father (see Phil 2:6-8), but it was about to be restored in full (Phil 2:9-11).[20] Some Evangelicals are even willing to admit an eternal subordination of the Son to the Father, noting that even before the incarnation the Father sent the Son (never the reverse). Even after Christ's exaltation and at the end of human history, Jesus "will be made subject to [God]" (1 Cor 15:28).[21] But historic Christianity has always insisted on balancing Christ's *functional* subordination with his onto-logical equality. In other words, in the very essence of Christ's being he is eternally equal with God, even if in playing certain roles he voluntarily submits himself to his Father (Jn 1:1, 14).[22]

How important is this issue? The answer to this question sets the stage for our final chapter on salvation. Christians have usually insisted that a correct formulation of the doctrines of God and Christ is important because the possibility of eternal life depends on it. If

Christ was ever less than fully God (even when he assumed a human nature), then he is by definition not the kind of infinite deity necessary to atone for our sins and to pay the infinite price required for our purification, so that we can live in his presence forever. It seems to me that Mormons and Evangelicals generally agree on the importance and the reality of Christ's substitutionary atonement for the sins of the world,[23] so presumably we should both be equally eager for our Christ really to have been able to make this atonement.

Athanasius, the champion of the perspective that triumphed at Chalcedon over Arius (who believed that Christ was the first creature God made), clearly understood this. He proclaimed, "If Jesus is not fully God, we do not truly receive salvation, for in salvation we participate in the divine nature." Ironically, it is precisely in this context that he wrote, "The Word was made man in order that we might be made divine."[24] So Lorenzo Snow actually differs from the point of the orthodox parallels to his famous couplet in *both* halves of his saying (see p. 94). Not only did the early church not blur the distinction between God and humanity the way Mormonism seems to have done (p. 81), but it also insisted that the God who became incarnate to make salvation and glorification for humanity possible had to have been part of the triune God from all eternity past—never merely mortal and never so distinct from the Father that anyone could see them as two entirely separate beings (to say nothing of two separate *human* beings).

Avoiding Misconceptions

Few Evangelicals claim that everything in the historic creeds of the early church is demonstrably biblical in derivation. Ultimately we do not base our beliefs on Chalcedon, Nicaea or even the Apostles' Creed, but on the Old and New Testaments. We do usually claim that the *heart* of these creeds' affirmations about God, Christ and the Spirit can be supported biblically and that other statements are the logical corollaries of the Bible's teachings. We reject the charge that we are merely quibbling over semantics, for as just noted, our salvation depends on having a God "big enough" to make atonement for us.

Few of us claim that we must affirm every detail of the creeds or be able to explain at length the doctrine of the Trinity in order to be saved and inherit eternal life. If that were the case, few of us would ever qualify for salvation! We resist the notion that we are merely "offenders for a word," arguing that at the level of objective reality (as distinct from our subjective understanding of it) the doctrine of the Trinity has to be true if salvation is really available for us. Not much depends on whether we can correctly articulate our *beliefs* in every detail, but everything depends on whether historic Christian beliefs are *in fact true.*

Translating ancient Greek and Latin discussions into English creates further misconceptions. Standard formulations often spoke of God as one "essence" *(ousia)* in three "substances" *(hypostaseis).* This has led modern English speakers to mistakenly think of each person of the Godhead as necessarily material or tangible.[25] But the meaning of the ancient formulations draws on the distinction in Greek philosophy between that which forms the metaphysical core of an entity and "independent realities" by which that entity manifests itself. The term *substance* can designate either materiality or immateriality; when referring to God, the church fathers always implied that God was immaterial. As theology moved from the Greek to the Roman world, Tertullian, among others, spoke of one substance *(substantia)* in three persons *(personae)* but intended by his Latin what the previous Greek writers had phrased somewhat differently.[26]

The language of one God in three persons can also mislead. It often conjures up, even among non-Mormons, the notion of three distinct personalities (if not bodies). It is a short distance from that notion to imagining some grotesque form of schizophrenia or multiple personality disorder! Closer to the original concept is the understanding of "person" as a center of personal consciousness.[27] In other words, we do not believe that Jesus prayed to himself. He was fully aware of a separate spiritual presence with whom he communed, but he also realized that he was more intimately linked with that presence than any other human ever can be.

Oxford Evangelical theologian Alister McGrath puts it another way: "Jesus is not *identical* with God in that it is obvious that God continued to be in heaven during Jesus' lifetime, and yet Jesus may be *identified* with God in that the New Testament has no hesitation in ascribing functions to Jesus which, properly speaking, only God could do."[28] McGrath goes on to illustrate his point with the analogy of an estuary, a stream and its source. All are part of a river, each part necessarily containing at some point the whole of the river, yet none of which by itself is the entire river.[29] In short, Jesus and the Spirit are each fully God, but neither constitutes all that there is to God.

Numerous other partial analogies to the Trinity have commended themselves to Christians over the years. Physical analogies illustrate diversity in unity (not every aspect of trinitarianism) in everyday life: one atom is made up of electrons, protons and neutrons; one body has many organs; a container of water can be turning to ice at one end and steam at another. Psychological analogies also illustrate enormous complexity and functional difference within unity: a person's inner and outer self; a Christian's sinful nature and new nature; the psyche's cognition, volition and emotion. Social analogies illustrate unfathomable diversity within unity involving persons, most notably in marriage and the church.[30]

Finally, Evangelicals regularly refer to the Trinity as a "mystery," but few of us believe it to be an absurdity. It is important to distinguish a concept that cannot be demonstrated to be completely understandable by finite minds from a concept that can be demonstrated to contain logical contradictions. One God in three persons falls into the former category; one God in three Gods or one person in three persons might fall more obviously into the latter. In other words, the doctrine of the Trinity does not affirm and deny the same thing at the same time *in the same respect.* What is more, should we not expect an omnipotent, omniscient, omnipresent God not to be fully comprehensible by mere mortals? "Indeed if we did not encounter deep mystery in God's nature there would be every reason for suspicion concerning the Bible's claims," writes Bruce Milne. And he adds, "For all its difficulty the Trinity is simply (!) the price to be paid for having a God who is great enough to command our worship and service."[31]

Misgivings About the LDS Understanding of Jesus as God's Son

Evangelicals have two basic reservations about the LDS perspective. First, it appears to them that the Father and the Son in the standard Mormon perspective are too separate. Second, it is not clear that either the Father or the Son, especially the Son defined as perpetually subordinate to God, can qualify as fully, eternally God. We get the impression, perhaps not quite as baldly as from the Jehovah's Witnesses, that Mormons see Christ as a created being, even if he is the first and highest of all creation. Thus the door at least remains open for polytheism and hence for worshiping created beings. B. H. Roberts's words, for example, are rather disconcerting:

In nothing have men so far departed from revealed truth as in their conceptions of God. . . . This was the revelation with which the work of God in the last days began. The revelation of God, the Father; and of God, the Son. *[sic]* They were seen to be two distinct personages. . . . That is, more than *one* God was engaged in the work of creation. . . . The revelation given to Joseph Smith challenged the truth of the conception of God held by the modern world—pagan, Jew, Mohammedan and Christian alike.[32]

If we are prepared to accept as inspired something that is so divergent from all other religions, what would ever disqualify an idea from being a true revelation from God? Where is there evidence of anyone "testing the spirits"? Which is more likely—that everyone in the entire modern world was wrong and Joseph Smith got it right or that the tenets of monotheism shared by Jews, Christians, Muslims and other theists are right and Mormonism is wrong?

All of the Mormon tenets about God and Christ seem to flow from this initial affirmation, based on Joseph's vision, of two distinct, divine men. So my misgivings about Mormon Christology cannot be separated from the concerns I expressed in chapter two. Without Joseph's vision there is no reason to reject the biblical teaching of "coinherence"—the Father *in* the Son and vice versa. There is no reason to postulate Christ as some antemortal spirit distinct from God who took on human flesh. There is no reason for the literal, biological interpretation of biblical language of sonship or the virgin birth.[33] Consider, for example, the exposition of Bruce McConkie:

> All men (Christ included) were born as the sons of God in the spirit; one man (Christ only) was born as the Son of God in this mortal world. He is the Only Begotten in the flesh. God was his Father; Mary was his mother. His Father was an immortal man; his mother was a mortal woman. He is the Son of God in the same literal, full, and complete sense in which he is the son of Mary. There is nothing symbolic or figurative about it. He is God's Almighty Son and as such is distinguished from the Father in the same way any son is a separate person from his father.[34]

Where is all this in the Old or New Testament (or even in the Standard Works)? All that Isaiah or Matthew ever says is that "the virgin will be with child and will give birth to a son" (Mt 1:23; compare Is 7:14). Luke is equally restrained. The angel tells Mary, "The Holy Spirit will come upon you, and the power of the Most High will overshadow you. So the holy one to be born will be called the Son of God" (Lk 1:35).[35] (Alma 7:10 clearly reproduces Luke's wording.) That is the sum total of Scripture's revelation about the nature of the virgin birth.[36]

Our misgivings continue as we see how other Scriptures are handled. Mormons have read much into the phrase "only begotten," which occurs frequently in the KJV (for example, Jn 1:14, 18; 3:16). This phrase is a misleading translation of the Greek adjective *monogenēs,* based on the KJV translators' mistaken assumption that the word was derived from the Greek verb *gennaō* ("to be born") plus the adjective monos ("only"). But then the adjective would have had to contain two *n*'s. Instead *monogenēs* comes from *monos* plus a form of the verb *ginomai* (the first *i* becomes an *e* in various tenses) meaning "to be" (or "to become")—hence "only existing." Modern translations therefore correctly render the term as "only" (NRSV) or "one and only" (NIV). There is nothing here to suggest God created (or "begat") Jesus.[37] First John 5:18 does use "begotten" (of God) for both Jesus *and* believers. Yet I am the biological offspring of my human parents, not God. So there is no reason to see *begotten* in either of its uses in this verse as anything other than an equivalent to "spiritually born."[38]

Mormons misunderstand the term *firstborn* as well (as in Col 1:15—Christ "is the firstborn over all creation").[39] The Greek term *prōtotokos* can mean first in a temporal sequence, but it can also mean first in rank, prominence or hierarchy. In the larger context in which all the fullness of Deity lives in Christ in bodily form (1:19; 2:9), it is highly unlikely that Paul would be calling Christ a created being, however exalted or ancient.[40]

First Corinthians 8:6 is another key text that we fear has been misunderstood: "for us there is but one God, the Father, from whom all things came and for whom we live; and there is but one Lord, Jesus Christ, through whom all things came and through whom we live." Verse 5 has just noted the existence of "so-called gods," indeed many of them, but in reality they are nothing at all (v. 4). "For us," therefore, does not mean that Christians disregard the other gods in the universe and focus exclusively on God in Christ, for *there are no other gods, objectively speaking,* even though people turn parts of creation into idols to worship. Rather, "for us" in this context is equivalent to "we know" (vv. 1, 4). That is, even though pagans do not know it, Christians recognize that there is one God and one Lord.

This is also an excellent text to demonstrate my earlier point about the development of trinitarian thought in the context of Jewish monotheism. Verse 4 is a direct allusion to Deuteronomy 6:4 ("we know . . . that there is no God but one"). Although we can understand why someone reading verse 6 all by itself might imagine that the "one Lord, Jesus Christ," set up as parallel to the "one God, the Father," is an entirely distinct God, in the larger context of Paul's writing and Jewish background this is most unlikely. Paul's experience of the risen Christ on the Damascus Road has forced him to make room for Jesus in his concept of monotheism, but he still insists on affirming "no God but one."[41]

I remember the first time I read the Book of Mormon cover to cover in response to an invitation to do so by a Mormon missionary. I already had learned that the LDS rejected the orthodox doctrine of the Trinity. I was surprised, therefore, as I found more instances of seemingly clear trinitarian language in the Book of Mormon than in the Old and New Testaments put together. I am still perplexed by this phenomenon as I read texts like 1 Nephi 19:10; 2 Nephi 10:3; 11:7; 25:12; 31:21; Mosiah 3:5-8; 7:27; 13:34; Alma 11:29-44; Helaman 14:12; 3 Nephi 9:15 and Mormon 7:7. If anything, it is *clearer* in several of these texts that it was the same God who was God the Father who became incarnate in the Son. Indeed, in several places the Son seems to be identified with the Father, as he is called "the Eternal Father," a direct equation the Bible never makes.

To cite just one example, consider Mosiah 3:5, 8:

> The Lord Omnipotent who reigneth, who was, and is from all eternity to all eternity, shall come down from heaven among the children of men, and shall dwell in a tabernacle of clay, and shall go forth amongst men, working mighty miracles, such as healing the sick, raising the dead, causing the lame to walk, the blind to receive their sight, and the deaf to hear, and curing all manner of diseases. . . . And he shall be called Jesus Christ, the Son of God, the Father of heaven and earth, the Creator of all things from the beginning; and his mother shall be called Mary.

These verses surely seem to affirm God's eternal existence *as omnipotent,* the incarnation of Jesus as the taking on of human form for the first time *by God the Father himself,* and a more direct equation of

Jesus with "the Father of heaven and earth" than any passage in the New Testament ever makes. How do we square these observations with the language of "Gods" that suddenly appears for the first time in the later book of Abraham's account of creation (chaps. 4—5) and similar language scattered throughout the Doctrine and Covenants (76:58; 121:28, 32, and esp. chap. 132)? Of course one can claim that what Joseph says more explicitly later is what he had in mind all along, just as Prof. Robinson explains the three ways in which Jesus can be considered Father.[42] One wonders, though, if it is not simply more probable that Joseph's views changed over time.[43]

But even if Joseph's later theology was implicit from the start, there is a second issue here. The LDS frequently accuse the early church of severely corrupting the pure gospel as soon as the apostles died off. All this trinitarianism, it is alleged, is the product of the Greco-Roman world as Christianity lost its moorings in Judaism. Yet the closest parallels to Mormon doctrine in the ancient world are found in the Arianism and tritheism that divided the early church *precisely in its Greco-Roman milieu.* The idea of Father and the Son, both fully God, but kept as separate as Mormonism wants to keep them, is entirely without parallel in the framework of Jewish monotheism. Further, if we are agreed not to rely on the later creeds but to stick with the form of "oneness in threeness" that the New Testament teaches, then where do we find *any* reference to the LDS distinctives about God's body, the eternal progression of the Father and the Son, a biological conception of the virgin birth, unity limited to "oneness of mind, purpose and intent," and so on *in the Bible?* To an outsider it certainly seems that these doctrines require the later "revelations" to Joseph Smith in a context that has long since lost sight of the Judaism of biblical times, for anyone to have thought of them.

It is ironic that the closest parallels to several Mormon doctrinal distinctives in the history of Christianity appear among the early Greek Orthodox theologians, distinctives of which contemporary Evangelicals are understandably suspicious. These parallels include such doctrines as the deification of believers, the eternal subordination of the Son, a chance to respond to the gospel after death, baptism for the dead and other esoteric "mystery" rites.[44] Not one of these doctrines finds significant precedent in the first-century Judaism that birthed the New Testament, and not one is unambiguously taught in the New Testment. But all are eminently paralleled in pagan Greek religious and philosophical thought. It is certainly not just historic Christianity that has been influenced in places by Hellenistic thought forms!

It is hard to imagine anyone concocting the orthodox doctrine of a triune God, with all its complexities. But it is entirely understandable that someone frustrated with those complexities should want to create a neater and tidier system. It has been tried, with variations, many times throughout church history. Tritheism even has numerous parallels in the history of pagan religions.[45] Pure biblical trinitarian thought is a unique "mutation" of Jewish monotheism. Millard Erickson sums it up this way: "We do not hold the doctrine of the Trinity because it is self-evident or logically cogent. We hold it because God has revealed that this is what he is like."[46] To be sure, the word itself does not appear in the Bible. But we believe that the concepts it implies are all there in a nutshell.

A More Positive Conclusion

Given all I have said about the mystery of God transcending our finite, human understanding, it would be presumptuous to claim that I have fully and satisfactorily articulated the doctrines of the person of Christ and the triune God. It would be equally presumptuous to condemn others who with good intentions try to articulate their Bible-based understanding of the same doctrines and yet come to different conclusions. It is hard to read the history of the debates in the first five centuries of church history without suspecting that at least in certain instances this is exactly what happened, especially given the ecclesiastical politicking that also played a major role in the development of events.[47] Martin Luther seems to have been more candid when he "admitted that . . . since the article of the Holy Trinity is so far beyond our human mind and language, God must pardon us if we stammer and prattle about it as well as we can, provided only that our faith is pure and right."[48] Still, if we err it ought to be in the direction of the unity of the Godhead, not in the direction of polytheism. Otherwise we are left with a Jesus who could not and therefore did not save us, and we would remain dead in our sins.

I am nevertheless profoundly grateful to read of Stephen Robinson's dissociation from various popular Mormon views, which are not clearly taught in the Standard Works. I hope that Prof. Robinson is part of a trend that will catch on widely at the grassroots level as well. If Robinson in good conscience can truly accept all of the New Testament witness concerning the "threeness in oneness" of God[49] and even the Apostles' Creed (see pp. 219-220 n. 8) without eccentric definition of terms, then there is hope for substantial progress in our discussion. Nicaea need not be the watershed; it is not canonical. We can hope that twenty-first-century dialogues on this topic between Evangelicals and Mormons will be far more charitable and informed than the nineteenth-century ones.

Christ & the Trinity

[R O B I N S O N]

What Latter-day Saints Believe

Since we have agreed to deal with the doctrine of the Trinity under the heading of Christology, let me address that first. There are some areas where Mormons are less careful in making fine theological distinctions than are Evangelicals (for example, in discussions of faith/works), but the tables turn when we come to the doctrine of the

Trinity, for in my experience "orthodox" Christians generally use the term *trinity* in a careless and ambiguous way to mean two different things at the same time. They use the term to mean (1) the biblical doctrine of the simultaneous oneness and threeness of God and (2) the nonbiblical attempts of fourth- and fifth-century councils to define exactly *how* God is at the same time one and three by using Greek philosophical concepts, categories and terms. My experience has been that most Evangelicals in practice recognize no distinction at all between (1) and (2), and simply equate the biblical data with the extrapolations of the councils, assuming that to believe one is necessarily to believe the other.

Mormons, however, do not equate the biblical data with the findings of the councils; we wholeheartedly accept the former and frequently reject the latter. And since most Evangelicals do not recognize the distinction between the two, when Mormons reject the councils and their creeds we are unfairly accused of also rejecting the New Testament. Though Evangelicals often refuse to believe it, Latter-day Saints accept all the biblical teaching on the nature of God and Christ, *provided these are stated in their biblical forms* rather than in their postbiblical, creedal forms.[1]

That God is somehow simultaneously three and one I have no doubt because the Bible and the Book of Mormon both tell me so, but I do not trust the intellectuals of the Hellenistic church to have figured out exactly *how* this is so (1 Cor 3:19), nor do I invest their theories and conclusions with the authority of Scripture.[2]

The threeness of God is quite literally an article of faith for Latter-day Saints: "We believe in God, the Eternal Father, *and* in his Son, Jesus Christ, *and* in the Holy Ghost" (Article of Faith One, emphasis added). I have no interest in arguing against either the threeness of God or the unity of God as witnessed in the biblical passages cited by Prof. Blomberg. *I accept them all.* In addition to these, among the LDS sources, the testimony of the Three Witnesses to the Book of Mormon concludes with the line "And the honor be to the Father, and to the Son, and to the Holy Ghost, which is one God. Amen." The Book of Mormon itself reads at 2 Nephi 31:21: "And now, behold, this is the doctrine of Christ, and the only and true doctrine of the Father, and of the Son, and of the Holy Ghost, which is one God, without end. Amen." Notice that these texts emphasize the unity of the Godhead by using a singular verb for the plural subject: the Father, Son and Holy Ghost *is* one God.

Also in the Book of Mormon the prophet Abinadi declares, "God himself shall come down among the children of men, and shall redeem his people. And because he dwelleth in flesh he shall be called the Son of God, and having subjected the flesh to the will of the Father, being the Father and the Son—the Father, because he was conceived by the power of God; and the Son, because of the flesh; thus becoming the Father and Son—and they are one God, yea, the very Eternal Father of heaven and of earth" (Mosiah 15:1-4). Additional LDS Scripture testifying to the threeness and oneness of God can be found in Alma 11:26-29, 44, Mormon 7:7, and in Doctrine and Covenants 20:21-28.

That Father, Son and Holy Spirit are one God is, as Prof. Blomberg has pointed out, a paramount doctrine of the Book of Mormon. His surprise to find it so makes my point: Latter-day Saints have believed in the simultaneous oneness and threeness of God since the beginnings of their faith—and Evangelicals have for just as long declined to believe this could be so. Like Evangelicals, Latter-day Saints also believe that Father, Son and Holy Spirit are separate and distinct *persons.* Many Evangelicals would be surprised to learn that Mormons can accept the formula of "one God in three persons." However, we believe that the oneness of these three is not an ontological oneness of being (this is a *creedal* rather than a *biblical* affirmation), but a oneness of mind, purpose, power and intent. The Godhead consists of God the Father, God the Son and God the Holy Ghost, "and these three are one" (1 Jn 5:7).[3] The three persons are one God. What is not said in the Bible, but is said at Nicaea and is rejected by Mormons, is that these three persons are ontologically one *being.*

Latter-day Saints believe the *biblical* concept of "oneness" or of "being one" is revealed at John 17:21-23, Romans 12:5, 1 Corinthians 12:12-13, Galatians 3:28, etc., where the individual disciples can also be "one" in the Father and the Son, or "one" in Christ, or even "one" with each other in Christ—though still remaining separate beings with separate and individual bodies. Mormons accept John 14:11 as much as Evangelicals do: "Believe me that I am in the Father, and the Father in me: or else believe me for the very works' sake." But 14:11 should probably be read together with 17:21-22, which illustrates the *nature* of their oneness: "That they all may be one; as thou, Father, art in me, and I in thee, that they also may be one in us: that the world may believe that thou hast sent me. And the glory which thou gavest me I have given them; that they may be one, *even as we are one*" (emphasis added). Professor Blomberg insists that this goes beyond oneness of mind, purpose, power and intent and affirms the doctrine of "co-inherence" (p. 117). But whatever it means that the Father is in Christ and Christ in the Father (14:11), it *cannot* be ontological oneness of being or "co-inherence," since the disciples, who are indisputably separate and individual beings, can also be one in the Father and the Son *in the same way* that the Father and Son are one in each other (17:22). And this is not a philosophical extrapolation from the text using nonbiblical terms formulated centuries later; it's what the text actually *says*.

Latter-day Saints are trinitarians in the sense that they truly believe in God the Father, in God the Son and in God the Holy Spirit, and also in that they believe these three are one God. But they are not trinitarians in the later creedal sense as defined at Nicaea and Chalcedon because those creeds imposed nonbiblical concepts on the biblical data, and they used nonbiblical terms—trinity, *homoousios,* consubstantial, ungenerated, indivisible and so forth—in doing it.

It is true that Mormons are thoroughly subordinationist in their theology of the Godhead, as were many of the early Church Fathers, but this does not constitute a rejection of the New Testament any more than it did for the Fathers. Rather, it is one logical and coherent way of understanding the New Testament data. In the LDS view, the Son is subordinate to the Father, and the Holy Spirit is subordinate to both the Father and the Son.[4] If the Father did not exist, neither the Son nor the Holy Ghost would be God, for their divinity comes through their relationship with the Father.[5] Professor Blomberg apparently feels this type of subordination would make Christ less than fully divine and therefore unable to atone and redeem, yet it was clearly the *mortal* Jesus Christ, in his subordinate state (or "lower position" or "state of humiliation," p. 117) *before* his ascension and glorification, who suffered for us, bled for us, atoned for us, redeemed us, and died for us.[6] If the Son was subordinate to the Father while in the flesh, and if he was in the flesh while performing the atonement, then is it wise to insist that a subordinate Christ could not have power to save?

An LDS type of subordinationism was common in the earliest Christian church and was not felt to be contrary to the orthodox Christian faith until after the fourth century.[7] The writings of the earliest Christians, the Apostolic Fathers, the Greek apologists, and even some of the Nicene Fathers, provide many examples of an understanding of God that would be "unorthodox" by later post-Nicene trinitarian standards—though no one would argue that they were "unbiblical" or "unchristian." Few would seriously accuse these early Christian writers of being heretics, yet I believe modern critics apply a different standard to post-Nicene Mormons in this regard than they do to the ante-Nicene Fathers. For if pre-Nicene mainstream Christians, like Justin Martyr, Irenaeus or Eusebius of Caesarea, can be thoroughly unorthodox in their view of the Godhead (by post-Nicene standards) without being declared heretical, then is it not unfair to demonize the LDS for the same point of view? Remember, I am not talking about departing from the biblical information—only from the creeds.[8]

Occasionally, some Evangelical will tell me that my belief in three separate and distinct divine beings adding up to only one God is illogical and therefore amounts to polytheism.[9] While it may seem illogical that Mormons believe a divine Father, Son and Holy Ghost who are separate and distinct beings still only add up to one God, it is nevertheless what we believe; for the divine Son and the divine Holy Spirit are subordinate to the Father and dependent on their oneness with him for their divinity. They cannot stand alone; they are "God" only as they are one with the Father in the Godhead. If their oneness with the Father should cease, so would their divinity.[10] Thus there are three divine persons, but only one Godhead. Clearly Prof. Blomberg feels that such a Godhead is unlikely and that defining the Godhead so runs a risk of polytheism—but that is not the LDS belief. It would horrify the Saints to hear talk of "polytheism." Surely our assertion of one God in three beings presents no greater challenge to comprehension or logic than the "mystery of the Trinity" as defined at Nicaea and Chalcedon, the difficulties of which are generally conceded (pp. 120-21, 126-27). Besides, I think we have already stipulated the fallacy of defining each other's beliefs in ways that violate each other's *self*-understanding.

Latter-day Saints also accept through modern revelation some propositions about God (in all three persons) not found in the Bible. This scandal to Evangelicals often causes them to conclude incorrectly either (1) that Mormons reject the biblical information or (2) that the Mormon view by being *different* in some respects must therefore necessarily contradict the Bible. Nevertheless, differences are not of necessity contradictions, and those who would insist otherwise in the case of the LDS are obliged to demonstrate contradictions (from canonical sources) and not just differences. Some Christians believe that Jesus will return soon, perhaps even in this generation, others believe that dancing is immoral, or that computer-scanned bar codes are the mark of the Beast. Their beliefs may or may not be correct, and they are certainly not stated in the Bible, but believing them does not necessarily *contradict* the Bible.

LDS beliefs *do* contradict the doctrine of the later councils and creeds, but these creeds are not Scripture. After all, if full and complete understanding of and agreement with the Chalcedonian/Nicene Christology is necessary for salvation, then most Evangelicals of my acquaintance will not be saved either! As I understand it, such a requirement would also violate the principle of salvation by grace, replacing it with salvation by right doctrine or salvation by creedal affirmation. I do not think that any knowledgeable Evangelical would insist on the necessity of adherence to the creeds for salvation in *theory,* but they often do lay such a necessity on the Latter-day Saints in *practice* without thinking about it, as when they demand Nicene or even Calvinist orthodoxy before Mormons will be considered even generically Christian.

How can Protestants who insist on *sola scriptura* do this in good conscience? I fear it is because they invest the creeds with the authority of Scripture, equating the Nicene and Chalcedonian Trinity with the biblical trinity, in effect adding to the Bible from the creeds in spite of *sola scriptura.* The bottom line is that for most "orthodox" it is not enough that Mormons accept the New Testament; we must also *interpret* it in the "traditional" manner—through the lenses of Nicaea and Chalcedon—even though technically that tradition is not vested with scriptural authority. This seems to us a grand contradiction.

Often I hear the creeds defended as merely "apt summaries" of the biblical information. How dearly I wish this were so! For then the gap between Evangelicals and Latter-day Saints could be closed in a single step. Evangelicals could just list the various Scriptures of which the creeds are "summaries," and then the LDS could affirm their belief in the un-"summarized" Scriptures. Bingo, instant agreement, instant orthodoxy! Of course it will not happen—because there is no combination of biblical passages that will yield the complete doctrines and fine distinctions of Nicaea and Chalcedon. These are not "summaries"—they are expansions and extrapolations.

The feelings of Latter-day Saints about Jesus Christ are ably summarized in the Book of Mormon at 2 Nephi 25:26: "And we talk of Christ, we rejoice in Christ, we preach of Christ, we prophesy of Christ, and we write according to our prophecies, that our children

may know to what source they may look for a remission of their sins."
According to Joseph Smith, "the fundamental principles of our religion are the testimony of the Apostles and Prophets, concerning Jesus
Christ, that He died, was buried, and rose again the third day, and
ascended into heaven; and all other things which pertain to our religion
are only appendages to it."[11]

It must be emphasized that Latter-day Saints believe in the full
divinity of Jesus Christ. Though subordinate to his Father, Jesus has
been fully God by the will of the Father from the beginning. For us
Christ is not a being separate from the Jehovah of the Old Testament—
we identify Christ *as* Jehovah, the God of Abraham, Isaac and Jacob
(1 Nephi 19:10). It was the Father of Jesus Christ who remained
"unseen" (Gk *aoratos*) and largely unknown before the atonement of
Christ restored human access to him. We believe that almost all
references to "God" or to "the Father" in the Old Testament, and many
in the New, refer specifically to God the Son, Jesus Christ, who is also
Jehovah or Yahweh. Though he is not his own Father, the Son rightly
receives the title "Father" in at least three ways.

1. He is the agent and representative of his Father to human beings.
He is also the agent and representative of human beings to his Father,
and thus all that we direct to the Father must be done in the name of
Jesus Christ our mediator.

2. Jesus is by the will of the Father the creator of heaven and earth,
and he is the power that keeps the created universe from flying apart from
second to second (Jn 1:3; Col 1:16-17; Doctrine and Covenants 88:41-42).

3. Through Jesus' suffering and death—a vicarious and substitutionary
atonement—human beings may be spiritually "born again" as sons and
daughters of God. Thus, Jesus is the divine parent of the saved, who then
become the sons and daughters of Christ (Mosiah 5:7).

Further, the Book of Mormon teaches that if Christ were not fully
God, he could not have brought about the infinite atonement by which
humans are saved (Alma 34:10, 14; 2 Nephi 9:7). For Latter-day
Saints, Jesus is not just the Son of God, he is God the Son, and we

insist on his full divinity and infinite atonement as much as Evangelicals do. It is misrepresentation to insist, using "orthodox" logic, that if Mormons believe A (the subordinate nature of the Son), then they can't believe B (the full divinity of the Son)—when Mormons, in fact, believe both A and B.

In regard to the virgin birth, Latter-day Saints believe everything that the Bible has to say on the subject. However, the Bible has less to say on this subject than many seem to wish it did. Certainly the gynecological expositions of the medieval church are as extrabiblical as they are tasteless and indelicate. Unfortunately, popular speculations on the LDS side have sometimes also been tasteless and indelicate. Still, on this subject official Mormonism makes four assertions.

1. Mary was a pure virgin (Alma 7:10; 1 Nephi 11:13-20).

2. Mary was in some unspecified manner made pregnant by God the Father, through the power of the Holy Ghost (Lk 1:32-35), "not in violation of natural law but in accordance with a higher manifestation thereof."[12] Hence Jesus is not a metaphorical Son, but a *begotten* Son.

3. Jesus of Nazareth, the offspring of that divine conception, is in his biological being the son of a mortal mother, Mary, and a divine father, God. Jesus is not the son of the Holy Ghost, but of the Father through the Holy Ghost. Jesus' divine paternity was necessary in order for him to have power over death and therefore to accomplish his saving mission (Jn 5:26; 10:17-18) and perform his atoning sacrifice. Only one with the power to live could truly die voluntarily.

4. The exact details of how Jesus' conception was accomplished have not been revealed, either in the Bible or in modern revelation.

While it is true that certain LDS leaders (mostly in the nineteenth century) have offered their opinions on the conception of Jesus, those opinions were never included among the official doctrines of the church and have, during my lifetime at least, not appeared in official church publications—lest they be taken as the view of the church.[13] Yet those who would misrepresent the LDS Church (and also a vocal minority of its own eccentrics) continue to insist on the unofficial speculations of nineteenth-century members rather than on the *official* views of the church then or now.

Latter-day Saints also insist on the preexistence of Jesus Christ and on his identity in his preexistent state as God (Jn 1:1-14). Thus, it was not only Jesus' incarnation that made him God the Son, but his designation by the Father to be the Son "in the beginning."

Finally, Latter-day Saints believe that Jesus will come again in the clouds of heaven in the day of the Lord to establish his kingdom (Acts 1:6, 11) and to rule for a thousand years on the earth (Rev 20:4-7). In that glorious kingdom, the prayers of millions of Christians that "thy kingdom come, thy will be done on earth as it is in heaven" will be positively answered. To use Evangelical terms, this makes Mormons premillennialists (just like Justin Martyr, Irenaeus or Hippolytus in the early church).

Avoiding Misconceptions

Evangelicals often accuse Latter-day Saints of worshiping a "different Jesus" because we believe some things about Jesus that cannot be proven from the Bible. However, I would point out that John thought Jesus was crucified the afternoon before Passover (Jn 19:14; 18:28), so that the Last Supper was not the Passover meal, while Matthew, Mark and Luke say Jesus ate the Passover with the disciples and was crucified the morning after (Mk 14:12; Mt 26:17-19; Lk 22:13-15).[14] Is John (or the Synoptics) writing about "a different Jesus," or do they simply disagree on the details concerning one Jesus? If some Christians think Jesus had siblings and other Christians think that he did not, or if some think he stayed in Egypt for years while others think it was merely for weeks or months, do they worship different beings? If I think Jesus liked his veggies and you think he didn't, are we therefore talking about two different people? Some Evangelicals, like the Mormons, do not accept the Nicene and Chalcedonian definitions, I am told, but limit their Christology to the New Testament data. Do these people also worship "a different Jesus" than other more creedal

Evangelicals, and are they therefore not Christian?

This charge, that people worship "a different Jesus" if they disagree over any detail of his character or history, is simply a rhetorical device, a trick of language.[15] All I can say to it is that Latter-day Saints worship that divine Son of God of whom the apostles and prophets of the Old and New Testaments bear record, and we believe all that they have to say about him. There is no biblical information about the Son of God that the Latter-day Saints do not affirm. If Evangelicals truly worship "a different Jesus" than this, I shall be greatly disappointed.

LDS Misgivings About Evangelical Belief

Basically, Latter-day Saints are troubled by the Evangelical reliance on the formulae of councils and creeds for their "standard of orthodoxy" instead of on the language of the New Testament. Professor Blomberg states correctly that it was the Council of Chalcedon that "defined what would remain the standard of orthodoxy" (p. 112). But why, the LDS would ask, does the Bible not provide this standard? The answer, of course, is that biblical language is inadequate for defining actual orthodox belief about the nature of God. It is less precise and less technical than that of the creeds, and it fails to make the fine distinctions that the philosophers wanted made. But I suggest that if God left some things undefined or unresolved in the Bible, then the lack of fine distinctions must not have bothered God as much as it bothered the philosophers. Moreover, the "standard of orthodoxy" provided by Chalcedon contains terms like *inconfusedly, unchangeably, indivisibly, inseparably* and *subsistence*—none of which can be found in the Bible. I frankly do not see how terms that cannot be found in the Bible can be made a test for *biblical* orthodoxy!

If the biblical teaching about the Trinity really is imprecise or ambiguous in some respects and may as a result be coherently interpreted in more than one way, then by what authority do the councils "amend" it? Were they "holy men of God" inspired to write additional Scripture? On the other hand, if the biblical information *is* adequate for defining God, then there is no need for clarifying creeds to restate what is already clearly stated.

Either the Bible is inadequate for defining Christian orthodoxy, or the creeds are redundant for defining Christian orthodoxy. Anyone who accepts the former option has in fact added the creeds to the Bible. While Mormons readily admit that we are not "orthodox" Christians in that we do not accept the councils and creeds, we do accept the Bible without its theological add-ons. On the other hand, LDS Christians feel that "orthodox" Christians, in the interest of truth in advertising, ought to clarify that they believe the Bible only as amended and interpreted by later voices.

For example, in support of the subordinationist view of the LDS and of the early Church Fathers, I can refer among many other passages of Scripture to John 14:28, where Jesus flatly states, "My father is greater than I." What *biblical* passages can the "orthodox" cite that state in equally plain and clear language the opposing view as formulated at Nicaea and Chalcedon, that the Father and the Son are "eternally co-equal?"[16] There are none. This view can be arrived at only by first accepting the Greek concept of deity and then working backward to reinterpret the Scriptures. Latter-day Saints perceive this as the tail of human reasoning wagging the dog of Scripture.[17]

It is true that there are Latter-day Saints who read too much into the term "only begotten," but on the other hand, Prof. Blomberg's interpretation of *monogenēs* (p. 123) also seems to me a bit overstated. However, the point is moot since there are other passages of Scripture that do refer to Jesus as "begotten," and from *gennaō* rather than *ginomai*. In fact, the Nicene Creed itself declares that Jesus is "begotten." Such prominent Evangelical scholars as F. F. Bruce and I. H. Marshall have held that "the One begotten by God" (1 Jn 5:18) is Jesus.[18] R. E. Brown lists no fewer than twenty-three other modern scholars plus the NEB and RSV as subscribing to the same view.[19] So it isn't just the Mormons standing alone here!

In Matthew 1:16, the final verse of the "begats" (Abraham begat

Isaac, etc.), Mary is referred to as she "out of whom was begotten (*egennēthē*) Jesus." In this verse the passive form of *gennaō* appears as the last in a string of forty consecutive occurrences of that verb, all unmistakably having the sense of paternal "begetting." As Abraham begat Isaac, so Jesus "was begotten" of Mary. That God "begot" Jesus (*gegennēka*) was also important to the author of Hebrews (applying Ps 2:7), as his begotten status set Jesus apart from and made him higher than the angels (Heb 1:5; 5:5). It is true that the root of *monogenēs* is *ginomai* rather than *gennaō*. However, *monogenēs* is still used in the New Testament to refer to "sole progeny" at Luke 7:12, 8:42 and 9:38, and at Hebrews 11:17, and is twice used in the same sense by Josephus.[20] Surely Evangelicals do not dispute the unique and literal sonship of the mortal Jesus. Are we really in disagreement here?

If Jesus was truly a *human* being, then he had forty-six chromosomes, a double strand of twenty-three. If he was truly human, he got one strand of twenty-three chromosomes from his mother. Where did the other strand come from, if not from his Father? I am not talking about a sexual conception (see n. 13), only a *divine* conception and a *divine* sonship. I would be shocked to learn that Evangelicals believe Joseph or somebody else to have been Jesus' father—that the Father was not *the* Father of the Son.

There can be no doubt that Mary was pregnant and that God caused her pregnancy (Mt 1:18; Lk 1:34-35). Latter-day Saints believe that this makes the mortal Jesus the "begotten" Son of God. For me it means God was the immediate cause of the conception of Jesus in the flesh, that is, as a physical, mortal and biological being. Exactly how God caused Mary to become pregnant is unknown (perhaps that is what Blomberg is getting at), but *that* God did indeed cause her to become pregnant is in my view a fundamental belief of historic Christianity. If Evangelicals do not believe that God was the Father of the mortal Jesus, the cause of his coming into biological existence, then Latter-day Saints would have misgivings about Evangelicals being truly Christian!

Finally, on the subject of Christ and the Trinity, as on most other subjects, Latter-day Saints are frustrated at the Evangelical use of nonauthoritative LDS sources to define LDS beliefs. The average Evangelical hears me say that such and such is true and sees me offer evidence from the LDS Scriptures to prove it. Then the same Evangelical listens to some anti-Mormon who says that such and such is *not* true and cites evidence from other LDS sources to prove it. Without the ability to distinguish authoritative Mormon sources from speculation and private opinion, it is natural to trust fellow Evangelicals— even if they are clearly polemical. But the proper standard for judging a religion is its authoritative, collective beliefs, not the private views of this or that individual member. If I were to define modern Evangelicalism by the proslavery rhetoric of *some* nineteenth-century Evangelical leaders, you might think it unfair. If I defined as basic, authoritative Evangelicalism *everything* I may hear *any* TV evangelist say on the air (which, unfortunately, some Mormons do), that would be unfair as well. If I labeled the murder of abortion doctors and the bombing of clinics as tenets of Evangelicalism just because *some* Evangelicals believe they are, you would undoubtedly think that was unfair also. And yet few Evangelicals are willing to judge the religion of the Latter-day Saints for what it *actually* teaches from its own *authoritative* sources in its *mainstream* twentieth-century persona.

The only binding sources of doctrine for Latter-day Saints are the Standard Works of the church: the Bible, Book of Mormon, Doctrine and Covenants, and Pearl of Great Price. The only official interpretations and applications of these doctrinal sources are those that come to the church over the signatures of the First Presidency or the Quorum of the Twelve Apostles (collectively). All the rest is commentary.[21]

A More Positive Conclusion

Latter-day Saints believe that Evangelicals worship Christ, and because they worship Christ, they are Christians. We believe that Evangelical doctrine is incorrect in some particulars, and this leads us to want to correct them, but it does not for us change the fact that Evangelicals are already Christians. Latter-day Saints who understand their religion will view committed Evangelicals in the same way that Aquila and Priscilla viewed Apollos: eloquent, mighty in the Scriptures, fervent in the spirit, and diligent, but needing to have the way of God expounded to him more perfectly (Acts 18:24-26). As a Latter-day Saint, I would be pleased to have Evangelicals think of me in the same manner: as one who worships Christ, but imperfectly by Evangelical standards. Unfortunately, that has not usually been my experience. If we would admit that we share a common acceptance of the Bible while rejecting each other's additions to it (the councils and creeds on your side and the revelations of Joseph Smith on mine), we would find that we share far more than we dispute. This could serve as a ground for cooperation, dialogue and increased tolerance and respect, though it would still be insufficient grounds for full fellowship. It is not the LDS aim to be accepted as "orthodox" or Evangelical Christians; we are not. But the frequent assertion of many Evangelicals that Latter-day Saints do not even worship Christ or believe in the Bible is untrue. In view of the real theological differences that exist between us, I would not think it appropriate to grant full fellowship to one another or to cease proselytizing on either side. But it is time to recognize each other's common devotion to the Christ of the New Testament—whichever of us may be the real Apollos in need of more perfect instruction.

Joint Conclusion

[BLOMBERG & ROBINSON]

BOTH EVANGELICALS AND THE LDS believe in the simultaneous oneness and threeness of God, though Evangelicals understand God's oneness as an ontological oneness of being, while the LDS understand it as a oneness of mind, will and purpose. Both sides accept the biblical data about Christ and the Trinity, but interpret them by different extrabiblical standards (the ancient creeds for Evangelicals, the modern revelations of Joseph Smith for Mormons).

Both communities accept the full divinity of Jesus Christ, his divine sonship, and his role as the only means of salvation for human beings. Latter-day Saints are subordinationists, making the Father greater than the Son, while Evangelicals generally find this a compromise of the divinity of the Son. Evangelicals insist on an eternal difference in kind between the human and the divine, whereas Latter-day Saints see the human and the divine as a single species. They believe that God and humans are reconciled in Christ, who makes it possible then by grace for humans to become what God is. We jointly affirm that Jesus Christ is the Son of God and the Savior of the world. We affirm that his death on the cross completed an infinite, vicarious atonement that paid for the sins of the world and that reconciled God and humanity. Jesus was resurrected from the dead and is now glorified in the heavens, and he will return at the last day to establish his rule fully and for all eternity.

4

Salvation

[ROBINSON]

What Latter-day Saints Believe

One of the most important components of the Christian confession is the knowledge that for fallen humanity Jesus Christ is the way to salvation and that besides Christ there is no other way. According to the Book of Mormon (Mosiah 3:17):

> And moreover, I say unto you, that there shall be no other name given nor any other way nor means whereby salvation can come unto the children of men, only in and through the name of Christ, the Lord Omnipotent.

Again from the Book of Mormon (2 Nephi 2:5-8):

> And by the law no flesh is justified; for by the law men are cut off.
> ... Wherefore redemption cometh in and through the Holy Messiah; for he is full of grace and truth. Behold, he offereth himself a sacrifice for sin, to answer the ends of the law, unto all those who have a broken heart and a contrite spirit; and unto none else can the ends of the law be answered. ... There is no flesh that can dwell in the presence of God, save it be through the merits, and mercy, and grace of the Holy Messiah, who layeth down his life according to the flesh.[1]

I readily grant that anyone who believes that it is possible to earn salvation apart from the merits, mercy and grace of Christ is not a true Christian nor, as the Book of Mormon clearly indicates (2 Nephi 2:8), a true Latter-day Saint. Such a doctrine is foreign to the religion I practice and teach, and I am not aware of any element within the LDS

Church that would propose any other name or any other way into the kingdom of God than through Christ Jesus.

It is fundamental to both the Bible and the Book of Mormon (for example, 2 Nephi 31:21 or Moroni 7:26) that there is no other name than Jesus Christ whereby humans can be saved. This is what I believe; it is what I was taught growing up; it is what I teach my students and what I teach my children. Faithful Latter-day Saints declare with Nephi, "I glory in my Jesus, for he hath redeemed my soul from hell" (2 Nephi 33:6).[2]

Latter-day Saints believe that God in his perfect justice cannot tolerate or condone sin in any degree (Doctrine and Covenants 1:31) and that all human beings have sinned in some degree and are therefore unworthy of the glory of God (Rom 3:23; Mosiah 5:21). This condition cannot be remedied by subsequent individual righteousness, since we have already *broken* the moral law and cannot justly claim innocence under a law we have broken. The curse of the law is that our very first sin renders justification by law or by works forever impossible to even the most subsequently righteous and upright human being.[3]

To overcome this obstacle, God through grace has provided the gift of his perfect Son. If humans accept this gift and enter the gospel covenant by making Christ their Lord, they are justified of their sins, not by their own works and merits, but by the perfect righteousness of Jesus Christ accepted in their behalf. As Father Lehi explained to his son Jacob, even though Jacob was a "good" boy: "I know that thou art redeemed, because of the righteousness of thy Redeemer" (2 Nephi 2:3).

Just as the covenant of marriage makes husband and wife one flesh, so the covenant of the gospel makes the Savior and the saved to be "one," a new creature no longer strictly one entity or the other, but both (2 Cor 5:17; Gal 6:15). In this oneness of the covenant relation, our sins become his to pay, and his righteousness becomes ours for atonement and justification. Thus I am both ransomed and justified by faith in Christ.

For Latter-day Saints Jesus is Jehovah. Jesus' actual Hebrew name Yeshua means "Jehovah saves" and thus depicts, in our view, both his identity and his function. The connection between Jesus and salvation is so close that it amounts to virtual identification of one with the other. Jesus may be assisted by apostles, prophets or disciples who spread his word, but the words that bring salvation are all his and not theirs. And the merits and mercy and grace by which salvation comes are likewise his and not theirs (2 Nephi 2:8). Mormons do not worship Joseph Smith or look to any source other than Jesus for salvation.

Christ invites *all* human beings, not just a select few, to enjoy the salvation he has prepared.[4] In the LDS view, we accept the offered salvation by believing in Christ, repenting of our sins and being baptized in the name of Jesus Christ for the remission of sins (Acts 2:38; 22:16; Tit 3:5; 1 Pet 3:21).[5] God then confirms the covenant by bestowing the gift of the Holy Ghost through the laying on of hands. This is, after all, the apostle Peter's prescription for those who have believed his preaching at Acts 2:38 (with Acts 8:17-18; 19:6). In accepting the gospel covenant we agree to make Jesus Lord of our lives and in our lives. To deny him his lordship and our subsequent obedience is to deny *him,* regardless of what we might profess to believe *about* him (Mt 7:21).

Latter-day Saints enthusiastically endorse the validity of salvation through grace by faith (Doctrine and Covenants 20:30) but insist that "faith" not be totally divorced from its Semitic origin meaning "faithful" (Hebrew *'āman*) and become watered down to mean mere mental assent (Jas 2:14-26, esp. v. 19). To have "faith" in Christ must in some degree imply subsequent "faithfulness" to Christ as Lord, and this seems agreeable to Prof. Blomberg (p. 169).[6] Consequently, the LDS concept of being "in Christ" (Paul's term) or being "perfect in Christ" (Moroni's term) is one of covenant relationship. While there are no preconditions for entering into the covenant of faith in Christ to be justified by his grace through faith, there are covenant obligations incurred by so entering. Those who have been justified by faith are *obliged* to serve Christ and to make him their Lord by imitating him in their behavior and keeping his commandments (Jn 14:15, 21; 15:8, 10; Rom 6:16; 1 Cor 6:9-10). As reflected in the LDS eucharistic prayers, the obligation of believers is that we are in principle *willing* to take his name on us, *willing* to always remember him and *willing* to keep his commandments. This willingness to remember and to serve him and not serve sin, a commitment of faith, in turn guarantees that we will have his Spirit with us.[7]

Once coming to Christ and assuming his yoke, the Christian must then "endure to the end" (Mt 24:13; Mk 13:13). Since Latter-day Saints reject the Calvinist doctrine of eternal security, or once-saved-always-saved, it follows that we also accept the possibility that one may "fall from grace" (Gal 5:4; 2 Pet 3:17) or fail to "endure to the end." This may come about if we rebel against God and refuse to serve him as promised, thus denying both our vassalage and Christ's lordship. Whoever we *want* to serve is our true master (Rom 6:16), be it Christ or Satan. So after being born again Christians may either "endure" in their commitment to Christ and their desire for him or "fall from grace" through willful rebellion, by withholding their promised hearts (Gal 5:4; Doctrine and Covenants 20:32).

The astute reader will recognize that in this (and many other theological points) the LDS view is thoroughly Arminian. Like the late sixteenth-century Dutch Reformer Jacob Arminius, Latter-day Saints reject the Calvinist doctrines of total depravity, unconditional election,[8] limited atonement, irresistible grace and the perseverance of the saints—the whole TULIP (an acronym for these five doctrines).[9] Like Arminius, the LDS insist on real free will, "agency" or "moral agency" as we call it. Calvinist Evangelicals frequently label LDS soteriology sub-Christian when it is in reality Arminian, so I am comforted by Prof. Blomberg's assurances (p. 175) that informed Evangelicals accept Arminian theology (the Wesleyan tradition among others) as fully Christian. Time and again I have been accused of heresy by Calvinist Evangelicals not only for the LDS distinctives but also for beliefs the LDS hold *in common with Arminian Evangelicals.*[10]

Calvinist Evangelicals insist that a "backslider" was never really converted, while Mormons and other Arminians say that the backslider "fell from grace." But both agree in principle that genuine Christian conversion must somehow be associated with Christian behavior. To argue otherwise is to join the antinomians castigated by Paul in Romans 6—8.

Whatever good works Christians manage to perform are not prerequisites for grace, for justification or for entering the covenant, since their works *follow* their conversion. But such works are the necessary fruits of conversion (Mt 7:19-20; Alma 7:24). Thus genuine Christians justified by faith in Christ may be found in many degrees of compliance with the commandments of God. In relative human terms some are "better" than others. We may serve Christ poorly and still be saved Christians with lots of room for growth, but if we *refuse* to serve him and serve sin instead, then we are no longer his and no longer saved (Rom 6:16). All true Christians must share in principle the desire to serve God. Where the obligation to live righteously is rejected, Jesus has not *really* been made Lord, and there is neither justification nor salvation. LDS belief in the necessity of commitment to Christ is well stated by John: "He that saith, I know him, and keepeth not his commandments, is a liar, and the truth is not in him" (1 Jn 2:4).

Unlike Evangelicals, Latter-day Saints see "being saved" at conversion as just the beginning of a process of becoming like Christ. At first—just after accepting Christ—we may not be very much like him. This does not really matter, for even then we are justified before God by Jesus' performance and not our own: "We know that justification through the grace of our Lord and Savior Jesus Christ is just and true" (Doctrine and Covenants 20:30). But as we worship Christ by imitating him, and as we move toward him drawn by his Spirit, the fruits of our conversion begin to appear. As we continue faithful to the covenant we get better; we become more and more Christlike in our personal lives. It is possible to say the words of commitment and not mean them (Mt 7:21-27), but salvation cannot be attained in this manner. It is even possible to say the words and merely *wish* that we meant them, but this is similarly futile.

It is quite true that Latter-day Saints emphasize the importance of works or behavior much more than some other Christians do. Beyond the clear teaching of Scripture, one motive for this has been a reaction to those Christians who teach "easy grace" as a license for wickedness. Sadly, a common stereotype among Latter-day Saints is that most Evangelicals believe just *saying* "Lord, Lord" will get them into the kingdom of heaven even if they refuse to *obey* the Father's will (Mt 7:22). I have learned that this perception is largely unfair, but there is at least as much truth in it as in the stereotype among Evangelicals that Mormons think we can save ourselves by our works.

Another factor that predisposes Latter-day Saints to stress the value of works is the cultural pressure of a Western, survivalist, do-it-yourself pioneer heritage in which work was a primary virtue. The social and cultural value of work can influence its theological value. Further, a theological focus on the *goal* of Christian commitment (to become like Christ), instead of on the *beginning* of Christian commitment (in justification through faith in Christ), has often tilted LDS attention toward ultimate perfection rather than toward conversion. Still, salvation by works without grace, making ourselves just and worthy without Christ, is a concept incompatible with LDS Scripture and LDS faith and has been identified by church leaders as a "heresy," even though it has at times been common at the popular level.[11]

The real sticking point between LDS and Evangelicals is not whether we are saved by grace (both affirm this) but whether we are saved by grace *alone,* that is, without individual, personal involvement or participation. Latter-day Saints find "salvation by grace *alone*" to be unbiblical[12] and, borrowing C. S. Lewis's analogy, like cutting cloth with only half of the scissors.[13] We would agree with Bonhoeffer or MacArthur that one cannot "have eternal life yet continue to live in rebellion against God."[14] I would judge the terms "being saved," "coming to Christ," "accepting the gospel," "entering the covenant," "making Christ Lord in my life" and "serving Christ" as being roughly equivalent. It follows, then, that saying "I have come to Christ, but I refuse to serve him" is self-contradictory. How does one accept Christ without accepting Christ *as Lord?* And to accept Christ as Lord is to accept myself as his vassal, and vassals do the will of their lord, not their own will.

Prof. Blomberg cites Paul (Gal 5:6), "the only thing that counts in God's eyes is faith *working* through love," and James (2:14, 17, 24, 26), "faith without the *works* that flow from receiving the gospel of Christ is dead and unable to save" (p. 167; emphasis added). These sound indistinguishable to me from the post facto requirement of faithful service that the LDS and other Arminians describe as "enduring to the end."

It is incorrect to state that Mormons believe baptism is necessary for all people in order to inherit the celestial kingdom of God. Children who die before the age of individual accountability (eight years) and those impaired mentally below roughly an eight-year-old level inherit the celestial kingdom by the grace of God without needing baptism (Doctrine and Covenants 137:10).[15] Also, persons who did not have the opportunity of baptism presented to them during their lives may still inherit that kingdom if, in the infinite foreknowledge of God, they *would* have received it given the opportunity. This is very similar to the view of the Arminian Evangelicals described by Prof. Blomberg (p. 171) and the view of some other Protestants and Catholics, though these would propose that God simply dispenses with the need for baptism under these circumstances and grants salvation without it.[16]

According to the perfect foreknowledge of God, "God will deal with people on the basis of divine awareness of how they would have responded had they heard the gospel" (Blomberg, p. 171). The LDS statement of this principle is found in Doctrine and Covenants 137:7: "All who have died without a knowledge of this gospel, who would have received it if they had been permitted to tarry, shall be heirs of the celestial kingdom of God." In the LDS view it is only those who have heard the gospel fairly and correctly presented, who understand it correctly, who feel a witness of the Spirit and who yet refuse to accept it who will bring their spiritual progress to a halt.[17]

The LDS doctrine of the afterlife is largely, though not entirely, biblical, and in part it is identical to the Evangelical view. That is, at death the spirits of all human beings are judged and consigned to one of two conditions. The spirits of the righteous are received into paradise, or Abraham's Bosom (which is *not* the same as heaven), and the spirits of the wicked suffer in a real hell where they are subject to the malice of the devil and his angels (Lk 16:19-31; Alma 40:11-14).

However, for the LDS this paradise and this hell are only temporary states to which spirits are consigned between death and resurrection. At the second coming of the Lord the righteous dead will be resurrected to glory (1 Thess 4:16), while the wicked will wait another thousand years until the *second* resurrection, when hell will finally deliver up its captive dead (Rev 20:5, 13). Only then will all humans be finally and permanently judged before the great white throne (Jn 5:29; Rev 20:11-15; Rom 2:6-8). Only then will the damned be cast out with the devil and his angels to suffer forever. The saved will be glorified and will receive rewards "according to their works" (Rev 20:13; 1 Pet 4:6).

A major difference between Evangelical and LDS views on the afterlife is that the LDS believe the period between death and resurrection is still a probationary or testing period for those in hell. If they repent and turn to Christ, they may yet be redeemed from Satan through the atonement and inherit some degree of glory among the many mansions of the Father. To this end, we believe the gospel is preached to the ignorant and rebellious spirits *(pneumata)* in prison,[18] that they may repent and accept Christ and live (Jn 5:25-29; 1 Pet 3:18-20; 4:6). Like the prodigal of the parable, they may yet reconsider, repent and be joyfully received among the mansions of the

Father although perhaps not to receive all that will be inherited by the more faithful.[19] Evangelicals who struggle with the fate of the unevangelized are forced to choose between the mercy of God on the one hand and the absolute necessity of accepting Christ on the other. Latter-day Saints have it both ways by making the period between death and resurrection probationary. In this way there is still only one name under heaven whereby people can be saved, and there is also an equal opportunity for all who will to hear the gospel and to confess the name of Christ.

Even the absolute need for the traditional Christian sacraments such as baptism and confimation may be maintained in this way without fear of excluding those who could not or did not receive them. Latter-day Saints believe that eventually, though before the resurrection, baptisms and the other Christian sacraments may be performed for the dead by living humans acting as proxies (1 Cor 15:29). Their theology in this regard allows Mormons to insist on the absolute necessity of Christian confession and even of the Christian ordinances, without fear of excluding any who might not have had an opportunity to hear and accept the gospel during their mortal lives.

These doctrines are usually rejected by Evangelicals, since they are not expressly stated in the Bible, but if an Evangelical like Sir Norman Anderson can suggest that God may enable those ignorant of the gospel "*somehow* to cast themselves on the mercy of God and cry out, as it were, for his forgiveness and salvation" (p. 171, emphasis added), may not the LDS suggest *how* this might be accomplished, consistent with 1 Peter 3:18-19, 4:6 and 1 Corinthians 15:29, as many other Christians have also done?[20]

After the resurrection of both the righteous and the wicked (Rev 20:4-5, 11-15) all human beings will be consigned to their final and permanent fate. From that verdict there will be no appeal or hope of release. Before the great white throne those who are filthy still through their own obdurate will are cast eternally into the lake of fire (Rev 20:13-15; 2 Nephi 9:15-16), and all those who, either in life or in the period between their death and resurrection, have accepted the gospel and the atonement of Christ will be allotted a degree of glory appropriate to their faithfulness (Jn 5:28-29; Rev 20:12-13).[21]

Strictly speaking, there will be as many degrees of glory among the mansions of the Father as there are degrees of individual behavior among the saved.[22] However, Mormons believe the saved will be divided into three broad divisions called kingdoms or glories.[23] The lowest of these is the telestial glory, which is reserved for those who were wicked in the flesh (both LDS and non-LDS) but who, like the prodigal, in some sense and to some degree turned to Christ in their suffering between death and resurrection. Even this least of the heavenly glories "surpasses all understanding" (Doctrine and Covenants 76:89).

The next highest glory, the terrestrial kingdom, is reserved for the honorable men and women of the earth, the "righteous," who rejected the fullness of the gospel and the witness of the Holy Spirit during their mortal lives but changed their minds in the spirit prison (Doctrine and Covenants 76:71-78). Their lot in eternity is to dwell with Jesus in glory forever, but without enjoying the separate presence of the Father and without enjoying continuing family relationships. From Prof. Blomberg I understand this to be a fair approximation of what Evangelicals expect heaven to be like: one being representing both the Father and the Son, no marriage or other family ties, glory beyond mortal comprehension, but with no chance of becoming literally like Christ. (This means that if the Mormons turn out to be right after all, most Evangelicals will *still* get just about what they had expected in an afterlife!) The terrestrial kingdom is also for those LDS who knew the "fullness of the gospel" in life but were not "valiant" in their commitment to Christ (Doctrine and Covenants 76:79).

The highest degree of heavenly glory is the celestial kingdom, which is *not* reserved for the LDS alone, since children and the mentally handicapped also inherit this kingdom. So also do those good people of every religious belief who never heard and understood the gospel during their lives or who never felt the Spirit bear witness to it, but who would have accepted it if they had. These will have the opportunity to hear, understand and feel the witness of the Spirit between death and resurrection and receive celestial glory.

The LDS believe there will be millions, even billions, of good souls who will come from the east and the west to sit down with Abraham, Isaac and Jacob in the celestial kingdom of heaven (Mt 8:11)—including, in my opinion, a very large percentage of Evangelicals. At the same time all who knew the gospel in some degree, the children of the kingdom, but who would not live it will be cast out. The celestial kingdom is reserved for those for whom no sacrifice was too great and who always moved toward the greater light. These are the ones who overcome *all* things through faith in Christ and are "made perfect through Jesus" (Doctrine and Covenants 76:69), who become sons and daughters of God and receive his image and glory. They are those who are called "gods, even the sons of God" (in the sense of Ps 82:6 and Jn 10:34-36). They are also the dead in Christ who are first to be raised up at his second coming (1 Thess 4:15-17). They will eventually enjoy the presence of the Father as well as the Son, and continuing family relationships, both with the Godhead (as sons and daughters) and with their own faithful spouses and children to whom they have been sealed forever (Doctrine and Covenants 76:50-70).

So the LDS believe the Evangelical view of the afterlife is essentially correct in this regard: immediately at death the spirits of the righteous and the wicked are separated and consigned either to a paradise of rest and comfort or to a hell of misery. But the LDS believe that between this preliminary judgment at death and the final judgment after resurrection there will be opportunity for justice and fairness— for those who never heard to hear, for those who were deceived to be reclaimed and, by the grace of God, for the repentant prodigals to come home.

Latter-day Saints do not derive their belief in the three degrees of glory primarily from the Bible, as Blomberg suspects (p. 182). The

doctrine is alluded to there (1 Cor 15:40-42; 2 Cor 12:2; most occurrences of "heaven" are actually plural in the originals), but not clearly
enough to arrive at the LDS view. The division of heaven into three
degrees comes from modern revelation, primarily Doctrine and Covenants 76 (see also 137 and 138). And if we Mormons are wrong about
heaven being subdivided, about the Father's house having many
mansions (Jn 14:2) and about people being rewarded according to their
works (Mt 16:27; Rev 2:23; 20:12-13), is that a sufficiently egregious
error to nullify the power of Christ's blood in our behalf? I don't think
so. If Arminian and Calvinist Evangelicals can disagree over free will,
election, irresistible grace, eternal security and so on, and yet both be
deemed Christians, I don't think merely believing in a subdivided
heaven or believing that Jesus can save even the dead should get the
LDS thrown out of Christendom.

Avoiding Misconceptions

For the record, there should be no disagreement between LDS and
Evangelical Christians that

    1. human beings are fallen from an Eden state through the trans-
gression of their first parents, Adam and Eve;

    2. the biblical Jesus Christ is the only way to salvation;

    3. Jesus lived a perfect and sinless life; then, though completely
innocent, he voluntarily suffered in Gethsemane and on the cross, the
pain, infirmities and guilt of all humanity, and freely offered up his
life as a vicarious sacrifice—all for our sakes;

    4. through his merit and his substitutionary atonement, Christ will,
if we accept his sacrifice and come to him in good faith, redeem us
from all our sins and errors, from all effects of the fall of Adam, and
will save us from suffering the pains of hell that would otherwise be
justly inflicted upon us;

    5. the opportunity to be born again in Christ is a total gift of grace,
and without the grace of God no one can be justified or saved;

    6. there are no prerequisites to accepting grace and coming to

Christ—other than accepting grace and coming to Christ. (You cannot *do* it without *doing* it!) However, to accept Christ and make him the Lord in our lives and of our lives *is by definition* to accept the obligation of his children to serve and obey him henceforth (Rom 2:8; 6:16). To refuse him service is to refuse him lordship.

Evangelicals and LDS use the term "salvation by works" quite differently. Evangelicals generally equate "salvation" with one's initial conversion to Christ (being born again) and being justified by his blood. When they say "salvation by works," they generally mean the false view that an individual can earn salvation or be justified by personal merit without needing to rely completely on Christ. On the other hand, Latter-day Saints generally use the term "salvation" to mean completed salvation or "glorification," that is, actually *receiving* the heavenly, resurrected glory which is now in the future, even for the born again. Thus "salvation by works" for Mormons usually means keeping our Christian obligation to serve Christ and make him Lord in our lives so as to finally receive our promised blessings at resurrection. The term in LDS usage is equivalent to "enduring faithful to the end" (Mt 10:22; 24:13; Mk 13:13) or not falling from grace (Gal 5:4; Heb 10:29) by abandoning Christ.

For Evangelicals "salvation by works" is something erroneous that someone might attempt *before* or *instead of* coming to Christ. For Latter-day Saints "salvation by works" is a positive term for serving and obeying Christ *after* conversion and not falling from grace. Latter-day Saints and Evangelicals are talking about different things even though they use the same term. Unfortunately, however, Evangelical antipathy to the term "salvation by works" (as they define it) is such that if the term even comes up, it ends the discussion and poisons the well—though the LDS usually mean something completely different than they think we do.

Paul used the phrase "work out your own salvation" (Phil 2:12) in the LDS sense, not meaning we should bring about initial justification by our own merits without Christ, but rather meaning we should continue in bearing the fruits or works of conversion until the end. Even though the LDS talk about works all the time and may even use the phrase "salvation by works," it always means serving Christ *after* being converted so as not subsequently to fall from grace.

LDS terminology often seems naive, imprecise and even sometimes sloppy by Evangelical standards, but Evangelicals have had centuries in which to polish and refine their terminology and their arguments in dialogue with other denominations. We Mormons have not been around nearly as long, and we have no professional clergy to keep our theological language finely tuned (thank heaven!). Our few conversations with other denominations have usually been highly polemical, and both sides have exploited what the other *says* without actually attempting to discover what the other *means*. The Bible condemns this as making someone "an offender for a word" (Is 29:21), and I do not think it pleases God when it is done on either side.

Now along comes Prof. Robinson who tries haltingly to use the Evangelical idiom to state what the LDS really *mean,* and for this I am sometimes accused either of lying or of not truly representing traditional Mormonism—simply because my version sounds different than Brigham Young or Orson Pratt do when left "untranslated." But we do speak two different theological languages, and it does not do any good to object to what Brigham Young or Bruce McConkie *said* in the Mormon idiom without first translating this into what they *meant* in Evangelical terms. This has seldom, if ever, been done in the past, and until we learn to do it, we will never understand each other.

Evangelicals seem to have a particularly hard time with the LDS claim that there are no prerequisites for being born again. Professor Blomberg finds "tension" among Mormons sources on this issue (pp. 175-82). However, as we see things, there is no such tension, for the Bible itself teaches that true faith includes obedience and that obedience is part of being in Christ. See, for example, Paul's use of the term "the obedience of faith" (Rom 1:5; 16:26), "obeying the truth" (Rom 2:8; 6:17; Gal 3:1; 5:7), "obeying the gospel" (Rom 10:16; 2 Thess

1:8), or the importance of the "obedience" that leads to righteousness (Rom 6:16-17). According to Peter, Christians are sanctified "unto obedience" (1 Pet 1:2), they "obey the gospel" (1 Pet 4:17), "obey the truth" (1 Pet 1:22), and "obey the word" (1 Pet 3:1). Luke quotes Peter as teaching that the Holy Spirit is given by God "to them that obey him" (Acts 5:32), and the author of Hebrews states that Christ himself "learned obedience" and is the author of salvation "unto all that obey him" (Heb 5:8-9). John sees the truth as something one *does* as much as something one believes (Jn 3:21; 1 Jn 1:6; 3:7), just as Jesus urges us to "*do* his word" rather than just to "hear" it in the Sermon on the Mount (Mt 7:24-27). I would suggest in view of all this that there is clearly a need for the born again to behave *and* obey—not as a condition for being born again, but as an obligation that being born again incurs. True faith includes obedience, and the true Christian obeys. The "tension" Dr. Blomberg detects here in Mormonism is nothing more than the "two strands" or "two broad camps" he easily accommodates in Evangelicalism (pp. 166-68).

Nevertheless, the LDS believe the only obedience necessary to be born again is obeying the commandments to have faith in Christ, to repent and to be baptized.[24] These are the only "laws and principles" on which being born again is predicated. The language in Article of Faith Three and in Elder McConkie's writings that so disturbs Prof. Blomberg ("through the Atonement of Christ, all mankind may be saved, by *obedience* to the laws and ordinances of the Gospel"; see pp. 177-78) is clarified in Article of Faith Four: "We believe that the first principles and ordinances of the Gospel are: first, Faith in the Lord Jesus Christ; second, Repentance; third, Baptism by immersion for the remission of sins." To those who obey these principles God gives the gift of the Holy Spirit (Acts 5:32), "fourth, laying on of hands for the gift of the Holy Ghost." In other words, it is impossible to be born again without faith in Christ, repentance and baptism (Acts 2:38; Jn 3:3-5). Most Evangelicals would agree with the first two, and some would agree with all three. But there is no quid pro quo here, no earnings being paid off; these things *constitute* being born again. The only "requirement" for coming to Christ is to come. Truly, there are other laws and principles after these "first" ones, but these refer to ways in which the saved may become more like Christ. They are not conditions for "being saved" initially, as Evangelicals use the term.[25]

Most LDS understand the requirements and obligations of the gospel as referring to the obligation of Christians to remain committed to Christ and to keep his commandments *after* they are born again. Evangelicals would call this process "sanctification," and would, I think, agree that "actual growth in tangible righteousness" (to use Prof. Blomberg's terms, p. 175) is necessary for sanctification. But *there are no prerequisites to being justified by faith.*

When Elder McConkie distinguishes between those who receive *some* glory and those who receive the *highest* degree of glory, he is describing the difference between being "saved" in the beginning and being "glorified" at the end. In the other examples cited by Blomberg (pp. 177-78), Elder McConkie uses the term *repentance* to mean *completed* repentance—that is, receiving forgiveness. Thus I understand him to say that in order to be forgiven of our sins, we must first obey the commandment to repent on which forgiveness is predicated (for example, Mt 4:17; Mk 1:15; 6:12; Acts 2:38; 3:19; Ether 4:18). Most Mormons understand his usage; most Evangelicals do not (an Evangelical would not normally use *repentance* to mean "forgiveness"). That is why we must either learn each other's idiom or be doomed to continue feeling that each other's theology "doesn't add up."

Prof. Blomberg similarly misunderstands my arguments in the book *Believing Christ* (pp. 180-82), which was meant to be a popular book using LDS language for LDS readers, not a work of theological precision using Evangelical terms for Evangelical readers. "Doing what we can" (or are able to do), "doing everything we can" and "doing the best we can" are intended to be synonymous terms for "being committed in principle to keeping his commandments" or "making Christ the Lord of our lives" or "making a Christlike life our highest aspiration." Once again, the LDS writer has in mind the process subsequent to conversion, while the Evangelical reader has in mind the initial event of conversion—and we are talking past each other. Is it synergism to insist that the saved must remain faithful and obedient to the will of God after they are saved, or that their future lives and choices must in some degree reflect their service to the Master? No, we have agreed on this already (pp. 169, 175). Salvation consists of both God's offer and the individual's acceptance of that offer.

In the parable of the bicycle from my book *Believing Christ,* the sixty-one cents Sarah contributed to the cost of the bicycle was an arbitrary figure symbolizing her acceptance of her father's offer, nothing more. Had she been broke, the offer would still have been made, but the terms would have asked for her heart in return. But if she had rejected my gracious offer or had demanded a better one—that would be different. Nevertheless, there are *still* no good works required for justification and remission of sins, of "being saved" in the Evangelical sense, other than accepting the offered gift in the manner specified by Peter (Acts 2:38).[26]

Continued faithfulness *is* required in order not to fall from grace after we have been saved. This is Arminianism, not synergism. The only obligations of the covenant are to *stay* in the covenant by obedience to the gospel and not to go wandering off. I trap my students with the question, Is it necessary to keep the commandments in order to enter the celestial kingdom? in order to show them the difference between what Mormons and John (Jn 14:15; 1 Jn 2:3) usually mean by "keeping the commandments" and what Evangelicals and Paul usually mean by "keeping the commandments" (Rom 3:9-11, 20, 23; Gal 3:10). Only a minority of my students really believe that exaltation requires perfect performance, for they have all been taught about the Fall and that Jesus was the only perfect person. But like most LDS, they are often unsophisticated in their terminology and sometimes have not paid attention to the words before. In any case, we do not want to throw out either John or Paul, though the LDS may favor one and Evangelicals the other!

Prof. Blomberg is quite right that my view of his eternal options is quite a bit less risky than his view of mine (pp. 183-84). He notes that if the LDS are correct, he may receive a tolerable reward, but were he to convert to Mormonism and then find that the usual Evangelical stereotype of Mormonism was correct, he would be damned. I point out that there is a third alternative he has at least understated. If the usual Evangelical stereotype of the LDS (that we do not worship Christ or that we do it so badly that he will decline to save us) is *not* correct—then he would be saved in *either* case! And that is more to the point of the present discussion. However, Blomberg seems to be assuming that if he converted to Mormonism his present confession of Christ as Lord and Savior would no longer be acceptable to God; that is, that the promises of God to Evangelicals and others is not valid for Mormons. Alternatively, he may be suggesting that he must repudiate his Christian confession in order to become LDS, something I dispute vehemently and in which case he *ought* to be damned—and would be by *both* our theologies.

Blomberg is also mostly correct in his application of Pascal's wager to this problem (p. 186). However, in the present case I would point out that while one's *losses* might be minimized by wagering on the exclusive truth of Evangelicalism and being wrong, one's possible *gains* are also minimized by this strategy. If one is willing to give up the possibility of celestial glory, of being fully joint heirs with Christ, in return for a guarantee of the lesser terrestrial glory, I say, "Go for it." In my opinion, it may be characteristic of terrestrial individuals that they will do this—and of celestial individuals that they will not.

I would be thrilled at the prospect of Latter-day Saints and Evangelicals who already know their own faith studying the faith of the other,[27] praying for divine guidance and then following the guidance they receive. I would have no reproach for anyone of either faith who converted or did not convert after employing such a procedure (Jas 1:5).[28]

Finally, Prof. Blomberg, like most Evangelicals of my acquaintance, misunderstands the LDS view of non-LDS Christians. The "great and abominable church" mentioned in the Book of Mormon and Doctrine and Covenants is not, as I understand it, any specific denomination or even group of denominations. It is an apocalyptic category that designates *all* those, both LDS and non-LDS, who fight against the Lamb. The term is roughly equivalent to the "Babylon" of the Apocalypse (see, for example, Rev 18—19). The opposite category, "the church of the Lamb," refers to *all* those, both LDS and non-LDS, who worship Christ and seek to do his will or who would if they knew him (1 Nephi 14:10; 22:23, 2 Nephi 10:16). And these are boundaries that cannot be defined denominationally.[29]

In Joseph Smith's first vision, the statement that all existing denominations are "wrong" is not an aspersion on the character of their members. These churches are not "depraved," "corrupt" or "abominations." They are just *wrong*—and therefore not the Lord's one true church. Despite the impression received by Prof. Blomberg, Joseph Smith's History says nothing to the effect that the religious worship of other Christians is "all a hypocritical pretense." It does say that their *creeds* are an abomination, but this is because creeds are philosophical idols created by human minds, imposed upon the Scriptures and then revered as God's word in place of God's Word. Those who believe such creeds are not "abominable." They are just wrong.[30]

However, those who offer these intellectual idols to their hearers as the word of God (in Joseph's words, "their [the creeds'] professors") *are* corrupt when "they teach for doctrines the commandments of men." If they would just stick to the Bible without filtering it through the creeds—and many do—they still would not have *all* the truth, but they would not be "abominable" or "corrupt" either. There is no insult here to non-LDS Christians who believe the Bible and refrain from dragging in the philosophers and theologians as equal or higher authorities. However, those who subordinate the Bible to the creeds are on thin ice, for they make the human product the standard for interpreting God's Word instead of vice versa, and this is, frankly, an abomination.

Misgivings About Evangelical Belief

The biggest dispute between Mormons and Evangelicals should not be over *what* Mormons believe, but over *why* we believe it and *whether* it is true or not. Yet with Evangelicals we seldom get past the *what* to the *why* or the *whether.* This is a clear sign of massive misunderstanding and also of misrepresentation of LDS beliefs, sometimes intentionally, by Evangelical "experts," usually anticultists. I *know* what I believe. Why won't Evangelicals believe I believe it?

When Calvinist Evangelicals tell me that they believe in irresistible grace or eternal security (doctrines with which Wesley and I would both disagree), I do not dispute that this is their belief. I may discuss with them why they believe these doctrines or whether or not they are correct, but I would find it silly to go searching through Evangelical literature back to Calvin looking for evidence that Evangelicals do not *really* believe what they *think* they do. And yet when I begin to explain to Evangelicals what Mormons believe, the discussion almost never centers on why I believe it or whether it is correct. Rather, it centers on whether or not I actually believe it.

For example, when I say that I believe in Jesus Christ or in justification by faith in Christ, I often hear in return, "Oh, no you don't, and I can prove it," accompanied by a flurry of prooftexts culled from sources supposedly more reliable than I am on the subject of what *I* believe. But it is just as absurd to try to prove to me by prooftexting LDS literature that I do not believe what I think I do as it is for me to try to argue to Calvinists that they don't really believe in irresistible grace or eternal security. Stop and think about it. If I could compile enough snippets of citations from Calvinist writings to support my thesis or make it credible, would I convince you that you do not really believe what you think you do? Of course not!

However, even when I occasionally do convince Evangelicals that I as a Mormon really do believe A, B and C, their next response is equally predictable and equally frustrating. "Yes," they will say, "I now believe that you believe these things. It is wonderful to see someone break away from those nasty Mormon beliefs and find Jesus." And once again I cannot convince them, no matter what I say, that I am not an aberration, but that I am actually fairly representative of contemporary LDS orthodoxy. I am certainly not aware of any rift between myself and Joseph Smith, Brigham Young or Gordon B. Hinckley, our present LDS leader. When we LDS do not speak your language, you do not understand us; but where a few of us have learned to speak your language and adjust accordingly, you accuse us of changing our story or of making a break with "traditional" Mormonism.[31] It is frustrating.

In the introduction Prof. Blomberg concedes quite correctly that Latter-day Saints believe in Jesus Christ, believe what the Bible says about Jesus, believe in the substitutionary and sacrificial atonement of Christ, the resurrection of Christ and the future second coming of Christ. This is just a sample of what we share with Evangelicals. Most LDS would not wish to be considered Christian in the historical, orthodox sense, and I would object to any claim that the differences between us are trivial or inconsequential. Nevertheless, Latter-day Saints worship God the Father in the name of the Son. We look to Jesus Christ as the way, the truth and the life: the only name given under heaven whereby we may be saved. We do not pretend to believe this—we believe it.[32]

Latter-day Saints often feel in their relationships with Evangelicals somewhat like Prince Rilian in C. S. Lewis's wonderful Chronicles of Narnia.[33] Prince Rilian is under an enchantment, and he is not really the monster he appears to be. But Jill, Scrubb and Puddleglum the Marsh-wiggle are so frightened by what they see that they will not approach him. Finally Prince Rilian appeals to them in the name of the great Lion, Aslan. This creates a dilemma, for Aslan's instructions were to aid whoever spoke in his name. But could Aslan really have meant *anyone?* Surely his instructions could not include this deranged lunatic! Finally the Marsh-wiggle, bless him, says, "That fellow will be the death of us, once he's up, I shouldn't wonder. But that doesn't let us off following the Sign."

Certainly the visage and reputation of the LDS as created for Evangelicals by anticultists are terrible to behold, and certainly we LDS are not what Evangelicals are used to. But it is possible that we are also not the monsters the Witch would have you believe. If Latter-day Saints read and accept the New Testament witness to Christ, if they do all they do in the name of Christ, if they confess Christ as Lord, call upon his grace, seek cleansing in his blood and attempt to serve him in this world—are not these "Aslan's signs," even if they are found in such an unexpected place and under such surprising circumstances?

I have frequently been assured by Evangelical Christians that if I would confess Jesus as my personal Savior and accept him as Lord, I would be saved. When I respond that I do so confess and accept him—on occasion even making confession (sincerely) on the spot—I am assured that heaven is mine. But when I mention I am also a Mormon, things change. Then the initial promise is usually amended with either (a) the confession won't work for Mormons, that in our case we must not only accept Jesus to be saved, but must also reject the Restoration and pass other doctrinal tests, or (b) that uniquely of all human beings Latter-day Saints are not able to confess Christ properly, even when we intend to.

Even if the rest of Mormonism—apart from our faith in Christ—is not true (though I firmly believe it is), then which is more potent, my theological "error" in believing the Book of Mormon or Christ's saving blood as I call upon his name? Was God's promise (Rom 10:9-13) truly unconditional, or is there an implied exception just for Mormons who might believe and confess? Are Christians saved by the grace of Christ or by "proper" theology—by the atonement or by catechism? If Evangelicals demand the latter of Mormons, then they have come full circle since the Reformation and have established a "new magisterium."

This is why anticultists must always insist that Latter-day Saints do not *really* believe in Jesus—even though we claim to. They insist, like Scrubb resisting the Marsh-wiggle, "It was [only] the *words* of the Sign," for there is no doubt that we *do* say the words, and if we actually *mean* them, well, then, we cannot remain the boogeyman any longer. To be sure, we Latter-day Saints, rightly or wrongly, believe many things that Evangelicals do not. But the fact remains that we also have faith in, confess, worship, love and serve Jesus Christ, the Son of God, the Lord of all. Whoever denies our devotion to Christ does not speak the truth.

A More Positive Conclusion

When Sidney Rigdon came to Joseph Smith in 1830, a month after converting to Mormonism from being a Campbellite minister, he was told that his ministry *as a Protestant* had been like that of John the Baptist, who prepared the way for the fullness of the gospel (Doctrine and Covenants 35:4-5).

That revelation to Sidney Rigdon still expresses the LDS view of other denominations: they have light, truth and knowledge, but not the fullness of these. Where most Evangelicals think of themselves as being in the light and all who disagree with them as being in the darkness, Mormons think of themselves—or at least should—as being one-hundred-watt bulbs and other denominations as being, say, forty-, sixty- or eighty-watt bulbs. Certainly from our point of view other denominations make errors and believe things that are not "light," but they are neither "abominable" nor "corrupt" on account of this.

Nevertheless, these same denominations have much light already, and we do not want to take away any of that light. We believe that we have additional light, which we would like to share with them (Prof.

Blomberg's "filling in the theological gaps"), but only to build on what truth we may already share. What we have in common, which is considerable, is good and true and necessary. We accept other denominations that worship Christ and confess his name as Christians, albeit as Christians who, like Apollos, need further instruction and, like John the Baptist, have not the fullness of the gospel.

Salvation

[BLOMBERG]

What Evangelicals Believe

Evangelicals discern two strands of New Testament texts in regard to salvation. The first group of texts strongly stresses God's grace, appropriated through faith (or belief), as the sole means of a restored relationship with our Maker. Ephesians 2:8-9 puts it most bluntly: "For it is by grace you have been saved, through faith—and this not from yourselves, it is the gift of God—not by works, so that no one can boast." Galatians and Romans were particularly instrumental in Martin Luther's conversion, which in turn provided the main impetus for the Protestant Reformation in the early 1500s, with such texts as Galatians 3:11 ("clearly no one is justified before God by the law, because 'the righteous will live by faith' "; compare Rom 3:21-28).[1] In the Gospels, Jesus repeatedly tells people, "Your faith has saved you" (Mt 9:22; Mk 10:52; Lk 7:50; 17:19).[2] In Acts 16:31 Paul and Silas explain to the Philippian jailer that the way he can be saved is to "believe in the Lord Jesus." And in perhaps the most famous verse in all the Bible, the apostle John writes, "For God so loved the world that he gave his one and only Son, that whoever believes in him shall not perish but have eternal life" (Jn 3:16).

Another set of passages, however, stresses that genuine faith inevitably demonstrates itself in good works. Following immediately after Ephesians 2:8-9, verse 10 continues, "For we are God's workmanship, created in Christ Jesus to do good works, which God prepared in advance for us to do." Galatians 5 describes the fruit of the Spirit's presence in our lives—"love, joy, peace, patience, kindness, goodness, faithfulness, gentleness and self-control" (vv. 22-23) and states explicitly that the only thing that counts in God's eyes is "faith working through love" (5:6). James makes this even clearer—while the works of the Old Testament law can save no one, faith without the works that flow from receiving the gospel of Christ is dead and unable to save (Jas 2:14, 17, 24, 26).[3] Jesus in the Sermon on the Mount declares, "Unless your righteousness surpasses that of the Pharisees and the teachers of the law, you will certainly not enter the kingdom of heaven" (Mt 5:20). In John's Gospel Jesus differentiates the saved from the lost on the basis of having done good or evil deeds (Jn 5:29), but then goes on to explain that the preeminent good work that separates those bound for heaven from those on their way to hell is believing "in the one he has sent" (Jn 6:29).

Evangelicals, like Protestants more generally, can be divided into two broad camps in terms of how they have synthesized these two strands of teaching. Calvinists, following the legacy of sixteenth-century Reformer John Calvin, stress the first set of texts, at times almost to the virtual exclusion of the latter, in strongly emphasizing the grace and sovereignty of God. Calvinists are known for their famous theological TULIP—five fundamental affirmations that form an acronym: total depravity, unconditional election, limited atonement, irresistible grace and perseverance of the saints. These doctrines maintain, respectively, that (1) humans are sinful and are wholly unable to merit salvation, (2) God has freely chosen (elected or predestined) those who will be saved, (3) Christ died only for the elect, (4) once God's Spirit begins to draw an elect person, he or she will of necessity respond with saving faith, and (5) those who have been truly saved can never lose that salvation—they will "persevere" to the end.[4]

Jacob Arminius, a Dutch Reformer who came after Calvin, rejected all five points of the TULIP, stressing the second group of texts cited above, as part of his emphasis on human free will.[5] Of course, both theological systems had to range much more broadly throughout Scripture in search of support for their beliefs on the specific doctrines debated.[6] Calvinism has influenced Presbyterian thought, while Arminianism played a major role in the Methodist movement founded by John Wesley in the 1700s. In fact, many Protestant denominations have aligned themselves with one or the other. For example, the nineteenth-century restorationist movement, which heavily influenced Joseph Smith and Sidney Rigdon, was thoroughly Arminian and roundly rejected Calvinist thought. It gave rise to the Disciples of Christ Church. Today, the intellectual wing of Evangelicalism is predominantly Calvinist (especially in its colleges and publishing houses), so it is easy for an outsider to equate the two (and for insiders to write off Arminians as sub-Christian!), but at the grassroots level, Arminianism is deeply entrenched in American Christianity. Most popular evangelistic crusades, as well as personal witnessing, say next to nothing about predestination and treat all who are addressed as being able to respond with faith in Christ if they so choose.

Mediating positions have also sprung up. Many Evangelicals do not find adequate biblical or logical evidence for "limited atonement," believing instead that Christ died for the sins of the whole world. Yet they still insist on "perseverance of the saints," often called "eternal security," embodied in the slogan "Once saved, always saved."[7] But virtually all Evangelicals agree that the proper way to harmonize the teaching of Scripture on faith and works is that only God's grace, received by faith, brings us into a right standing before God ("justification"), a new birth—the beginning of new life with Christ ("regeneration"), liberation from bondage to past sin and its eternally damning consequences ("redemption"), and a new relationship with God and others ("reconciliation"). At this moment of conversion, the time of our salvation, God's Spirit comes to live in us and begins a process of moral transformation, unique to each person, often frustratingly slow and filled with setbacks, but nevertheless one that inevitably leads to perseverance in good works of all different kinds, though never quantifiable and never adequate to merit eternal life with God in and of themselves.[8]

A second issue that divides some Evangelicals arises over the question of whether we can first accept Jesus merely as Savior and then later as Lord, or whether we must accept both simultaneously at the new birth. Proponents of the former option are rightly concerned not to make it seem as though we do anything to merit salvation: we merely accept a free gift. Proponents of the latter option are afraid of preaching "cheap grace": the gift comes only as we entrust ourselves to a new master.[9] Increasingly, Evangelicals are recognizing truth in both "camps" and the need for mediating positions. The one group is right to stress that we cannot possibly know everything that Christ will demand of us when we come to him and that even what we do know will not always be easy for us to follow. So our acceptance of salvation cannot be dependent on our own performance in any area of Christian living. The other group is right to stress that we cannot claim to have really surrendered control of our lives to Jesus if we consciously refuse to obey him in certain areas of our lives. We have to be willing, at least in principle, to turn over everything to him.[10] The paradoxical conclusion that perhaps captures the correct balance here is that "salvation is absolutely free, but it will cost us our very lives." Our old natures must be crucified with Christ regularly.

A third issue on which Evangelicals differ involves the relationship of baptism to salvation. Luther, Calvin and Wesley all preserved, to varying degrees, the practice of infant baptism that had come to dominate the Roman Catholic Church, while often redefining its significance. The sixteenth-century Anabaptists experienced severe persecution and even martyrdom for returning to what they believed was the uniform, biblical position of restricting baptism to believers only. Contemporary Evangelical descendants of these various Protestant traditions continue to differ on who should be baptized but generally agree that baptism by itself, especially when administered to infants, does not confer salvation on anyone. Children must grow up and trust Christ for themselves. Churches that practice believers' baptism generally agree that it is faith in Christ, not baptism, that saves a person. Baptism is an important act of obedience to a command of Christ, but failure to obey it (or any other individual command) could not make a person forfeit salvation unless salvation were after all by works and not faith. Baptists, like the restorationist movement of the nineteenth century, usually stress the close connection between repentance and baptism, so that the terms can be used almost interchangeably in various contexts (as in Rom 6:1-4) or as a "package" of what happens relatively simultaneously when one comes to faith in Christ (as in Acts 2:38; Mk 1:4).[11] Still, a passage like 1 Corinthians 10:2-5 alerts us to the danger of claiming that baptism by itself saves anyone, and the example of the thief on the cross (Lk 23:43) is often held up as a reminder that genuine trust in Christ, even without baptism, suffices to save a person.

A crucial part of any discussion of salvation is the life to come. Evangelicals see death as the irreversible point in time at which our eternal destiny is fixed. The Bible describes only two options for all of humanity—heaven or hell. Those who have trusted in Jesus will enjoy eternal bliss with God and Christ in a re-created earth and heaven (Rev 21—22); those who have rejected the gospel will spend eternity separated from God and all things good (2 Thess 1:9).

The vexing question, What about those who have never heard of Jesus? receives a variety of answers. Clearly it was an important one in pioneer America as Christians wrestled with the fate of the Indians; Joseph Smith was not the only person to propose a story about the migration of some lost tribes of Israel to North America, with a second appearance of Jesus Christ.[12] Historic Christian orthodoxy, however, has taken different approaches. Probably the best known is the most restrictive position: All who die apart from conscious acceptance of Christ are lost forever because God through "general revelation" (the witness of nature, design in the universe, conscience and moral accountability, etc.) has not left himself without testimony (Acts 14:17). Unsaved humanity freely rebels against that witness and therefore bears accountability for its sins (Rom 1:18-32). Because of sin, all people deserve eternal death (Rom 6:23). Thus the question is not, How can God condemn those who have not explicitly heard and rejected the gospel? but rather, How is it that God graciously chooses to accept those who do hear and respond, even though they have done and can do nothing to merit such acceptance?

A second common answer to the question, which is less restrictive, is based on Romans 2:13-16, Paul's discussion of the heathens' consciences alternately accusing or excusing them. Some Christians have proposed that God judges those who have not heard the gospel on the basis of "the light" (i.e., spiritual illumination) that they have received. They suggest that there may be some who do not try to save themselves by good works but trust in the grace of God to the extent that they know God and are accepted by him. A leading British Evangelical scholar of world religions, Sir Norman Anderson, put it this way:

> What if the Spirit of God convicts them, as he alone can, of something of their sin and need; and what if he enables them, in the darkness or twilight, somehow to cast themselves on the mercy of God and cry out, as it were, for his forgiveness and salvation? Will they not then be accepted and forgiven in the one and only Saviour?[13]

Note that Anderson is referring to a personal response to God in this life, not to an opportunity for salvation after death.

Still others, particularly in the Arminian camp (which stresses God's advance knowledge of all things more than his predestination of individuals), argue that God will deal with people on the basis of divine awareness of how they would have responded had they heard the gospel.[14] A more conservative variation on this view is the belief that all who so cry out to God will in fact hear the gospel in this life, if not through the witness of other people then by a direct, special revelation of Jesus himself (as has occasionally happened throughout church history).

Generally rejected as unbiblical, however, are theories that have people receiving an opportunity for salvation after death or that have God eventually saving everyone. The latter position, known as universalism, often appeals to Philippians 2:10-11, "That at the name of Jesus every knee should bow, in heaven and on earth and under the earth, and every tongue confess that Jesus Christ is Lord." But this passage is a partial quotation of Isaiah 45:23, which goes on to declare that "all who have raged against him will come to him and be put to shame" (v. 24). Isaiah concludes (v. 25) by contrasting the fate of the faithful in Israel to make it clear that while one day all people who have ever lived will be forced to acknowledge that God in Christ is who God said he was, that does not mean everyone will experience the joy of spending eternity with God.[15]

People who hold to the idea of a second chance after death often appeal to 1 Peter 3:19-20, which describes Christ, after dying on the cross, preaching "to the spirits in prison who disobeyed long ago when God waited patiently in the days of Noah." This interpretation presupposes that the preaching was an offer of salvation and that the spirits in prison were those of dead humans. But the Greek word Peter uses here is *kēryssō,* a neutral term for announcing a message, not *euangelizō,* the common New Testament verb for preaching the gospel. The word for "spirits," *pneumata,* in every other unqualified use in the Bible, *in the plural,* refers to angelic or demonic—not human—spirits. Thus it is more likely that this passage describes Christ's announcement of victory over the demonic world (so directly involved in that particularly wicked era just prior to the flood, 2 Pet 2:4) than any postmortem offer of repentance to the unevangelized.[16] After all, Hebrews 9:27-28 declares plainly:

Just as man is destined to die once, and after that to face judgment, so Christ was sacrificed once to take away the sins of many people; and he will appear a second time, not to bear sin, but to bring salvation to those who are waiting for him.

First Peter 4:6 clearly *is* talking about dead humans, but it is not likely that the preaching referred to (this time using *euangelizō* and referring to the offer of salvation) took place after their deaths. The immediate context (vv. 4-5) makes the point that people will be judged for the things they do while they are alive, even if they die before the judgment day. So verse 6 most likely implies that believers, too, are judged on the basis of the response they made to the gospel while they were alive. The NIV brings this out in its translation of the first half of the verse: "For this is the reason the gospel was preached even to those who are *now* dead."[17]

Notwithstanding widespread Evangelical agreement on the fact that this life is the only occasion for settling our eternal destiny, diversity of opinion returns when we raise the question of what heaven and hell are like. More specifically, are there degrees of reward in heaven or degrees of punishment in hell? Some Evangelicals believe that although salvation (and thus "getting into" heaven) is entirely by God's grace, there will be different ways in which believers experience that salvation based on how godly their lives were. Some speak of different crowns, different mansions, varying responsibilities or capacities to appreciate heavenly bliss. I have elsewhere argued, however, that the biblical texts that speak of the different experiences we will all have before God on the judgment day (such as 1 Cor 3:10-15) never suggest that such differences are perpetuated for all eternity. Indeed, the whole notion of heaven as a perfect place for people with perfectly glorified resurrection bodies logically precludes such gradation in reward. Historically, the idea of differing levels in heaven was an early Protestant attempt to salvage something of the Roman Catholic doctrine of purgatory.[18] Luther, however, never accepted it and recognized that for believers the judgment seat of Christ was entirely a "mercy seat." In a famous sermon on the topic, he concluded that

> if that were the way faith were preached, men would be justified and all the rest; a pure heart and good conscience through genuine, perfect love would follow. For the man who through faith is sure in his heart that he has a gracious God, who is not angry with him, though he deserves wrath, that man goes out and does everything joyfully. Moreover, he can live this way before men also, loving and doing good to all, even though they are not worthy of love. . . . This is the highest security, the head and foundation of our salvation.[19]

On the other hand, the idea of degrees of punishment in hell does fit biblical teaching (Lk 12:47-48), and it makes sense logically. After all, the lost will be judged on the basis of works, not by grace, and unsaved people vary greatly in the amount of evil they perpetrate. It is not fair to imagine the Idi Amins and the Adolf Hitlers of this world experiencing the same punishment as the friendly, hardworking non-Christian homeowner down the street. However metaphorical or literal the biblical pictures of hell may be (another matter of debate among Evangelicals), the Bible is clear that if in this life people have heard the true gospel and have consciously rejected it, they will spend an unpleasant eternity apart from God and all his people.[20]

Avoiding Misconceptions

To begin with, faith or belief is much more than intellectual assent to a set of doctrines, that is, the assertions of the gospel—the affirmations of what we believe. Biblical faith must also involve trust in the person of Christ; it involves a personal relationship with him based on our convictions about *who* he is and what he did.[21] It is an act of *commitment,* as we progressively replace our ambitions with his and seek to live a life of service to him *out of profound gratitude for the death he died in our place.* We do not to try to earn any additional favors or to work our way up some celestial ladder—even those who believe in degrees of reward in heaven point out that work done with that motivation in view by definition disqualifies itself (Lk 14:12-14). But we surely do seek to obey Christ's commands, to do that which pleases him and to grow in Christlikeness. Any evangelist who claims that we can come to Jesus and do nothing for him for years on end, exhibiting no transformed lifestyle and yet being saved, has not accurately represented the biblical gospel.

Second, although there are some who speak of accepting Jesus as Savior without immediately also acknowledging him as Lord (and I am not one of these), they never pretend that this is a desirable state of affairs. All Evangelicals agree that we are commanded to recognize Christ in both roles. The branch of Evangelicalism that most strongly insists on the possibility of salvation without immediate lordship[22] is also one of the wings of the church that has most stressed the need for growth in sanctification, or Christian holiness. They have maintained merely that justification (a legal declaration of "not guilty" because Christ has served our sentence) and sanctification (actual growth in tangible righteousness) should be kept sharply separate, both logically and chronologically.[23]

Third, despite the scant attention paid to Arminianism in some circles, it should not be assumed that rejecting doctrines such as predestination, original sin and eternal security places anyone outside the Evangelical camp, or, conversely, that we must believe in those doctrines to be Evangelicals. As one with Calvinist leanings, I personally believe that Calvinist doctrines help make sense of Scripture, but I cannot with integrity make them the watershed of what defines true Christian faith. Mormons should understand that there are other legitimate options within historic Christianity, if their primary concerns about Christian orthodoxy involve Calvinist distinctives. We do not have to throw the baby out with the bath water.

Misgivings About Mormon Doctrines of Salvation
Evangelicals fear that Mormons believe in salvation by works (or by

faith plus works), attempting to earn salvation through personal merit rather than giving God all the credit for the process from start to finish. At the same time, we perceive various tensions within Mormon teachings on the topic.

One is a historical tension within the LDS Scriptures. Numerous texts in the Book of Mormon seem to teach perfectly orthodox views about salvation. One of the most extensive and encouraging is 2 Nephi 2:4-8:

> Salvation is free. And men are instructed sufficiently that they know good from evil. And the law is given unto men. And by the law no flesh is justified; or, by the law men are cut off. . . . Wherefore, redemption cometh in and through the Holy Messiah; for he is full of grace and truth. Behold he offereth himself a sacrifice for sin, to answer the ends of the law, unto all those who have a broken heart and a contrite spirit, and unto none else can the ends of the law be answered. Wherefore, how great the importance to make these things known unto the inhabitants of the earth, that they may know that there is no flesh that can dwell in the presence of God, save it be through the merits, and mercy, and grace of the Holy Messiah, who layeth down his life according to the flesh, and taketh it again by the power of the Spirit, that he may bring to pass the resurrection of the dead, being the first that should rise.

And 2 Nephi 31:19 declares, "Ye have not come thus far save it were by the word of Christ with unshaken faith in him, relying wholly upon the merits of him who is mighty to save." Mosiah 3:12, Alma 22:14-16, Helaman 13:6, 3 Nephi 9:22 and Moroni 7:24-28 and 8:3 all say much the same thing, stressing the need for faith and repentance but giving no hint of good works as a necessary part of the salvation package. Indeed, one passage in the Book of Mormon seems to shut the door explicitly to human effort as a contributing factor to salvation. Mosiah 4:9-12 highlights the need for belief, repentance, sincerity of faith and humility and then commands people to "always retain in remembrance, the greatness of God, and your own nothingness, and his goodness and long-suffering towards you, unworthy creatures, and humble yourselves even in the depths of humility, calling on the name of the Lord daily, and standing steadfastly in the faith of that which is to come" (Mosiah 4:11).

There seems to be a little tension between these passages and the Book of Mormon's insistence on baptism as a prerequisite of salvation (such as 2 Nephi 9:23) or a text like 2 Nephi 25:23 ("for we know that it is by grace we are saved, after all we can do"; see Prof. Robinson's explanation, p. 222 n. 24).[24] But there is little here to prepare the reader for Joseph Smith's later, *seemingly* wholesale endorsement of salvation by works in Article of Faith Three: "We believe that through the Atonement of Christ, all mankind may be saved, by obedience to the laws and ordinances of the Gospel." It is true that Article Four defines "the first principles and ordinances of the Gospel" as faith, repentance, baptism and the laying on of hands, but, to the outsider at least, it sounds as though these are only the *first* commandments—to be followed by others. I am delighted if in fact I am wrong in that perception!

So, too, Doctrine and Covenants 76 hits us like a bolt out of the blue with its elaboration of *four* possible destinies of humanity: the celestial, terrestrial and telestial kingdoms, as well as hell. More than supplementing previous revelation, this passage provides a substantial modification (if not outright repudiation) of it (contrast Jn 5:29; Mt 25:31-46; Dan 12:2 and even the Book of Mormon—for example, Mosiah 2:38-41; Alma 11:40—12:18). It is hard not to come to the conclusion that Joseph Smith simply changed his mind over time about what he believed on these matters.[25] I hope and pray that influential modern LDS authors like Prof. Robinson are indeed shifting the balance back toward grace, but conversations with numerous Mormon missionaries, Mormon friends and ex-Mormons suggest to me that an orientation toward works is still well entrenched. It is more than slightly disconcerting, for example, to read Bruce McConkie's clear distinction between mere resurrection (which all humanity experiences) and exaltation (reserved for the LDS):

> Immortality is one thing, eternal life another. . . . Both come by the grace of God. One comes as a free gift; the other is earned by obedience to the laws and ordinances of the gospel. . . . Those who work by faith must first have faith; no one can use a power that he does not possess, and the faith or power must be gained by obedience to those laws upon which its receipt is predicated.[26]

These are not stray quotations. McConkie repeatedly makes statements to the effect that "repentance is a gift of God conferred upon those who earn the right to receive it. It comes by obedience to law." Or again, it is a gift "reserved for those who abide the law that entitles them to receive it."[27] Although Prof. Robinson believes that millions if not billions of people, including many Evangelicals, can make it to the celestial kingdom (see p. 153), the reader can understand why I am concerned on this point.

A related tension in LDS thought, or so it appears to the outsider, involves the relationship between faith and good works (or "fruit"). Passages like Alma 5:54 and 12:15 borrow language from the KJV to exhort people to "bring forth works which are meet for repentance" (compare Mt 3:8 [JST 3:35]; Acts 26:20). In the biblical contexts, and in the Elizabethan English of the KJV, "meet for" means "befitting," "appropriate to" or "proper and right." The expression refers to God's people doing those good deeds that are appropriate for men and women who have already claimed to repent. I have no idea whether Joseph Smith understood this, but it seems clear that McConkie did not. He writes, "In order to repent, men must 'do works meet for repentance' (Acts 26:20)."[28] This puts the cart before the horse—doing good works in order to repent. Rather we must repent first—confessing our sins and our sorrow for them, and pledging to change our ways—so that Christ can then empower us to live in a manner that pleases him. But if the faith that produces good works must itself be preceded by obedience, as McConkie argues, it is hard to see how *repentance* can mean only the completion of repentance at the end of one's Christian pilgrimage as Robinson argues (p. 158).

Classic Mormonism, on the other hand, seems to reflect a surprising mixture of very conservative, works-oriented, "legalistic" religion, perilously close to what Paul condemns in Galatians as a false gospel that damns (Gal 1:8), and an unusually optimistic or "liberal" view of human nature and human potential.[29] Other Utopian communities have reflected similar combinations, but confronting the reality of human sin caused them to change their views or to disappear. Mormonism has clearly not died out; the question remains how much it has changed (is changing or will change) in order to adapt to the realities of human experience. Again, I am happy to be told that I have misunderstood the Mormon position on this issue because I am not adequately fluent in LDS terminology. An elucidation of my (mis-)perceptions (widespread among Evangelicals) would further our mutual quest for a common theological vocabulary (or will at least articulate definitions of terms we use differently), so that we can each truly understand the other's affirmations.

Professor Robinson's various writings suggest that some of the current LDS positions, whether constituting "developments" away from an earlier period of history or a "return to basics," may be quite significant. Over and over again he comes tantalizingly close to historic Christian affirmations of salvation by grace alone but then stops just short of them. In *Are Mormons Christians?* for example, he declares up front that "it is impossible to earn or deserve any of the blessings of God in any sense that leaves the individual unindebted to God's grace,"[30] a statement with which every Evangelical should agree. But then he adds, "Our best efforts to live the laws of God are required, but not because they earn the promised rewards— our efforts are infinitely disproportionate to the actual costs. Rather our best efforts are a token of our good faith."[31] This too is potentially acceptable, but I remain concerned about the language of "best efforts." Who of us ever gives a best effort, especially throughout our lives? And if such efforts are "required," what happens when we inevitably fail to meet those requirements?

Robinson substantially elaborates his view in *Believing Christ.* Here he tells the story of his daughter, who had been saving up to buy an expensive bicycle. When the day came for father and daughter to go to the store, the little girl became crestfallen because she had still accumulated only sixty-one cents, while the bike cost over a hundred dollars. With a stroke of parental genius and compassion, Robinson told his daughter, "You give me everything you've got, the whole sixty-one cents, and a hug and a kiss, and this bike is yours." He then uses this story to describe how Christ saves us: "only . . . when we finally realize our inability to perfect and save ourselves, when we finally realize our truly desperate situation here in mortality and our need to be saved from it by some outside intervention—only then can we fully appreciate the One who comes to save."[32]

So far so good. But Robinson continues,

At that point the Savior steps in and says, "So you've done all you can do, but it's not enough. Well, don't despair. I'll tell you what, let's try a different arrangement. How much do you have? How much *can* fairly be expected of you? You give me exactly that much (the whole sixty-one cents) and do all you *can* do, and I will provide the rest for now. . . . Between the two of us, we'll have it all covered. You will be one hundred percent justified."[33]

Despite the wonderful wisdom of this approach for a human parent dealing with a child who wants something almost entirely out of her reach, the analogy raises two serious concerns for theological discussion. First, this approach seems to advocate "synergism" (the cooperation of faith and works to produce salvation) rather than an understanding that works come *after* a fully completed salvation by grace through faith alone. This is the old Judaizing (Galatian) heresy in modern garb, and one that orthodoxy has rightly condemned each time it has manifested itself. Second, how do we translate the sixty-one cents onto a spiritual plane? How much can *fairly* be expected of humans? No matter what standard of obedience God might set up, sinful humans inevitably fall short. Then what?

Similar questions are raised by the rest of *Believing Christ*. Each time Prof. Robinson refers to human inability to merit salvation, he backs away from the statement and speaks of us doing everything we can do. So, for example, we rejoice and our spirits soar when we read that he feels

> very strongly that in most cases the belief that we must save ourselves by our own good works is not merely misinformed, it is evil. It is evil in the first place because it places an impossible burden on people—the burden of being perfect. Eventually they will despair and give up. Second, it is evil because it keeps people from admitting their need of a savior and accepting the merits and mercy of the Holy Messiah.[34]

Martin Luther could have written these words. Yet just three pages earlier Robinson wrote, "In simple terms this is the arrangement—we do what we are able to do, and Jesus Christ, the object of our faith, out of his love and mercy and grace, does what we are not yet able to do."[35] So the outsider remains puzzled. What if Robinson's daughter had come to the store flat broke? What if she had squandered her sixty-one cents and even incurred a small debt by borrowing and frittering away some small change from her friends? These analogies correspond more closely to the actual spiritual state of humans apart from Christ.[36]

I am greatly encouraged by Prof. Robinson's clarification that salvation would still be possible even in these revised versions of his bicycle parable (p. 159). Here he insists that what counts is our *desire* to follow Christ, and with that I heartily concur. I would also want to be reassured that my salvation was not lost whenever my desire waned, as it inevitably does from time to time. But I have no quarrel whatever with the insistence that for the one who *repeatedly and consistently* rejects God's moral standards (a word I think more appropriate than "laws" in the age of the gospel, which is never called a law in the New Testament), "Jesus has not *really* been made Lord, and there is neither justification nor salvation" (p. 147).

I would be thrilled to discover that Robinson's views, when clarified, actually do fall within the parameters of New Testament teaching about salvation. I would be overjoyed if I learned that there might be an "Evangelical Mormonism," just as increasing numbers of Roman Catholics or Seventh-day Adventists are abandoning their legacies of works-centered religion.[37] But then I would need to raise a further important question: How widespread in LDS circles are views like Robinson's? On the one hand, he perceives himself (and has been accepted) as remaining well within the bounds of current LDS orthodoxy. And I have no reason to doubt him. On the other hand, he admits in his writings, "It is true, I suppose, that some Latter-day Saints do not adequately understand this aspect [salvation by grace] of their own religion."[38] Later, he makes an even more telling admission:

> When I ask my students if it is necessary to keep the commandments to enter into the celestial kingdom, they all answer with absolute certainty that it is. They know that this is true because they have heard Church leaders and teachers tell them so all of their lives. But when I ask them if they've ever broken a commandment, or if they are not now living any commandments one hundred percent, most of them answer in the affirmative. They don't usually see the major problem implied by these two answers.[39]

If this description reflects Robinson's uniform experience with his students and what they have heard in their churches all their lives, then perhaps the reader can understand why I ask if it is really only a minority of the LDS who do not adequately understand salvation by grace.

Two other misgivings about the LDS doctrine of salvation need brief mention before I conclude. First, the whole elaboration of three kingdoms (celestial, terrestrial and telestial) into which the majority of humanity will one day enter is based on a fundamental misunderstanding (and rewriting) of 1 Corinthians 15:40.[40] The intent of the original Greek is well captured by the NIV: "There are also heavenly bodies and there are earthly bodies, but the splendor of the heavenly bodies is one kind, and the splendor of the earthly bodies is another." The context of Paul's remarks is his response to those who doubt that there is a resurrection at all (vv. 35-58). An imagined objector is asking him, "How are the dead raised? With what kind of body will they come?" (v. 35). By way of reply, Paul has his interlocutor consider a plant. It is the same life form as the seed from which it sprouted, even though it has an entirely different appearance (vv. 36-37). Then he states that God has created many different kinds of "flesh" (animal life—humans, other mammals, birds, and fish, vv. 38-39) and points out the diversity in God's creation in the universe—from the earthly bodies described in verses 38-39 to the heavenly bodies—sun, moon and stars (v. 41). Since God can create all this diversity, surely God knows how to create resurrection bodies for his people. In other words, the heavenly bodies of verse 40 (KJV "celestial") refer to all three of the categories mentioned in verse 41—sun, moon and stars. The earthly bodies of verse 40 (KJV "terrestrial") refer to all of the categories of animal life mentioned in verse 39. There is thus no basis for distinguishing different types of resurrection bodies from this passage.[41]

My final concern in this section is what happens to me according to LDS thought. I am an ordained Protestant (Baptist) minister, seminary teacher and biblical scholar who trusted in Jesus Christ as my Savior and Lord at the age of fifteen. I have sought to follow him faithfully ever since (however imperfectly I may have succeeded). LDS friends have challenged me to read the Book of Mormon prayerfully to see if it is true. But the more I read, the more I feel it to be the product of nineteenth-century religious fervor, however well intentioned. I am greatly reassured by Prof. Robinson in personal conversation that he does not feel compelled to try to convert me to Mormonism and that he believes I can look forward *at least* to a very pleasant eternity with Jesus in his terrestrial kingdom. Perhaps, since I have never knowingly rejected a "testimony" from the Spirit that Mormonism is true, I might even believe the LDS gospel after death and make it to the celestial kingdom.

So that raises two questions for me. First, why should I ever consider the risk of converting to Mormonism? If I stay as I am, *and Mormonism is right,* I will receive, they tell me, eternal, resurrected happiness with my Savior Jesus and perhaps even something much better. But should I convert to Mormonism and to my horror discover too late that traditional Christian fears about the LDS Church are correct, then I am damned for all eternity. Surely that risk is too great to take simply for the possibility of progressing into a somewhat nicer paradise.

Second, while I sincerely appreciate Prof. Robinson's generosity in assessing my current spiritual state (and fate), there are many more ominous overtones in the LDS Scriptures that trouble me. In 1 Nephi 13:5-6 I read that I am part of "a church which is most abominable above all other churches," whose founder is the devil. In Doctrine and Covenants 29:21, that "great and abominable church" is called the "whore of all the earth," and it is predicted that she "shall be cast down by devouring fire" (compare Doctrine and Covenants 1; 10:68; 88:94). The "Personage" who spoke to Joseph Smith told him to join no existing Christian denomination, "for they were all wrong" and "all their creeds were an abomination in his sight," their "professors were all corrupt," and their religious worship all a hypocritical pretense (Joseph Smith History 2:19). This reads like a rejection of more than postbiblical creeds.[42] Would Joseph Smith have looked kindly on modern LDS evaluations of me as the next best thing to a Mormon? Other passages have me barely making it into the bottom of the telestial kingdom (see Doctrine and Covenants 76:99-101). Still, I am grateful for the current attitude among contemporary LDS and hope it is widespread! (See Robinson's response on pp. 160-62.)

Finally, it is worth stressing one last time that the Book of Mormon's strong language against the corruption of traditional Christianity fits perfectly into an early nineteenth-century pioneer American context. This age saw the greatest proliferation of new denominations in the history of Christianity. Morality in many places had reached an all-time low, leading many thoughtful religious leaders to want to begin again. Optimism about the possibility of starting fresh was high, given the vast uncharted wildernesses yet to be settled. We need not look to any ancient setting to find a context perfectly suited to the composition of the Book of Mormon. On the other hand, it is difficult to identify *any* earlier time in human history when all these factors were present and when a revelation like the one in the Book of Mormon would have been as appropriate.

So Where Has All This Brought Us?

The doctrine of salvation brings us to the heart of any interreligious dialogue. The first three chapters of this book, while important, are not as crucial as this one. Accepting as Scripture something that humans have added to the Bible is only as dangerous as the content of those additions. Inadequate understanding of God or the Trinity does not affect the triune God's ability to provide salvation for those who sincerely trust in him, through Christ, however imperfect their understanding may be. (Only if, *in reality,* God in Christ were not what trinitarian orthodoxy has historically claimed would God be unable to save those who come to him.)

It is the doctrine of salvation that truly distinguishes orthodox Christianity from all other world religions. Humans in their sinful pride universally desire to merit acceptance by God or reward in an afterlife. Students of comparative religion have often remarked how deeply embedded "works righteousness" is in all the major religions of the world.[43] Being saved by grace just does not seem fair. And that's the whole point! *We should not want God to be fair* because we know, when we are honest about the depth of our sin (failure, inadequacy, imperfection, etc.) in light of God's infinitely perfect and holy stand-ards, that we would never stand a chance of making it into any kind of heaven on those terms. On these points Robinson and I seem to agree. Because Christendom is made up of sinful humans, it too has struggled to keep the doctrine of salvation by grace alone free from corruption. There have been and still are many church-going Protestants and Catholics who have so relied on their own behavior as the criterion for entrance into heaven that they, like avowed non-Christians, will discover themselves excluded.[44]

The question that must be put to anyone in any religious system who relies on some combination of faith plus works is the one made famous by French philosopher Blaise Pascal.[45] Whenever two representatives of differing religions or worldviews disagree, it is crucial to ask, "Who has more at stake? What if I am wrong and my partner in dialogue is right? What if I am right and the other person is wrong?" When I asked that question earlier in this chapter, the answer that emerged was that the cost of the standard Mormon position being wrong and the standard Evangelical position being right is infinitely high, while the cost of a godly Evangelical being wrong and the Mormon being right is relatively low. Of course, we could both be wrong—on a variety of points—which could lead to both or neither of us being saved.

But surely the logical conclusion of Pascal's "wager" is that Evangelical commitment to Christ is the more sensible (and safe) option. However "apostate" aspects of the church may have become down through the centuries, we stand among millions of other Christians who have tried to be faithful to the apostolic faith of the New Testament.[46]

Joint Conclusion
[B L O M B E R G & R O B I N S O N]

HERE IN THE AREA OF soteriology we have again found much more in common than we had expected to find. Both Mormons and Evangelicals trust that they will be brought into a right relationship with God by Jesus Christ, who is both the Son of God and God the Son. Both believe in the substitutionary atonement of Christ, justification by faith in Christ, and salvation by grace.[1] Both believe in the power of his redeeming blood, and both hold the conviction that there is no other way to be right before God than through faith in Christ. Both believe that our relationship with Christ begins through faith, but that evidence of the transformation brought about by the indwelling Spirit must inevitably ensue. If we do not demonstrate good works, some sign, over time, of a changed life, our professions of faith are ultimately futile. Many Evangelicals (though not Blomberg) anticipate degrees of reward in heaven, not entirely unlike the three distinct heavens or kingdoms in Mormon thought, though without the watertight compartmentalization of telestial, terrestrial and celestial. Many of the apparent distinctives of LDS soteriology are actually shared by Arminian Evangelicals, who also reject the TULIP and strongly emphasize human free agency.

Differences between most Evangelicals and Mormons include our respective assessments of (1) the possibility of responding to the gospel after death, (2) how crucial a role baptism actually plays in a believer's life and (3) many of the specific details about the nature of the life to come. But all of these pale in comparison with one fundamental question each group asks the other. For the Evangelical, it is the question of whether or not the LDS have so elevated the role of human good works in the process of salvation that they deny (wittingly or unwittingly) the unique role of God's saving grace appropriated entirely by faith. Evangelicals believe that those who persist in this error fall under the biblical condemnation addressed to anyone who tries to merit God's favor. For the Mormon, it is the question of whether or not Evangelicals have so elevated the role of God's grace in the process of salvation that they deny (wittingly or unwittingly) the necessary response to God's initiative in bringing us to himself, namely, a transformed life. If they do, Mormons believe they fall under the biblical condemnation addressed to those whose faith is dead because it produces no works.

If members of both our communities can avoid these twin pitfalls, substantial progress in dialogue is possible. If there is not enough in all this for reciprocal fellowship, there may at least be enough to recognize in each other's traditions a joint legacy (however misshapen in our individual estimations) of the same basic theological traditions and of the same basic commitment to Christ and his gospel (especially as filtered through nineteenth-century restorationism), however differently we may understand them. And if even that proves too ambitious, there is at least enough common ground to begin talking to one another, learning each other's theological language, and treating one another civilly in the process.

Conclusion

[ROBINSON & BLOMBERG]

JUST BEFORE WE BEGAN TO DRAFT this joint conclusion, Prof. Blomberg was describing our project to a young man in his Sunday-school class, who nodded with approval. "All through junior high and high school," he explained, "my best friend was a Mormon. We shared the same interests in school, the same favorite sports, and the same moral standards. We talked a lot about our spiritual beliefs. Neither of us ever convinced the other to 'convert,' but we liked each other anyway. We each discovered that not everything our churches had taught us to believe about the other 'side' was true, though some of it certainly was. But we also both found that most of our friends in our respective youth groups couldn't understand why we would want to be such good friends when we didn't share the identical faith."

That conversation epitomizes some of the discoveries we made as we worked together on this project: having more in common than we expected, sharing numerous social and moral standards as well as many of the same theological doctrines, recognizing that not everything Evangelicals and Mormons say about each other is true, though some of it is. We have both explained to each other in some detail what we believe, but neither of us has "converted" the other. We have sought to debunk stereotypes, to correct misinformation, to separate peripheral issues from central ones, to trust that neither of us is lying to the other or trying to deceive the other, and to do it all in a spirit of mutual respect and consideration. Yet we have found many in our respective circles who are suspicious of the project, some even encouraging us to abandon it.

Why is this? Why do people oppose dialogue like ours, particularly in print? There are no doubt many factors, both historical and sociological. Joseph Smith first shared his visions with a Methodist minister, who then demonstrated great animosity toward him (Joseph Smith History 1:21). But what would have happened had that minister responded with love and understanding instead of hostility (even while disagreeing with Joseph's views)? Perhaps the last 175 years would have turned out quite differently.

One barrier to better understanding between Mormons and Evangelicals today is the fact that in many parts of the country and the world Mormons are so few in number that most Evangelicals may never interact with them at any length. Evangelicals' concept of Mormonism has usually been drawn from anticultists. In those regions where the LDS are strong, Evangelicals often feel like an embattled minority; where Evangelicals are strong, Latter-day Saints often feel the same way.

There is yet another factor. Family members often fight fiercely with each other, and the historical roots from which contemporary Mormonism and North American Evangelicalism derive are exceedingly close. The religion of Old and New Testaments filtered through a uniquely American grid that was deeply indebted to nineteenth-century restorationist movements and was imbued with a heavy dose of pioneer optimism and rugged individualism. But the descendants of this common religious and national heritage have differed on some of the most deeply cherished doctrines of the faith, and the predictable quarrels have erupted.

As we have made clear throughout this book, we do *not* claim to have settled all of our differences. Neither do we believe that Mormons and Evangelicals would, or even ought to, accept one another's baptisms. We harbor no delusions that this modest dialogue will in any way diminish the extent to which LDS missionaries bear testimony to Evangelicals or to which Evangelicals witness to Mormons, *nor do our respective beliefs convince us that such activity should diminish.* But we can hope and pray that as sincere, spiritual men and women (who all *claim* the name of Christ) talk about their beliefs and life pilgrimages with each other, they might do so with considerably more accurate information about each other and in a noticeably more charitable spirit than has often been the case, after the pattern set by Aquila, Priscilla and Apollos in the New Testament. After all, it is the common *intent* of both "sides" to confess, to worship, and to serve that Jesus Christ who is described in the New Testament as our Lord.

We hope that we have modeled these goals in this book. Neither of us has pulled any punches. We have gone to the heart of the issues on each topic as we see them, and unfortunately that has involved discussing our differences considerably more than our commonalities. It would have been much more enjoyable simply to stress what we agree on, but our respective constituencies would have immediately noticed that we were avoiding the hardest questions. Yet each of us has prompted the other to indicate where the tone of writing or choice of words sounds polemical or overly sharp, so that we can avoid gratuitously offending each other. No doubt some imperfections remain, but we hope that we have opened the door to further conversations that can go beyond ours.

Might we look forward to the day when youth groups or adult Sunday-school classes from Mormon and Evangelical churches in the same neighborhoods would gather periodically to share their beliefs with each other in love and for the sake of understanding, not proselytizing? (This has already happened in some places.) Can we allow ourselves to envision high-level conferences of Evangelical and LDS scholars and church leaders trying to determine in what ways they really do agree and disagree or trying to work together toward common social goals, as so many other ecumenical groups have done?

Surely the God who brought down the Berlin Wall in our generation is capable of such things.

The LDS have a hierarchy in place that enables them to move their entire church when they so desire and as they believe themselves moved on by the Spirit. Evangelicals, precisely because they have no magisterium, could choose to act relatively quickly, as individuals, individual churches and denominations, to begin a new era of cordiality in interreligious conversation and cooperation in social and political action, working together in an increasingly secular and decadent society. If we do not receive one another in full spiritual fellowship, can we not at least become allies in the service of God in temporal affairs?

Perhaps there are a few other lessons to be learned along the way. First, we must treat individuals as individuals, finding out what they believe and what they have experienced. There is considerable diversity among the LDS and bewildering diversity among Christians who attach to themselves the label "Evangelical." We must avoid stereotyping people we meet or trying to tell them what they believe (as if we know better than they do!).

Second, we ought surely to take people who have a track record of upright, moral living at face value, at their word, accepting what they say for what it is, not judging it to be willfully deceptive or mean-spirited unless we discover convincing reasons to do so. Many of the differences between Mormons and Evangelicals involve divergent use of common terminology. People get confused as they try to talk to each other, and it is understandable how one "side" or the other may come to be thought of as hiding something or as being less than straightforward. But an atmosphere dominated by mutual suspicion is not likely to advance the discussion.

Third, we must pay better attention to the differences between us in theological terminology. Latter-day Saints must try to understand Evangelical terms by Evangelical definitions. For example, most Evangelicals do *not* believe that we may come to Christ, but then rebel and subsequently pursue wickedness until death, and still be saved in the kingdom of God. "Saved by grace" does not mean license to sin. In fact, adjusted for differences in terminology, the LDS doctrines of justification by faith and salvation by grace are not as different from Evangelical definitions as many on either side believe. On the other hand, Evangelicals must take into consideration the LDS definitions of terms. "Being saved by works" to a Latter-day Saint means "enduring to the end," "being faithful to Christ" or "pursuing sanctification" in Evangelical terms. A necessary prerequisite to better relations between the two communities is the preparation of more "theologically bilingual" representatives.

Fourth, and perhaps most important, we can beware of the labels we apply to one another. Prof. Robinson has demonstrated that Walter Martin's definition of a "cult" applies equally as well to the original Jesus movement as to the origins of the LDS (small, new, withdrawing from society, led by a charismatic leader, etc.).[1] Many of these characteristics no longer apply to Mormonism, yet Evangelicals continue to group the LDS together with Moonies and Masons, Nichiren Shoshu and New Agers, and all kinds of other religious groups, calling them all "cults." Unless the term "cult" is to be so broad as to be meaningless (that is, equivalent to anything that is not Evangelical— including most Catholicism, Eastern Orthodoxy and liberal Protestantism, not to mention entirely separate world religions like Hinduism, Buddhism or Islam), then it should be reserved for the kind of small, bizarre fringe groups sociologists more technically label as cultic (such as those led to their deaths by Jim Jones or David Koresh).[2] As applied to contemporary Latter-day Saints, the term is technically incorrect.

Likewise, LDS rhetoric could greatly alleviate Evangelicals' fears by refraining from using exaggerated language. Referring to traditional Christians and their churches as utterly "false religion," "abominable" or "apostate" poisons the atmosphere, when what LDS actually reject are Evangelicals' creeds. Evangelicals are grateful for so simple a concession as voluntarily removing a negative portrayal of Protestant ministers from the LDS temple ceremony. It was not too many years ago when Prof. Blomberg was assured by Mormon acquaintances, more than once, that ordained Protestant ministers (such as himself) were "tools of the devil."

The Bible, to be sure, is filled with strong rhetoric against false apostles, prophets and other religious leaders. But in every instance this is *in-house* language for those within the church (or Judaism) who should have known better (Jesus against the scribes and Pharisees; Paul against the Judaizing Christians). Both LDS and Evangelicals need to "clean up their own houses," particularly in sweeping out their most legalistic and polemical elements. As Paul put it, "What business is it of mine to judge those outside the church? Are you not to judge those inside?" (1 Cor 5:12). Conversely, in the New Testament God's people, when obedient, consistently bent over backward to relate to the outsider (Jesus with the "tax-collectors and sinners," as in Lk 15:1-2; Paul with his philosophy of being all things to all people so as to save as many as possible, as in 1 Cor 9:19-23). If we Mormons and Evangelicals both believe that the other side needs to hear the gospel *as we understand it,* then it becomes all the more incumbent for us to treat each other in love as we share our respective convictions. Against our critics who would say that we should spend our time overtly proselytizing one another rather than "merely" dialoguing, we can each affirm that we have a far clearer understanding of each other's belief system and its consequences (if true) than we would have received from typical proselytizing encounters.

At the suggestion of our editors, we have entitled this book *How Wide the Divide?* We leave it to our readers to fully answer that question for themselves. Our own answer in part has been "Not nearly as wide as we once thought, but still wide enough to separate us on significant issues." The following lists summarize the most important points of agreement and disagreement that we have discovered within the scope of the issues addressed in this book.

On the one hand, we jointly and sincerely affirm the following foundational propositions of the Christian gospel as we both understand it.

1. The Father, the Son and the Holy Spirit are one eternal God.

2. Jesus Christ is Lord. He is both the Son of God and God the Son.

3. There is no other name and no other way by which any individual may be saved other than through Jesus Christ.

4. Jesus Christ suffered, bled and died on the cross to perform a substitutionary atonement for the sins of the world.

5. Jesus Christ was resurrected on the third day and raised up in glory to the right hand of God.

6. We enter into the gospel covenant and are saved by the preaching of the word and by the grace of God.

7. We are justified before God by faith in the Lord Jesus Christ.

8. We are progressively sanctified by yielding our lives to God's Holy Spirit, who enables us to obey God's commands.

9. All the gifts of the Spirit manifested in the New Testament church continue in God's church today.

10. The Bible is God's word and is true and trustworthy within those parameters that the Chicago Statement on Inerrancy and the eighth LDS Article of Faith share.

11. Jesus Christ will publicly and visibly return from heaven to establish his millennial kingdom on earth.

12. The God of heaven is a God of love, and those who desire to be with him must also seek to be motivated in all their relationships by love.

On the other hand, the following important issues continue to divide us.

1. Are the Old and New Testaments the sole inspired, authoritative canonical books that God has revealed to guide his people, or should the Book of Mormon, Pearl of Great Price, and Doctrine and Covenants be included as well?

2. Does God the Father currently have a physical body or not?

3. Was God at some point in eternity past a human being like the mortal Jesus, or has he always been the infinite Supreme Being?

4. Can exalted humans one day share by grace all the attributes of God or only the so-called communicable attributes?

5. Is God a Trinity in essence or only in function?

6. Do the classic early Christian creeds accurately elaborate biblical truths about God and Christ, while admittedly rephrasing them in later philosophical language, or have they so imported Hellenistic concepts into their formulations as to distort biblical truth?

7. Is "justification by faith" or "justification by faith *alone*" the more appropriate summary of the Bible's teaching on that topic?

8. Do good works function solely as a response to God's gracious act of saving us, or do they also determine the level of our eternal reward?

9. Do people have a chance to respond to the gospel after death or not?

10. Is heaven, the abode of the "saved," subdivided into three degrees of glory or not?

11. How serious are the consequences for each of us if one belief system turns out to be wrong and the other turns out to be right?

We remind our readers, in closing, that there are numerous areas of doctrine we have not discussed at all, so that our views on those topics will not appear in either of these lists. Still, if any among either Evangelicals or Latter-day Saints are surprised to discover that those on the other "side" can honestly assent to some of the twelve joint affirmations listed above, or still incorrectly insist that they *do not,* we shall have succeeded in establishing the need for this book. That we can readily formulate a list of eleven important disagreements establishes the need for even further dialogue. As we have repeatedly stressed, we can only hope that such dialogue may be characterized by speaking the truth to one another in love.

Notes

Introduction/Robinson

[1]A recent example is provided in the case of Aaron Walker, an LDS high-school student in Franklin, Tennessee, who was selected to receive the Male Athlete of the Year award by a local chapter of the Fellowship of Christian Athletes, to which he had belonged for years and in which he then served as vice president. Two weeks before the awards dinner, Walker's nomination was rescinded by state and national FCA offices because he was a Mormon.

[2]This evil is compounded by the fact that being "born again" and being "saved by grace" are vital doctrines of the LDS Church, which have in some individual cases become internal casualties of an unlovely antagonism toward Evangelicalism generally. Some LDS have thrown out the baby with the bath water.

[3]See D. Peterson and S. Ricks, *Offenders for a Word* (Salt Lake City: Aspen, 1992), pp. 1-21.

[4]See William O. Nelson, "Anti-Mormon Publications," in *Encyclopedia of Mormonism* (New York: Macmillan, 1992), 1:45-52.

[5]Reminders of the atrocities committed against the Saints are often included in General Authority messages to the Church in much the same way that other Christians remind themselves of what the early martyrs suffered for their faith. See, for example, Dallin H. Oaks, *Conference Reports,* April 1987, pp. 43-48, or Gordon B. Hinckley, "A City upon a Hill," *Ensign,* July 1990, pp. 2-5.

[6]This is the watershed of Walter Martin's virulent attacks on the LDS (see the example cited by Blomberg, p. 23). Martin was unable, or unwilling, to learn LDS definitions and adjust for them, preferring instead his own theory of willful deceit.

[7]Stephen E. Robinson, *Are Mormons Christians?* (Salt Lake City: Bookcraft, 1991), pp. 1-7.

[8]I would suggest the *Encyclopedia of Mormonism* (New York: Macmillan, 1992) as the most accessible introduction to the religion of the Latter-day Saints currently

available. Though published by a non-Mormon press, this work was produced with the cooperation of many competent LDS scholars. Even here, however, some definitions would not receive the unreserved endorsement of all Church leaders.

[9]Paul H. Thompson, "Lay Participation and Leadership," *Encyclopedia of Mormonism*, 2:814-16; Bruce R. McConkie, *Mormon Doctrine* (Salt Lake City: Bookcraft, 1966), pp. 170-72, 504-5; Joseph Fielding Smith, *Teachings of the Prophet Joseph Smith* (Salt Lake City: Deseret, 1938), p. 327.

[10]See Spencer Condie, "Missionary, Missionary Life," in *Encyclopedia of Mormonism*, 2:910-13, and Richard Cowan, "Missionary Training Centers," in *Encyclopedia of Mormonism*, 2:913-14.

[11]Taken loosely from the Articles of Faith by Joseph Smith found at the end of the Pearl of Great Price and in *History of the Church* (1951; reprint, Salt Lake City: Deseret, 1980), 4:535-41.

[12]In fact, "to take his name upon them" has been one of the covenant obligations of members and part of the liturgy of the Lord's Supper since the founding of the LDS Church in 1830 (Doctrine and Covenants 20:77).

Introduction/Blomberg

[1]There are, of course, exceptions. *A Guide to Cults and New Religions* (Downers Grove, Ill.: InterVarsity Press, 1983), by Ronald Enroth et al., is very irenic in spirit. It surveys the groups and recognizes that not all of them deserve to be called cults (see further our conclusion at the end of this book). See also Richard Kyle, *The Religious Fringe: A History of Alternative Religions in America* (Downers Grove, Ill.: InterVarsity Press, 1993).

[2]Walter R. Martin, *The Kingdom of the Cults,* 3rd ed. (Minneapolis: Bethany, 1977), pp. 181-82.

[3]Bruce R. McConkie, *A New Witness for the Articles of Faith* (Salt Lake City: Deseret, 1985), pp. 141-42.

[4]There have been pleasant exceptions from time to time. In the 1960s, for example, the Evangelical pastor Wesley P. Walters had a courteous and effective dialogue with key Mormon leaders, even publishing a study, "New Light on Mormon Origins from the Palmyra Revival," in both the Mormon journal *Dialogue* (4 [1969]: 60-81) and the *Bulletin of the Evangelical Theological Society* (10 [1967]: 227-44).

[5]All quotations from the Old and New Testaments in the sections of this book authored by Blomberg will be taken from the New International Version unless otherwise noted. Any significant differences between the NIV and either the King James Version (KJV) or Joseph Smith's Translation (JST) will, however, be mentioned.

[6]For example, see, respectively, Peter Williamson and Kevin Perrotta, *Christianity Confronts Modernity* (Ann Arbor, Mich.: Servant, 1981); Marc H. Tanenbaum,

Marvin R. Wilson and A. James Rudin, eds., *Evangelicals and Jews in Conversation on Scripture, Theology and History* (Grand Rapids: Baker, 1978); and Richard Quebedeaux and Rodney Sawatsky, eds., *Evangelical-Unification Dialogue* (Barrytown, N.Y.: Rose of Sharon, 1979). Overshadowing all of these now is the recent document "Evangelicals and Catholics Together" (*First Things* 43 [May 1994]: 15-22). Unlike that document, this book does not intend to address the question of whether Evangelicals and Mormons are both, in certain instances, bona fide Christians, however worthwhile that issue might be to discuss.

[7]See especially David L. Edwards and John Stott, *Evangelical Essentials: A Liberal-Evangelical Dialogue* (Downers Grove, Ill.: InterVarsity Press, 1988); and Del Brown and Clark H. Pinnock, *Theological Crossfire: An Evangelical-Liberal Dialogue* (Grand Rapids: Zondervan, 1990).

[8]See especially Lesslie Newbigin, *The Gospel in a Pluralist Society* (Geneva: World Council of Churches; Grand Rapids: Eerdmans, 1989).

[9]For an excellent survey of the breadth of North American Evangelicalism, see Donald W. Dayton and Robert K. Johnston, eds., *The Variety of American Evangelicalism* (Knoxville: University of Tennessee Press, 1991). For a definition of progressive Evangelicalism, see Timothy P. Weber, "Premillennialism and the Branches of Evangelicalism," in *The Variety of American Evangelicalism,* p. 13. For a briefer survey of a number of perspectives that I welcome (without necessarily endorsing all of them), see Roger E. Olson, "Postconservative Evangelicals Greet the Postmodern Age," *Christian Century,* May 2, 1995, pp. 480-83.

[10]Again, see Dayton and Johnston, *Variety of American Evangelicalism.* My own convictions combine the perspectives of Alister E. McGrath, *Evangelicalism and the Future of Christianity* (Downers Grove, Ill.: InterVarsity Press, 1995), with those of Stanley J. Grenz, *Revisioning Evangelical Theology* (Downers Grove, Ill.. InterVarsity Press, 1993).

[11]Because *fundamentalist* has taken on such negative connotations, many who qualify for this label theologically and sociologically also prefer to call themselves "Evangelical," thus blurring the historic distinction between these terms. For example, a fair number of Southern Baptists who until recently would have strongly resisted the label Evangelical (as a "Yankee" word that does not reflect their distinctives) are now welcoming it, even though their spirit and behavior are clearly fundamentalist. Little wonder those outside our movement get confused!

Chapter 1: Scripture/Blomberg

[1]For a helpful, thorough discussion, see Wayne A. Grudem, "Scripture's Self-Attestation and the Problem of Formulating a Doctrine of Scripture," in *Scripture and Truth,* ed. D. A. Carson and John D. Woodbridge (Grand Rapids: Zondervan, 1983), pp. 19-59.

[2]For details see John Wenham, *Christ and the Bible,* 2nd ed. (Grand Rapids: Baker, 1984).

[3]Published, for example, in *Inerrancy,* ed. Norman L. Geisler (Grand Rapids: Zondervan, 1979), pp. 493-502.

[4]Paul D. Feinberg, "The Meaning of Inerrancy," in *Inerrancy,* ed. Geisler, p. 294.

[5]I myself have addressed a number of these in the Gospels in my book *The Historical Reliability of the Gospels* (Downers Grove, Ill.: InterVarsity Press, 1987).

[6]Conservative estimates would suggest that more than 97 percent of the New Testament and over 90 percent of the Old Testament can be reconstructed beyond any measure of reasonable doubt. See, for example, Norman L. Geisler and William Nix, *A General Introduction to the Bible* (Chicago: Moody Press, 1968), pp. 365-66; Geisler and Nix also describe the science of textual criticism more generally.

[7]One of the best and most readable introductions to principles of interpretation for all the biblical genres is Gordon D. Fee and Douglas Stuart, *How to Read the Bible for All Its Worth,* 2nd ed. (Grand Rapids: Zondervan, 1994). For a more detailed treatment see William W. Klein, Craig L. Blomberg and Robert L. Hubbard Jr., *Introduction to Biblical Interpretation* (Dallas: Word, 1993).

[8]Stephen E. Robinson, *Are Mormons Christians?* (Salt Lake City: Bookcraft, 1991), pp. 49-51, rightly recognizes that it is "an extreme form" of biblical inerrancy that declares that "all religious truth is found in the Bible." But he also ascribes to this extremism the statement "The Bible is sufficient for salvation," which in fact was the rallying cry of all the Protestant Reformers and is held by large numbers of Christians today who would not otherwise affirm inerrancy at all.

[9]For a representative treatment, see Bruce A. Demarest, *General Revelation* (Grand Rapids: Zondervan, 1982).

[10]The JST conceals part of this by replacing Luke's statement "since I myself have carefully investigated everything from the beginning" (Lk 1:3) with "having had perfect understanding of all things from the very first." No manuscript evidence anywhere supports this change.

[11]John B. Noss, *Man's Religions* (New York: Macmillan, 1980), p. 507 n.

[12]The standard editions are produced by the United Bible Societies and are known as the *UBS Greek New Testament,* 4th ed. (identical in text to an edition called *Nestlé-Aland,* 26th ed.) and the *Biblia Hebraica Stuttgartensia,* 4th ed.

[13]For a full history of the English translation of the Bible since the KJV, see Jack P. Lewis, *The English Bible from KJV to NIV,* 2nd ed. (Grand Rapids: Baker, 1991). Against those in our circles who defend using only the KJV, see James R. White, *The King James Only Controversy* (Minneapolis: Bethany, 1995).

[14]KJV and JST both follow a very poorly attested textual variant, "book of life," rather than "tree of life," but otherwise reproduce the same sense.

[15]The Apocrypha comprises Jewish books written for the most part between the Old and

New Testaments and includes histories of that five-hundred-year period, psalms and proverbial wisdom, legendary exploits of Jewish heroes and heroines, apocalyptic literature articulating hopes for a coming messianic age, and so on. These books were never accepted as canonical by the rabbis, but they became increasingly influential and authoritative in the emerging Greek and Roman churches of the early Christian era. The Protestant Reformers' insistence on not including these books in the Old Testament canon was based on the composition of the biblical canon in the time of Jesus, the first-century Jew. For a standard English edition, see Bruce M. Metzger, ed., *The Oxford Annotated Apocrypha,* 3rd ed. (New York: Oxford University Press, 1977).

[16]Bruce M. Metzger, in a panel discussion at the 1994 Society of Biblical Literature meetings in Chicago. See also his *The Canon of the New Testament* (Oxford: Clarendon, 1987), pp. 271-75.

[17]See especially Sir Norman Anderson, *Christianity and World Religions* (Downers Grove, Ill.: InterVarsity Press, 1984).

[18]It does quote *other* nonapocryphal Jewish and Greek writers in places. For example, Jude 14-15 cites *1 Enoch* (a Jewish "pseudepigraphical" work), Paul quotes a Cretan proverb in Titus 1:12, and both texts can refer to their quotations as "prophecy." But this means not that Jude and Paul believed the works they were quoting from to be Scripture, but merely that these individual statements were strikingly true. Compare the unwitting "prophecy" of the Jewish high priest Caiaphas in John 11:49-51.

[19]See especially Roger Beckwith, *The Old Testament Canon of the New Testament Church* (Grand Rapids: Eerdmans, 1985).

[20]See especially James D. G. Dunn, "Prophetic 'I' Sayings and the Jesus Tradition: The Importance of Testing Prophetic Utterances Within Early Christianity," *New estament Studies* 24 (1978): 175-98.

See, for example, R. Laird Harris, *Inspiration and Canonicity of the Bible* (Grand Rapids: Eerdmans, 1957). Harris recognizes the problem with nonapostolic New Testament writers such as Mark and Luke but still maintains, "If it was part of the New Testament, it was recognized as inspired if it had been written by an apostle—either by himself or with the help of an understudy or amanuensis [scribe]" (p. 284). Although early church tradition closely associates Mark with Peter and Luke with Paul, it never makes as strong a claim as this. Luke's own testimony (Lk 1:1-4) is a more reliable explanation of why his work (and presumably the other Gospels and Acts) should be deemed trustworthy—he functioned as a careful historian following previously written accounts and interviewing eyewitnesses. The doctrine of inspiration merely affirms that God superintended the process to insure that the results were exactly what God wanted to communicate.

[22]Robinson, *Are Mormons Christians?* p. 47.

[23]On these texts specifically and on the role of New Testament prophecy more generally, with reference to the most relevant secondary literature, see Gordon D.

Fee, *The First Epistle to the Corinthians* (Grand Rapids: Eerdmans, 1987), pp. 641-46, 595-96.

[24]For this whole line of reasoning and for guidelines for testing modern Christian prophecy, see especially Wayne A. Grudem, *The Gift of Prophecy in the New Testament and Today* (Westchester, Ill.: Crossway, 1988). Some extreme manifestations of Pentecostalism at times transgress these boundaries, making Evangelicals as nervous about their claims as about Mormon claims of receiving new revelation.

[25]The same is true of *apostles*. The New Testament uses this term to denote (1) Jesus' closest followers during his lifetime, who witnessed his resurrection, and (2) one who was divinely commissioned by God for mission—a "church planter" as we might say today. The twelve "apostles" in the first sense (along with Paul who received a belated but equally significant audience with the resurrected Jesus) had a unique authority and played a foundational role in the church as spokespersons for God, but no text of Scripture ever draws a *direct* link between an individual's apostolic status and his authoring of a New Testament *book*. See further D. Müller and C. Brown, "Apostle," in *New International Dictionary of New Testament Theology*, ed. Colin Brown (Grand Rapids: Zondervan, 1975), 1:126-37.

[26]The amount of internal evidence that allows us to date each document varies from book to book, but those who take the claims of authorship and other historical circumstances seriously are forced to date all of these writings to the first century. Liberal scholars have questioned these conclusions in several instances, but Evangelicals do not find their arguments compelling. See, for example, D. A. Carson, Douglas J. Moo and Leon Morris, *An Introduction to the New Testament* (Grand Rapids: Zondervan, 1992).

[27]For the full history of the development of the New Testament canon, see F. F. Bruce, *The Canon of Scripture* (Downers Grove, Ill.: InterVarsity Press, 1988), pp. 115-251. Debates occasionally continued into the fourth century concerning seven books: Hebrews, James, 2 Peter, 2-3 John, Jude and Revelation. Two other writings, an epistle falsely attributed to Barnabas and a book known as the *Shepherd of Hermas,* seem to have gained brief followings among some Christians who prized them as highly as other books that eventually became part of our New Testament. But there is no evidence of any significant skepticism concerning the Gospels, Acts or major letters of Paul.

[28]For the points in this paragraph, see further Bruce, *Canon of Scripture,* pp. 255-69.

[29]For surveys of a variety of these claims, see Per Beskow, *Strange Tales About Jesus* (Philadelphia: Fortress, 1985), and Douglas Groothuis, *Jesus in an Age of Controversy* (Eugene, Ore.: Harvest House, 1996). For the last of these claims, assuredly the most bizarre of all, see James W. Deardorff, *Celestial Teachings: The Emergence of the True Testament of Jmmanuel (Jesus)* (Tigard, Ore.: Wild Flower, 1990).

[30]For a history of the major doctrines of the church that displays continuity and discontinuity with the apostolic witness, see Louis Berkhof, *The History of Christian*

Doctrines (London: Banner of Truth Trust, 1969).

[31]See also the parable of the wheat and the tares (Mt 13:24-30, 37-43), in which the "sons of the kingdom" and the "sons of the devil" grow together until the end of the age. This seems to leave no room for a period of church history in which no true people of God existed at all.

[32]All quotations from the Book of Mormon in Blomberg's sections are taken from the 1982 edition, published by the Church of Jesus Christ of Latter-day Saints in Salt Lake City.

[33]Sidney B. Sperry, *Answers to Book of Mormon Questions* (Salt Lake City: Bookcraft, 1967), pp. 131-36.

[34]Blomberg, *Historical Reliability of the Gospels,* pp. 149-50. This is not, however, to say that I am aware of any evidence outside the Book of Mormon that "Jerusalem" was ever similarly used as the name of a region.

[35]Another famous example is Alma 46:15, in which Nephites at the time of Moroni (73 B.C.) are called Christians, even though Acts 11:26 teaches that "the disciples were called Christians first at Antioch." Sperry, *Answers to Book of Mormon Questions,* pp. 171-72, seems to suggest that this is a more loose translation on the part of Joseph Smith. Whatever the actual term, Smith recognized that it was equivalent to what would later be called "Christians" and so used the term appropriately. This is not dissimilar to one Evangelical solution to the problem of Exodus 3:15, in which God seemingly reveals his name, the LORD ("Yahweh" or "Jehovah"), for the first time to Moses, even though this term has frequently appeared already in Genesis. G. J. Wenham, "The Religion of the Patriarchs," in *Essays on the Patriarchal Narratives,* ed. A. R. Millard and D. J. Wiseman (Leicester, England: Inter-Varsity Press, 1980), pp. 157-88, argues that the earlier references are merely a retrojection of the title from Moses' day into narratives of earlier times, since it was clearly the same God in each case.

[36]As argued in Sperry, *Answers to Book of Mormon Questions,* pp. 197-98.

[37]According to Anthony A. Hutchinson ("LDS Approaches to the Holy Bible," *Dialogue* 15 [1982]: 108), "most LDS commentators" go beyond Robinson and interpret 1 Nephi 13—14 "as speaking of the textual corruption of the Bible, and they see the modern LDS Scriptures and sources as part of the restoration of the true form of the text." Such claims are even more unsubstantiated.

[38]For more details on these three passages see, respectively, Donald A. Hagner, *Matthew 1—13* (Dallas: Word, 1993), pp. 144-45; William L. Lane, *The Gospel According to Mark* (Grand Rapids: Eerdmans, 1974), pp. 601-5; and I. Howard Marshall, *The Epistles of John* (Grand Rapids: Eerdmans, 1978), pp. 235-37.

[39]For a full list of differences between the JST and KJV, presented in two-column format, see *Joseph Smith's "New Translation" of the Bible,* with an introduction by F. Henry Edwards (Independence, Mo.: Herald, 1970). I am told that the Utah-based

LDS (unlike the Reorganized Church) incorporate only parts of the JST into the footnotes of the currently authorized edition of the KJV, a curious inconsistency viewed from an outsider's perspective.

[40]See, for example, H. Michael Marquardt, *The Book of Abraham Papyrus Found* (Sandy, Utah: Author, 1975); F. S. Spalding, *Joseph Smith Jr. as a Translator* (New York: Presiding Bishop and Council, Department of Missions, 1922).

[41]It is not necessary to argue that Smith took over someone else's work wholesale, as with the theory that he plagiarized much of the work of Solomon Spaulding. A Mormon author, writing under the pseudonym Robert C. Webb, in *The Real Mormonism* (New York: Sturgis and Walton, 1916), pp. 400-426, while debunking theories of direct dependence of the Book of Mormon on other religious literature of the nineteenth century, nevertheless demonstrates how many of the themes of the book were being discussed and written about more generally.

[42]Something seems amiss, however, when a "translation" need not correspond in any material way to the literal content of a scroll—as in the case of the Book of Abraham—especially when the nineteenth-century LDS insisted so strongly that the book *was* a more literal rendering.

[43]For a brief introduction to these events, see David F. Wells, *Revolution in Rome* (Downers Grove, Ill.: InterVarsity Press, 1972).

[44]Notwithstanding the important warnings of texts like 2 Corinthians 11:13-15, it strikes me as curious that Evangelical apologists often insist that the Book of Mormon must be either divine or demonic, as if there were no intermediate alternatives (such as a human origin, possibly well-intentioned even if consistently misguided). It is even more curious that Mormon apologists seem to welcome and even demand this either-or mentality. See, for example, Bruce R. McConkie, *A New Witness for the Articles of Faith* (Salt Lake City: Deseret, 1985), p. 413: "Among devout people whose souls are filled with fervor for one cause or another, it [the Book of Mormon] is rated as either a good or an evil book. There is no middle ground. True it is that there are indifferent and unconcerned souls who could not care less whether it is a divine or a devilish book. But they are the ones who have the same thoughtless feelings about the Bible and the things of the Spirit in general." But I am told that McConkie usually represents the most rigorous position possible within the bounds of LDS orthodoxy.

Chapter 1: Scripture/Robinson

[1]Latter-day Saints have the same biblical canon as Protestants. While there are many good things in the Apocrypha that one might benefit from reading and studying, Latter-day Saints, like Evangelicals, do not consider the Apocrypha Scripture. See Doctrine and Covenants 91 for the official statement of this position.

[2]Latter-day Saints sometimes use the term *Scripture* in a loose sense for any inspired

communication (Doctrine and Covenants 68:4), but such "Scripture" is private and its applicability confined to the one who receives it. It does *not* become part of the canon and has no normative force on the doctrines of the Church. For this reason, a more exact equivalent for what Evangelicals mean by "Scripture" is the LDS term "the Standard Works," which refers only to the normative, canonized LDS Scriptures—the primary source of official doctrine for the Church. See Stephen E. Robinson, *Are Mormons Christians?* (Salt Lake City: Bookcraft, 1991), pp. 13-18.

[3]For example, it is possible for an inexperienced, unskilled or dishonest translator to misconstrue or misrepresent the meaning of the Greek words. Some Bible translations now on the market in fact do this very thing.

[4]See the text-critical work of Royal Skousen, *Book of Mormon Critical Text: A Tool for Scholarly Reference* (Provo, Utah: F.A.R.M.S., 1984-87), in three volumes, and "Toward a Critical Edition of the Book of Mormon," *BYU Studies,* Winter 1990, pp. 41-69, by the same author.

[5]Words like *inerrancy, plenary* and *infallible* are not scriptural, nor are they part of the LDS vocabulary, so Latter-day Saints prefer not to use them, even when we understand how Evangelicals mean them.

[6]Doctrine and Covenants 1:24: "These commandments are of me, and were given unto my servants in their weakness, *after the manner of their language,* that they might come to understanding" (emphasis added).

[7]See, for example, the title page of the Book of Mormon where the prophet declares, "And now, if there are faults, they are the mistakes of men." That is, the revelation itself is not at fault but may be vulnerable to human error in the course of transmission.

[8]*Translation* is a broad term for Latter-day Saints, which, when applied to the Scriptures, refers to the whole process by which they have come into our hands, including copying, editing, redacting, revising, clarifying, translating, printing, transmitting or even interpreting (see pp. 64-65).

[9]Not everything, or even most things, said by the apostles and prophets has the authority of Scripture, only those things that are *theopneustos,* which are revealed to them by God and transmitted to the church in God's name and by God's direction.

[10]This is the *real* intent of 2 Peter 1:19-21. Peter points out, after reminding his readers that he has the "more sure word of prophecy" which they should heed, that the interpretation of Scripture is not a private (that is, individual) venture. Rather, Scripture is best interpreted as it was given—when holy men of God (apostles and prophets) are moved by the Holy Ghost. Far from prohibiting prophetic interpretation of the texts, this Scripture mandates it.

[11]See, for example, Dallin H. Oaks (one of the LDS apostles), "Apostasy and Restoration," *Ensign,* May 1995, p. 85: "We affirm that this divine declaration [i.e., that their creeds were an abomination] was a condemnation of the creeds, not of the faithful seekers who believed in them." See also L. Dahl, "The Theological Signifi-

cance of the First Vision," in *Studies in Scripture,* ed. R. Millet and K. Jackson (Salt Lake City: Randall Book, 1985), 2:326-27.

[12]See F. L. Cross and E. A. Livingstone, *The Oxford Dictionary of the Christian Church* (New York: Oxford University Press, 1978), p. 1256.

[13]Cf. Robinson, *Are Mormons Christians?* pp. 47-48.

[14]Certainly all apostles were "prophets" in the sense described in Revelation 19:10, "For the testimony of Jesus is the spirit of prophecy."

[15]See Robert J. Matthews, *A Plainer Translation: Joseph Smith's Translation of the Bible—A History and Commentary* (Provo, Utah: Brigham Young University Press, 1975).

[16]Although this clearly did occasionally happen to the biblical text, and the LDS believe the JST corrects many of these instances. The *completed* process of adding and subtracting can be seen in the Johannine comma (1 Jn 5:7-8) and in the last twelve verses of Mark (16:9-20) respectively. The process *under way* is witnessed by the adulterae pericope (Jn 7:53—8:11): according to Augustine the passage offended his Christian contemporaries and was even then being excised from the text (*De Coniugiis adulterinis* 2.6). The present result has been that many modern scholars, on the basis of so many excised copies, now doubt the authenticity of the pericope—despite the clear testimony of Augustine. Both the NIV and the NRSV make note that the earliest texts of John do not contain this pericope. Joseph Smith does not usually correct interpolations (the Johannine comma, for example). I suspect this is because these are usually not *incorrect* doctrinally speaking, but only *unoriginal.*

[17]I readily grant that the art of textual criticism provides good evidence that the present biblical text is a reasonably accurate representation of what the Bible was in the late second or early third century. However, to say that the present text faithfully preserves the *first*-century Bible is to say more than we know. I would date whatever changes were made in the present text to between A.D. 55 and 200 (i.e., between 2 Thess 2:2 and 3:17 on the one hand, and the Chester Beatty and Bodmer papyri on the other). Prof. Blomberg's correct insistence that there is no textual evidence of material being deleted from the text begs the question—since it is the LDS contention that the evidence *was* deleted.

[18]The major exception being the book of Moses, which is JST Genesis 1—6, and which was independently canonized as part of the Pearl of Great Price.

[19]Or, expressed differently, the JST plus the KJV does *not* equal "the fullness of the gospel" as Mormons usually define it. That requires the addition of the Book of Mormon, the Doctrine and Covenants, and the Pearl of Great Price—the other canonical texts of Mormonism.

[20]For example, Paul's other epistles or the genuine book of Enoch cited by Jude as a prophetic work (Jude 14-15), and which is not in my opinion found among the extant Enoch material.

[21]The reader is reminded that this is how *I* interpret the data and does not represent

an official view of the LDS Church—which takes official positions on very few issues beyond what the Standard Works themselves assert.

[22]Certainly Paul thought his letter to the Laodiceans worthy of circulation in the church even if later compilers did not (Col 4:16). I would dearly love a peek at the *real* first epistle to the Corinthians (cf. 1 Cor 5:9). Luke describes "many" accounts of the story of Jesus written in the first century according to eyewitness testimony—even though of the present Gospels he could only have known Mark. Where are the others? Most "orthodox" Christians extend their faith in inspired *authorship* of the biblical books to include faith in inspired *editorship* of both text and canon in later centuries—a biblically unwarranted leap.

[23]See Matthews, *A Plainer Translation,* pp. 7, 253. Despite Prof. Blomberg's feeling that this is a "stretch," it is a matter of record that Joseph used the term this broadly to mean even "render," "interpret" or "adapt." How else than by granting this broader meaning of "translate" can the JST, which starts with the KJV English and ends up *still in English,* be considered a "translation" at all? See "translate" in Noah Webster, *An American Dictionary of the English Language* (San Francisco: Foundation for American Christian Education, 1967). This volume is a reprint of Webster's 1828 first edition.

[24]3 Nephi 13:12, for example, *supports* KJV Matthew 6:13, where the JST reads differently, and yet the LDS accept both readings as inspired. A JST reading does not necessarily imply that the received text is in error.

[25]See Robert Funk, *The Five Gospels: The Search for the Authentic Words of Jesus—A New Translation and Commentary* (New York: Macmillan, 1993).

[26]See Alexander Di Lella, *The Book of Daniel* (Garden City, N.Y.: Doubleday, 1977), pp. 42-45, or John Goldingay, *Daniel,* Word Biblical Commentary 30 (Dallas: Word, 1982), pp. 326-29.

[27]See Galatians 3:19, 24-26; Doctrine and Covenants 84:23-27; Exodus 32-34; JST Exodus 34:1-2.

[28]See, for example, Ezra Taft Benson, *Conference Reports,* October 1986, pp. 3-4, and Dallin H. Oaks, "Another Testament of Jesus Christ," *Ensign,* March 1994, pp. 60-67.

[29]As stated in Doctrine and Covenants 84:54-57.

[30]In the Reformers' struggle against the authority claims of Roman Catholics for the magisterium, or authoritative tradition, of the Roman Church, they often appealed to the principles of *sola scriptura* ("the Scriptures alone") and *ad fontes* ("to the sources"). These slogans were shorthand for the doctrine that *the Scriptures alone,* God's written word, were authoritative for the declaration and definition of doctrine, and that Christians who wanted to understand the gospel should turn back from the traditions of the Roman Church to the (real) sources of doctrine.

[31]To be "historically orthodox" Christians, perhaps, but not to be *biblical* Christians. It is highly unlikely that the first generation of Christians would have understood

the issues at stake at Nicaea, let alone agreed with its conclusions.
[32]The exceptions being official statements of the First Presidency and/or the Quorum of the Twelve Apostles.

Chapter 1: Joint Conclusion
[1]Bearing in mind, of course, that the LDS might at any time add to their Standard Works through continuing revelation to the president of the Church.

Chapter 2: God & Deification/Robinson
[1]*Aoratos* is derived from the Greek alpha privative (*a-*), meaning "un-", "dis-" or "non-," plus the participle of *horaō*, a verb of seeing, to create the participial adjective meaning literally "unseen." Its derivative nuance of "incapable of being seen" is due largely to its use in Platonism (Wilhelm Michaelis, "ὁρατός, ἀόρατος," in *Theological Dictionary of the New Testament,* ed. Gerhard Kittel and Gerhard Friedrich, 10 vols. [Grand Rapids, Mich.: Eerdmans, 1981], 5:368). In the Septuagint (Is 45:3) *aoratos* is used to translate *mistārîm,* which means "hidden," that is, "not seen," rather than "incapable of being seen." *Aoratos* cannot be used to prove God is "invisible" rather than just "unseen," for the word contains both meanings.
[2]See Stephen E. Robinson, *Are Mormons Christians?* (Salt Lake City: Bookcraft, 1991), pp. 60-65.
[3]It does not matter that Paul is here quoting Aratus of Soli. Paul quotes this passage only because it makes his point—and it is *still* the word of God. See F. F. Bruce, *The Book of the Acts,* New International Commentary on the New Testament (Grand Rapids: Eerdmans, 1988), p. 339.
[4]*Stromateis* 7.10.
[5]As B. Studer notes in *The Encyclopedia of the Early Church* (New York: Oxford University Press, 1992) under "Divinization": "There is no doubt that the d[ivinization] of man was one of the fundamental themes of patristics, esp. the Greek." See also Symeon Lash, "Deification," in *The Westminster Dictionary of Christian Theology,* ed. A. Richardson and J. Bowden (Philadelphia: Westminster Press, 1983), p. 147: "Deification is for Orthodoxy the goal of every Christian."
[6]Though, once again, "incommunicable attributes" is *not* a biblical term. And if Peter says we partake of God's nature, by what authority can later theologians limit that to mean only *some* of God's nature?
[7]It is the Neo-Platonic extension of Plato's distinction between being and becoming, between the *one,* absolute and unchangeable, and the *many* (see, for example, *Timaeus* 28).
[8]See the discussion in Robinson, *Are Mormons Christians?* pp. 84-87.
[9]For example, in the ancient church Irenaeus (*Against Heresies* 4.38; 5.pref.), Clement of Alexandria (*Exhortation to the Greeks* 1; *Instructor* 3.1; *Stromateis*

7.10), Justin Martyr (*Dialogue with Trypho* 124), Athanasius (*Against the Arians* 1.39; 3.34) and Augustine (*On the Psalms* 50.2), and in the modern church C. S. Lewis (*The Weight of Glory* [New York: Macmillan, 1980], p. 18; *Mere Christianity* [New York: Macmillan, 1952], pp. 153-54, 164, 174-75). While one might coherently argue that Latter-day Saints misunderstand the traditional doctrine of deification, one cannot with honesty assert that we invented it.

[10]B. H. Roberts, a General Authority of the Church, once stated the principle this way: "The Church has confined the sources of doctrine by which it is willing to be bound before the world to the things God has revealed, and which the Church has officially accepted, and those alone. These would include the Bible, the Book of Mormon, the Doctrine and Covenants, the Pearl of Great Price; these have been repeatedly accepted and endorsed by the Church in general conference assembled, *and are the only sources of absolute appeal for our doctrine.* . . . As to the printed discourses of even leading brethren, the same principle holds. They do not constitute the court of ultimate appeal on doctrine. They may be very useful in the way of elucidation and are very generally good and sound in doctrine, but they are *not* the ultimate sources of the doctrines of the Church, and are *not* binding upon the Church. The rule in that respect is—What God has spoken, and what has been accepted by the Church as the word of God, by that, and that only, are we bound in doctrine" (Tabernacle Sermon, July 10, 1921, printed in *Deseret News,* July 23, 1921, sec. 4, p. 7; emphasis added).

[11]And even here, note the use of the lower-case *g,* employed to distinguish between those who are gods by grace and that God by whose grace they have become what they are.

[12]See, for example, *Deseret Weekly* 49 (November 1894): 610: "As man now is, God once was; As God now is, man may be."

[13]Joseph Fielding Smith, *Teachings of the Prophet Joseph Smith* (Salt Lake City: Deseret, 1938), p. 345: "God himself was once as we are now, and is an exalted man, and sits enthroned in yonder heavens! That is the great secret."

[14]See, for example, Frederick H. Borsch, *The Son of Man in Myth and History* (Philadelphia: Westminster Press, 1967), esp. pp. 60, 87, 114, 138, 397-401.

[15]In fact, if the LDS used Evangelical vocabulary and definitions, they could probably not refer to exalted beings as "gods."

[16]Particularly since so many others in the Christian tradition have used the term *gods* to refer to the glorified saints. Evangelicals are always telling me that these authors used the term *gods* differently from the way the LDS do—but I can never understand the basis of the claim. When I read Clement or Irenaeus or C. S. Lewis and say, "There! That's *exactly* what I believe," Evangelicals usually answer, "No, that's not what you believe at all."

[17]The generally accepted view of scholars is stated thus by J. A. Emerton in *Journal of Theological Studies* 11 (April 1960): 329, 332: "Most exegetes are agreed that [Jesus'] argument is intended to prove that men can, in certain circumstances, be

called gods . . . that the word 'god' can, in certain circumstances, be applied to beings other than God himself, to whom he has committed authority."

[18]See W. D. Davies, *Paul and Rabbinic Judaism* (New York: Harper, 1967), 288.

[19]Unless, of course, we grant scriptural authority to the fifth-century doctrine of the two natures in Christ (Chalcedon, A.D. 451)—from the LDS point of view a doubtful addendum to the Word of God.

[20]See, for example, in the Library of Early Christianity, vol. 7, the judgments of Shaye J. D. Cohen, *From the Maccabees to the Mishnah* (Philadelphia: Westminster Press, 1987), pp. 44, 86-87.

[21]As for Nicaea being a "summary" of the biblical view, my English professors made it quite clear to me that a summary may not introduce arguments or assertions not already found in the material being summarized. Show me *homoousios* or even *Trinity* in the New Testament and I have a problem, but there is no biblical passage or combination of passages that asserts what the Nicene Creed asserts. It is *not* a summary; it is an extrapolation.

[22]See the marginal note for this passage in the 1979 LDS edition of the Bible.

Chapter 2: God & Deification/Blomberg

[1]Stephen E. Robinson, *Are Mormons Christians?* (Salt Lake City: Bookcraft, 1991), p. 60.

[2]Millard Erickson, *Christian Theology* (Grand Rapids: Baker, 1983), 1:263-300.

[3]Gordon R. Lewis and Bruce A. Demarest, *Integrative Theology* (Grand Rapids: Zondervan, 1987), 1:193-201, 231-40. The sentences quoted form section headings; the bracketed words correspond to Lewis's addition in a personal communication.

[4]The term *generation* in this context refers merely to successive periods of time and implies nothing about whether creatures continue to be born for all eternity. See Walter Bauer, *A Greek-English Lexicon of the New Testament and Other Early Christian Literature,* ed. and rev. William F. Arndt, F. Wilbur Gingrich and Frederick W. Danker, 3rd ed. (Chicago: University of Chicago Press, 1979), p. 154.

[5]The KJV, following a few late manuscripts, omits the key phrase "before all ages," and the JST, knowing only the KJV, reproduces this error. Modern translations often read "before all time." There is no way in Hebrew, Greek or English to speak of people acting outside of time without engaging in a formal linguistic contradiction (if there were no time, there would be no before and after), since action as we conceive of it requires a succession of moments (compare Robinson's phrase "before the beginning," pp. 89-91). Jude's point nevertheless is that "the ascription of glory, greatness, might and power belongs to God; it is a statement of fact, not a prayer that these things may be ascribed to the Almighty." Further, "they always have done. They do now. They always will—hence the certainty of the final 'Amen' " (Michael Green, *The Second Epistle General of Peter and the General Epistle of*

Jude [London: Tyndale, 1968], p. 192). To argue that so absolute a claim leaves room for God to have been otherwise at some prior time simply fails to understand the inspired author's intent. The expression means "always—for all eternity past."

[6]Again, the JST alters the original Greek by translating "For unto such hath God promised his Spirit." Here there is no support even in the KJV for such an alteration. If what Joseph Smith believed was consistent with the KJV rendering of this verse, why did he change its wording so radically?

[7]The most widely acclaimed, up-to-date dictionary of New Testament vocabulary, recognized internationally for its linguistic excellence, is Johannes P. Louw and Eugene A. Nida, eds., *A Greek-English Lexicon of the New Testament Based on Semantic Domains,* 2 vols. (New York: United Bible Societies, 1988). For *aoratos* Louw and Nida give merely "pertaining to that which cannot be seen—'what cannot be seen, invisible' " (1:278). Conversely, *horatos* means "pertaining to that which can be seen—'what can be seen, visible' " (1:277).

[8]Again without any manuscript support, but betraying clear awareness that his doctrine could not be derived from the Scriptures he possessed, Joseph Smith adds "except them who believe."

[9]JST v. 19, which gratuitously adds "except he hath borne record of the Son."

[10]B. H. Roberts tried to harmonize these seemingly discrepant data differently. First he quoted John 6:46 that no one has seen the Father except the one who is of God. Then, countering the orthodox limitation of "the one who is of God" to Jesus, he cites Acts 7:55-56, in which Stephen sees the glory of God and Jesus standing at God's right hand in heaven. But even this text does not say that Stephen ever saw a human likeness of the Father. Roberts's next remark is telling: "Undoubtedly, for reasons that are wise, God the Father has been 'invisible' to men except under very special conditions" (*The "Mormon" Doctrine of Deity* [reprint Bountiful, Utah: Horizon, 1975], p. 81). Roberts seemingly admits that the vast majority of Scripture and of the personal experience of God's people supports the idea that the Father is immaterial and invisible. Why not then prefer the harmonization that grants this as God's essential nature and explains the exceptions as something temporary in service of God's revelation to humanity, rather than vice versa?

[11]For an excellent popular-level study of the significance of each of these in its scriptural setting, see Earll C. Sheridan, *When God Stands Up* (Grand Rapids: Zondervan, 1939).

[12]Again, it seems clear that Joseph Smith felt he could not support his doctrine without altering this text, so the JST reads, "In the beginning was the gospel preached through the Son. And the gospel was the word, and the word was with the son, and the Son was with God, and the son was of God." Historic Christianity's point is precisely the opposite: in the beginning was *not* the gospel preached through the Son; this did not (and could not) take place until the immaterial God incarnated

himself in the person of Jesus approximately two thousand years ago.

[13]Millard J. Erickson, *God in Three Persons: A Contemporary Interpretation of the Trinity* (Grand Rapids: Baker, 1995), p. 228. Pages 228-38 go on to discuss ancient and modern formulations of this doctrine of coinherence (Greek *perichōrēsis*)—"that each of the three persons [of the Godhead] shares the life of the others, that each lives in the others" (p. 229).

[14]Bruce Milne (*Know the Truth: A Handbook of Christian Belief* [Downers Grove, Ill.: InterVarsity Press, 1982], p. 61) observes, "Christian writers use the word 'God' in two ways; sometimes they mean the Father in particular, at other times, the entire Godhead.... Many sects miss this important distinction and so fall into difficulties with the biblical teaching concerning the full Godhead of the Son and the Spirit."

[15]Merely to note that Seth is created in Adam's image (Gen 5:3) does not prove that the "image" is his physicality; we have to ask what aspect of Adam's being is in view and derive that information from other texts that more explicitly answer the question.

[16]See further R. Ward Wilson and Craig L. Blomberg, "The Image of God in Humanity: A Biblical-Psychological Perspective," *Themelios* 18 (1993): 8-15, and the literature there cited.

[17]For a sympathetic overview from an Evangelical perspective, see Daniel B. Clendenin, *Eastern Orthodox Christianity: A Western Perspective* (Grand Rapids: Baker, 1994), pp. 117-37.

[18]See even the influential contemporary Greek Orthodox theologian Christovoros Stavropoulos, *Partakers of the Divine Nature* (Minneapolis: Light and Life, 1976), pp. 17-38, reprinted in Daniel B. Clendenin, ed., *Eastern Orthodox Theology: A Contemporary Reader* (Grand Rapids: Baker, 1995), pp. 183-92. Commenting on this verse and the historic Orthodox docrine of *theōsis* (deification), Stavropoulos writes (p. 184), "We are transformed into his [God's] likeness. *However, this union is not absolute. It is relative, for it is not the transformation of our essence. Rather, it is natural, ethical, and in accordance with grace.* It is the union of the whole person with God as unrestricted happiness in the divine kingdom." Stavropolous then quotes the ancient Greek theologian Anastasios of Sinai: "That which is of God is that which has been lifted up to a greater glory, *without its own nature being changed*" (italics mine in both instances).

[19]For full details and the range of options, see D. A. Carson, *The Gospel According to John* (Grand Rapids: Eerdmans, 1991), pp. 397-99; Carson himself follows numerous early rabbis in a third view—seeing the "gods" as Israel at the time of the giving of the law.

[20]Ironically, although it seemingly would have bolstered his position, Joseph Smith alters the word *god* (referring to Moses being like God to Pharaoh) to "prophet" in the JST.

[21]Even simple logic should suggest that it is contradictory to have more than one omnipotent being; otherwise, for example, not only would God be able to judge me

but I would be able to judge God. Both of us could theoretically destroy each other, and then there would be no eternally existing God.

[22]For a helpful overview, see Ronald H. Nash, *The Concept of God* (Grand Rapids: Zondervan, 1983).

[23]William Rowe, *Philosophy of Religion* (Encino, Calif.: Dickenson, 1978), p. 9.

[24]See, for example, Leon Morris, "Hebrews," in *Expositor's Bible Commentary,* ed. Frank E. Gaebelein (Grand Rapids: Zondervan, 1981), 12:50: "There is a certain quality involved when one has performed a required action—a quality that is lacking when there is only a readiness to act. Innocence differs from virtue."

[25]Donald G. Bloesch, *Essentials of Evangelical Theology* (New York: Harper & Row, 1982), 1:46.

[26]For a representative, informed Evangelical treatment of "heaven" see Peter Toon, *Heaven and Hell* (Nashville: Thomas Nelson, 1986).

[27]*A Topical Guide to the Scriptures of the Church of Jesus Christ of Latter-day Saints* (Salt Lake City: Deseret, 1977), pp. 140-41.

[28]In some of the literature I read, Jesus' references to himself as "Son of Man" were used as further support for the physicality of God the Father. But this was an established Hebrew idiom, used to mean "human" (see throughout the book of Ezekiel), including as a quasi-messianic title for a very exalted human (in Dan 7:13-14). While a massive debate among Bible scholars of all traditions rages as to which of these backgrounds is more important for Jesus' use of the term, all agree that it predicates nothing about the God who is Jesus' Father. See, for example, Seyoon Kim, *The Son of Man as the Son of God* (Grand Rapids: Eerdmans, 1985).

[29]By "finite" I mean merely what Stephen E. Robinson affirms in "God the Father: Overview," in *Encyclopedia of Mormonism,* 2:548, when he writes, "The Father became the Father at some time before 'the beginning,' as humans know it, by experiencing a mortality similar to that experienced on earth." The word is freely used by Mormon philosopher Blake T. Ostler throughout "The Mormon Concept of God," *Dialogue* 17 (1984): 65-93.

[30]On which see especially Christian philosopher Richard Swinburne, *The Coherence of Theism* (Oxford: Clarendon, 1977), p. 222; Swinburne adds "omnipresent spirit."

[31]Thus, in the example of $10 + \infty = \infty$, someone has to add ∞ to 10. But who added infinity to a finite god, unless there were even higher powers than that god?

[32]See further Francis J. Beckwith and Stephen E. Parrish, *The Mormon Concept of God: A Philosophical Analysis* (Lewiston, N.Y.: Edwin Mellen, 1991).

[33]On the parallels see Sterling M. McMurrin, *The Theological Foundations of the Mormon Religion* (Salt Lake City: University of Utah, 1965), p. 35: "Here [in its 'finitistic conception of God'] Mormonism reveals the radical nature of its heresy and its tendency toward the kind of common-sense liberalism that so deeply affected the nineteenth-century English-speaking world." For more explicit parallels, see

Reorganized LDS writer Garland E. Tickemyer, "Joseph Smith and Process Theology," *Dialogue* 17 (1984): 75-85. For an overview and Evangelical critique of contemporary process theology, see Ronald H. Nash, ed., *Process Theology* (Grand Rapids: Baker, 1987).

[34]Nash, *Concept of God,* pp. 22-35.

[35]Indeed, Moroni 8:18 would seem to exclude the original finitude of God when it declares, "For I know that God is not a partial God, neither a changeable being; but he is unchangeable from all eternity to all eternity."

[36]For a collection of such pronouncements, see Walter Martin, *The Kingdom of the Cults* (Minneapolis: Bethany, 1977), 178-79, which also excerpts Joseph's famous funeral sermon.

[37]Robinson, *Are Mormons Christians?* pp. 19-20.

[38]Ibid., pp. 60-65. C. S. Lewis's comments, in context, are designed to counter claims that Christ was only a moral example for people to follow. Lewis insists that God in Christ comes to live in us and to transform us into new creatures. His reference to a Christian as "god" or "goddess" (*Mere Christianity* [New York: Macmillan, 1943], p. 175) is immediately explained as a "dazzling, radiant, immortal creature, pulsating all through with such energy and joy and wisdom and love as we cannot now imagine, a bright stainless mirror which reflects back to God perfectly *(though, of course, on a small scale)* His own boundless power and delight and goodness" (italics mine). It is clear that Lewis still recognizes the categorical distinction between God and humanity.

[39]See, for example, Bruce R. McConkie, *Mormon Doctrine* (Salt Lake City: Bookcraft, 1966), p. 239: "Exalted persons gain the fulness of the Father; they have all power, all knowledge, and all wisdom."

[40]Robinson, *Are Mormons Christians?* p. 65.

[41]More reassuring is K. Codell Carter, "Godhood," in *Encyclopedia of Mormonism,* 2:554: the LDS doctrine "does not mean that any person would or could supplant God as the Supreme being in the universe; but it does mean that through God's plan and with his help, all men and women have the capacity to participate in God's eternal work," particularly by righteous living, begetting children, and leading them and others to Christ.

[42]Mormon sympathizer Robert Webb (*The Real Mormonism* [New York: Sturgis and Walton, 1916], pp. 187-88) unwittingly concurs with this logic when he writes that "the doctrine of the Godhead, as presented in Mormon theology, differs in little from the general lines of belief held to be orthodox, except in the fact that it carefully avoids the evident contradiction involved in the assumption of a God without body, parts or passions." Again, "instead of the utterly baffling, and really meaningless, formulation of the doctrine of the Trinity, as found, for example, in the Athanasian Creed, we find here an intelligible effort to make the essential truths of that doctrine clear to the human mind." Apart from Webb's overstatement regarding just how

contradictory and baffling orthodoxy is, we take his point, but it is precisely because the LDS doctrine reads like a clarification of previous enigmas that we find it most likely to be a conscious revision of God's original, true revelation.

[43]For modest moves in some of these various directions, applauded by many, see Stanley J. Grenz, *Theology for the Community of God* (Nashville: Broadman, 1994); for more radical and controversial ones, but still within Evangelicalism, see Clark H. Pinnock et al., *The Openness of God* (Downers Grove, Ill.: InterVarsity Press, 1994).

Chapter 3: Christ & the Trinity/Blomberg

[1]For example, there seems to be a discrepancy between the LDS claim that the Holy Spirit is a personal yet immaterial entity, while elsewhere Mormons exclude the possibility of a similar combination of traits for God the Father. See Walter Martin, *The Kingdom of the Cults* (Minneapolis: Bethany, 1977), pp. 183-84.

[2]See Roger Nicole, "The Meaning of the Trinity," in *One God in Trinity*, ed. Peter Toon and James D. Spiceland (Westchester, Ill.: Cornerstone, 1980), pp. 1-2: "The Christian doctrine of the Trinity is the simultaneous affirmation of three propositions—1) There is one God and one only. 2) This God exists eternally in three distinct persons: the Father, the Son and the Holy Spirit. 3) These three are fully equal in every divine perfection. They possess alike the fullness of the divine essence."

[3]Philip Schaff, *The Creeds of Christendom* (New York: Harper, 1877), 2:45. This is what is called the "received form," a standardized version eventually adopted by the church regularizing slightly variant predecessors. None of the earlier variations affects the meaning of the christological section germane to this chapter.

[4]Ibid., pp. 58-59.

[5]Ibid., pp. 62-63.

[6]The most detailed survey of these various claims is found in Arthur W. Wainwright, *The Trinity in the New Testament* (London: S.P.C.K., 1962).

[7]In Hebrew the word *before* means "besides" (as in the NIV margin). This text therefore does not suggest that there are lesser gods under the Lord.

[8]For these (and less widely held) options and their relative merits, see Gordon J. Wenham, *Genesis 1—15* (Waco, Tex.: Word, 1987), pp. 27-28.

[9]Jack B. Scott, "'lh," in *Theological Wordbook of the Old Testament*, ed. R. Laird Harris, Gleason L. Archer Jr. and Bruce K. Waltke (Chicago: Moody Press, 1980), 1:41-45. The plural again most likely reflects a plural of majesty or diversity within the unity of the *one* God. There is no solid historical support for the more liberal Christian or non-Christian hypothesis that human religion in general evolved from polytheism to monotheism. Both Genesis 1—11 and Romans 1:18-32 allege the reverse sequence—an original monotheism degenerated in many cultures into later polytheism—and there are numerous tantalizing missiological evidences in support of this claim. See especially Don

Richardson, *Eternity in Their Hearts* (Ventura, Calif.: Regal, 1981).

[10]See Herbert Wolf, " 'ehad," in *Theological Wordbook of the Old Testament*, 1:30; Paul R. Gilchrist, "yāḥîd," in *Theological Wordbook of the Old Testament*, 1:372-73.

[11]On the generation of Spirit from both Father and Son, which separated the Western (Roman) from the Eastern (Greek) church that believed only in the procession of the Spirit from the Father, compare Matthew 10:20 with Galatians 4:6, and note John 20:22.

[12]A popular modern, liberal reconstruction of early Christology, of course, has been to deny that it did. This hypothesis alleges that Judaism never compromised its monotheism and that belief in Christ's deity emerged only in a *Hellenistic* Christian milieu. For a recent exponent of this hypothesis see P. Maurice Casey, *From Jewish Prophet to Gentile God* (Louisville, Ky.: Westminster/John Knox, 1991). But a resurgence in study of the Jewish background to the New Testament has made this view not nearly as common as it once was. For detailed demonstration of the remarkable extent to which *Jewish* Christians were identifying Jesus with God within a few years (if not months) of his death and resurrection, see Richard N. Longenecker, *The Christology of Early Jewish Christianity* (Naperville, Ill.: Allenson, 1970).

[13]In brief, see E. Calvin Beisner, *God in Three Persons* (Wheaton, Ill.: Tyndale House, 1984), pp. 23-42; in detail, Larry W. Hurtado, *One God, One Lord* (Philadelphia: Fortress, 1988).

[14]B. H. Roberts, *Mormon Doctrine of Deity* (reprint Bountiful, Utah: Horizon, 1975), pp. 187-94.

[15]See Roger Haight, "The Point of Trinitarian Theology," *Toronto Journal of Theology* 4 (1988): 195: "The two outer limits of the trinitarian controversy, however, never existed on an equal footing. The polytheistic or tritheistic side of the dilemma was never a viable option. It served rather as a kind of negative limit, a fear on the part of theologians, or a suspicion about the positions of opponents. No theologian intended a tritheistic conception of God, whereas all theologians wanted to preserve the monarchy of God or more particularly the Father. . . . One can say then that, for the most part, all parties always accepted the oneness and unity of God even when their language tended to compromise their intentions."

[16]See classically Martin Hengel, *The Son of God* (Philadelphia: Fortress, 1976).

[17]For this concept, see F. F. Bruce, *The Epistle to the Hebrews* (Grand Rapids: Eerdmans, 1990), pp. 49-53.

[18]See Robinson's discussion of this subject on pp. 129-30.

[19]On the doctrine of coinherence, Gerald Bray (*The Doctrine of God* [Downers Grove, Ill.: InterVarsity Press, 1993], p. 242) writes, "Each of the divine persons manifests perfection whilst containing and manifesting the perfection of the others. This doctrine of co-inherence is perhaps the most important single teaching of the Bible in an age which finds it hard to reconcile individual freedom and dignity with

corporate commitment and responsibility."

[20]For an outstanding exposition of this important and controversial passage, see Paul D. Feinberg, "The Kenosis and Christology: An Exegetical-Theological Analysis of Phil. 2:6-11," *Trinity Journal* 1 (1980): 21-46.

[21]See, for example, Robert Letham, "The Man-Woman Debate: Theological Comment," *Westminster Theological Journal* 52 (1990): 65-78.

[22]See, for example, Robert M. Bowman Jr., *Why You Should Believe in the Trinity* (Grand Rapids: Baker, 1989), p. 15. "Christ in his divine nature is *essentially* equal to the father, though *relationally* (or functionally) subordinate or submissive to the Father, especially since becoming a man."

[23]Extensive sections of Stephen E. Robinson's *Believing Christ* (Salt Lake City: Deseret, 1992) deal with Christ's atonement and present little if anything Evangelicals should find objectionable. Indeed, much of the book is highly biblical and edifying.

[24]Athanasius *De Incarnatione* 54.

[25]For example, Robert C. Webb (*The Real Mormonism* [New York: Sturgis and Walton, 1916], p. 181) cites language in the Anglican articles of faith about the Son's being "of one substance with the Father" as support for the claim of Doctrine and Covenants 130:22 that "the Father has a body of flesh and bones as tangible as man's."

[26]See further Stanley J. Grenz, *Theology for the Community of God* (Nashville: Broadman, 1994), pp. 79-80.

[27]Gordon R. Lewis and Bruce A. Demarest, *Integrative Theology* (Grand Rapids: Zondervan, 1987), 1:272. Compare Donald G. Bloesch, *Essentials of Evangelical Theology* (New York: Harper & Row, 1978), 1:35: "It should be recognized that *persons* in the early church did not mean personalities in the modern sense (which indicates autonomy) but objective modes of being . . . that pertain to the inner life of God himself, not merely to dimensions of his activity (as in the heresy of Modalism)."

[28]Alister E. McGrath, *Understanding the Trinity* (Grand Rapids: Zondervan, 1988), pp. 121-22.

[29]Ibid, pp. 140-42.

[30]I am indebted to Prof. Gordon R. Lewis, in a personal communication, for several of these examples.

[31]Bruce Milne, *Know the Truth* (Downers Grove, Ill.: InterVarsity Press, 1982), p. 63. Compare Alister E. McGrath, "Making Sense of the Trinity," *Princeton Seminary Bulletin* 12 (1991): 2: "We need to respond to God as he has revealed himself—not invent simple ideas of God which, although much easier to believe, do not actually correspond to God. Augustine once wrote, 'If you can understand it, it's not God.' "

[32]Roberts, *Mormon Doctrine of Deity,* pp. iii-iv.

[33]Robinson's third affirmation about the official Mormon doctrine of the virgin birth, based strictly on the LDS Scriptures, inserts the words "in his biological being" to his affirmation of Jesus as son of the Father, which do not clearly follow from

any of the texts cited (p. 135).

[34]Bruce R. McConkie, *A New Witness for the Articles of Faith* (Salt Lake City: Deseret, 1985), pp. 67-68.

[35]The JST omits the part about the Holy Spirit "coming upon" Mary and the power of the Most High "overshadowing" her. This omission is consistent with the claim of recent Mormon president Ezra T. Benson: "Jesus was not the son of Joseph, *nor was he begotten by the Holy Ghost.* He is the Son of the Eternal Father!" (italics mine), as quoted in Robert L. Millet, "Jesus Christ: Overview," in *Encyclopedia of Mormonism,* 2:725.

[36]The classic Evangelical study of this doctrine (particularly in its historical setting), which compares various Jewish and pagan "parallels," remains J. Gresham Machen, *The Virgin Birth of Christ* (New York: Harper, 1930).

[37]Compare Leon Morris, *The Gospel According to John* (Grand Rapids: Eerdmans, 1971), p. 105 and n. 93.

[38]Matthew 1:16 says that Jesus was begotten of Mary, breaking the otherwise consistent pattern in the genealogy of referring to biological *fathers,* thus suggesting that Jesus had no literal, physical paternity. He is the eternal, uncreated incarnation of God himself.

[39]The KJV is less clear, rendering "firstborn of every creature," though at least this is a *possible* translation of the Greek.

[40]Compare, for example, Peter T. O'Brien, *Colossians, Philemon* (Waco, Tex.: Word, 1982), pp. 44-45.

[41]See the excellent study of this passage in its historical context by N. T. Wright, *The Climax of the Covenant* (Minneapolis: Fortress, 1992), pp. 120-36. Here is perhaps an appropriate place to comment also on the frequent biblical expression "God of gods" or "Lord of lords" (for example, Deut 10:17). It is a standard Hebrew superlative construction implying "the supreme God and absolute Lord." Nothing may legitimately be inferred from this expression about the objective existence of other beings worthy of worship. See Peter C. Craigie, *The Book of Deuteronomy* (Grand Rapids: Eerdmans, 1976), p. 205.

[42]See the scathing reply of Sidney B. Sperry (*Answers to Book of Mormon Questions* [Salt Lake City: Bookcraft, 1967], pp. 215-22) to Arthur Budvarson (*The Book of Mormon—True or False?* [Grand Rapids: Zondervan, 1961], pp. 31-35). Robinson's views, phrased graciously, appear in this chapter (p. 134).

[43]See the classic study by G. B. Arbaugh (*Revelation in Mormonism* [Chicago: University of Chicago Press, 1932]) on the development in Joseph Smith's thought throughout his career. The Mormon writer Boyd Kirkland seems to concede as much ("Elohim and Jehovah in Mormonism and the Bible," *Dialogue* 19 [1986]: 77-78), even referring to Joseph's earlier revelations as reflecting " 'trinitarian' perceptions."

[44]See Stephen E. Robinson, *Are Mormons Christians?* (Salt Lake City: Bookcraft,

1991), pp. 60-109.

[45]See Christopher Kaiser, "The Ontological Trinity in the Context of Historical Religions," *Scottish Journal of Theology* 29 (1976): 301-10.

[46]Millard J. Erickson, *Christian Theology* (Grand Rapids: Baker, 1983), 1:342.

[47]For a succinct overview of all the different perspectives denounced as heretical, in their historical context and sequence, see Millard J. Erickson, *The Word Become Flesh* (Grand Rapids: Baker, 1991), pp. 41-86. For later and especially modern attempts to formulate doctrines of Christ, see pp. 89-379.

[48]John T. Mueller, *Christian Dogmatics* (St. Louis: Concordia, 1955), p. 155.

[49]Robinson, *Are Mormons Christians?* pp. 12-18, 65-69, 71-79.

Chapter 3: Christ & the Trinity/Robinson

[1]The apostle Paul himself was often "unorthodox" by the standards of the fourth century. For this defect, later theologians have often referred to Paul's theology as "unclear," "undeveloped" or even "naive" (for example, J. Fitzmyer, *Pauline Theology* [Englewood Cliffs, N.J.: Prentice-Hall, 1967], p. 42). Finding the apostle to be congenial company, Latter-day Saints are pleased to be accused of this same lack of clarity.

[2]W. D. Davies's evaluation of Mormonism is that it attempts to return to a New Testament Christianity as it was before the Gentile Hellenization of later centuries, that it "challenged a too Hellenized Christianity to renew its contact with its roots in Israel." See his "Israel, Mormons and the Land," in *Reflections on Mormonism,* ed. Truman Madsen (Provo, Utah: Religious Studies Center, 1978), pp. 91-92.

[3]I realize this is the famous Johannine comma, but it doesn't matter. I think both Evangelicals and LDS accept it as *correct,* whether scholars think it original to the text or not.

[4]Many passages in the New Testament reflect a subordinationist point of view like that of the Latter-day Saints, for example, Mark 13:32; 14:36; John 5:30; 6:38; 14:28; Hebrews 5:8.

[5]See, for example, John 5:26-27, which clearly states that the power and authority of the Son are given to him by the Father.

[6]Of course the "orthodox" doctrine of the two natures in Christ from Chalcedon would insist that the divine Son of God *never* suffered, bled or died for humanity.

[7]See M. Simonetti, *Encyclopedia of the Early Church* (New York: Oxford University Press, 1992), p. 797. A subordinate deity runs afoul of the Platonic definition of God as "absolute" (a definition not found in Scripture). To the Greek philosophers a subordinate deity was an impossibility *by definition,* an oxymoron. Blomberg accepts the Platonic categories and logic (p. 118), but I think if the Father wants to make his subordinate Son fully divine—he probably can.

[8]I should probably make an exception here for the Apostles' Creed, which Latter-da Saints could affirm if allowed to define "holy catholic church" as "true Christianity,

as I believe Evangelicals also define it.

[9]I find it somewhat ironic that anyone who accepts the "mystery" of the Nicene Trinity could at the same time find fault with the LDS understanding of God's oneness and threeness on the grounds of *logic* or *comprehensibility.*

[10]For the subordinate position of the Son to the Father, see John 5:30 and 14:28; Mosiah 15:7; Doctrine and Covenants 19:24. For ceasing to be God should he change his present nature or position, see Mormon 9:19.

[11]Joseph Fielding Smith, *Teachings of the Prophet Joseph Smith* (Salt Lake City: Deseret, 1968), p. 121.

[12]James E. Talmage, *Jesus the Christ* (Salt Lake City: Deseret, 1915), p. 81.

[13]Prof. Blomberg's language (pp. 122-23 with notes) makes me suspect he has this bit of LDS speculation in mind, but the institutional church does *not* teach that the conception of Jesus was accomplished by a sexual act. See, e.g., Clyde Williams ed., *The Teachings of Harold B. Lee* (Salt Lake City: Bookcraft, 1996), pp. 13-14.

[14]See Raymond E. Brown, *The Gospel According to John* (Garden City, N.Y.: Doubleday, 1970), 2:555-56.

[15]Unfortunately, some Latter-day Saint authors have also resorted to this rhetorical device in describing "the false Jesus of the apostate sectarians" and the like.

[16]Scriptures affirming that the Father and the Son are one will not help here since "oneness" does not necessarily mean "eternal coequality."

[17]Revising the clear meaning of Scripture to accommodate the theologians in my view risks the censure recorded in Mark 7:9, "And he said unto them, Full well ye reject the commandment of God, that ye may keep your own tradition."

[18]See F. F. Bruce, *The Epistles of John* (Grand Rapids: Eerdmans, 1970), p. 126, and I. H. Marshall, *The Epistles of John,* New International Commentary on the New Testament (Grand Rapids: Eerdmans, 1978), p. 252 n. 37.

[19]Raymond E. Brown, *The Epistles of John,* Anchor Bible 30 (Garden City, N.Y.: Doubleday, 1982), p. 620. Brown himself concludes otherwise, but it is still hardly a discredited or indefensible interpretation.

[20]*Antiquities* 1.222; 5.264.

[21]See the discussion in Robinson, *Are Mormons Christians?* pp. 13-18, 21.

Chapter 4: Salvation/Robinson

[1]Though these passages are taken from the uniquely LDS Scriptures, Evangelicals need to remember that for Latter-day Saints the Bible is also the Word of God. Latter-day Saints would believe these same doctrines on the basis of Acts 4:12 or Galatians 2:16 even if the Book of Mormon did not exist.

[2]Notice the past tense. Not "will redeem," not "is redeeming with my help" and not "might redeem if I am worthy," but "*hath* redeemed."

[3]See Stephen E. Robinson, *Believing Christ* (Provo, Utah: Deseret, 1992), pp. 37-44.

[4]This includes those who commit the so-called unpardonable sin, who are unpardonable because they *will not* repent, not because they *cannot* repent.

[5]Mormons understand the Bible to teach that baptism is part of the good news (see Heb 6:1-2, where both baptism and the laying on of hands are represented as foundation principles of "the doctrine of Christ"). One is baptized into Christ (Rom 6:3; Gal 3:27; Col 2:12), and both salvation and the remission of sins are connected to baptism (Acts 22:16; Eph 5:26; Tit 3:5; 1 Pet 3:21). The belief that baptism is necessary is not peculiar to the LDS but is also held by some Evangelicals. Neither they nor the LDS understand it to be a *prerequisite* to conversion, but rather a *part* of conversion (Acts 8:12-17; 19:1-6). One's faith, repentance and submission to the lordship of Christ are expressed by submitting to baptism. Jesus' grand commission to his disciples was not just to teach, after all, but to teach *and* to baptize (Mt 28:19).

[6]Latter-day Saints thus line up with those Evangelicals who, like Prof. Blomberg (p. 175), insist that Jesus must be accepted as both Savior and Lord.

[7]See Doctrine and Covenants 20:77-79 or Moroni 4:3—5:1.

[8]Latter-day Saints believe that we may unconditionally enter into the covenant and be "in Christ," justified before God by the grace and blood of Christ. However, receiving the promised blessings of the covenant at the end time is conditioned on "enduring" in Christ from now until then (Mt 10:22; 24:13) or on subsequently repenting and returning to the fold. Thus, for the LDS, election depends both on God's grace and on the individual's choice not to throw it all away. Election has no conditions beyond the choice of the elect to remain elect, and this choice is revealed by whom they choose to serve with their behavior (Rom 6:16).

[9]"Arminianism," of course, does not describe a particular religion but an approach to these and other theological questions characteristic of many Protestant (even Evangelical) groups. See pp. 167-68.

[10]At present very few LDS or Evangelicals realize that the Arminian elements in Mormonism actually constitute common ground between the LDS and historical "orthodoxy."

[11]See Bruce McConkie, "Seven Deadly Heresies of the Modern Church," in *BYU Speeches of the Year* (Provo, Utah: Brigham Young University Press, 1980), pp. 77-78.

[12]The term "grace *alone*" is not found in the Bible, and the similar term "faith alone" is found only once—in a Scripture hostile to the idea (Jas 2:17).

[13]C. S. Lewis, *Mere Christianity* (New York: Macmillan, 1943), p. 129.

[14]John MacArthur, *The Gospel According to Jesus* (Grand Rapids: Zondervan, 1988), pp. 15-16; but read the whole introduction—with which the LDS would heartily agree. See also Dietrich Bonhoeffer's famous rejection of "cheap grace" in *The Cost of Discipleship* (New York: Macmillan, 1963), p. 45.

[15]This is also the view of Charles Hodge, *Systematic Theology* (New York: Scribner, 1872), 1:26-27.

[16]That is, salvation for the ignorant dead without baptism. Compare the various theories of "middle knowledge," "divine perseverance" or "postmortem evangelization" cited in John Sanders, ed., *What About Those Who Have Never Heard?* (Downers Grove, Ill.: InterVarsity Press, 1995), pp. 12-15.

[17]See, for example, Bruce R. McConkie, *Mormon Doctrine* (Salt Lake City: Bookcraft, 1966), p. 686.

[18]*Pneuma* is used in the Bible many times to mean the individual human spirit. Mary declares, "My *pneuma* rejoices in God my savior" (Lk 1:47), and the *pneuma* of Jairus's daughter "returned" to her body (Lk 8:55).

[19]It is my private belief that the parable of the prodigal should be read on one level as referring also to those who rebel against God, squander their lives and suffer for their mistakes in hell. But they turn again and, humbled and contrite, come back to God before their resurrection. Thus for our lost lambs, until the final judgment there is still hope.

[20]Gabriel Fackre and Leonhard Goppelt have both proposed an exegesis of 1 Peter 3:18-19 and 4:6 that is essentially the LDS view; see Goppelt, *A Commentary on I Peter* (Grand Rapids: Eerdmans, 1993), pp. 255-65, and Fackre, "Divine Perseverance," in *What About Those Who Have Never Heard?* ed. Sanders, pp. 81-85, 152-53. Fackre lists a half dozen contemporary theologians, including leading Evangelicals, who accept some form of "divine perseverance" or "postmortem evangelization" (p. 162).

[21]For this reason, those who repent in the spirit prison do not really get a "second chance." Their initial wickedness will be justly reflected in a reward "according to their works."

[22]Using the term "the saved" to mean those redeemed from the devil, whether in life or in the spirit prison between death and resurrection.

[23]The usual LDS interpretation of 2 Corinthians 12:2 sees Paul being caught up to the third heaven, or highest degree of glory, in his wonderful vision of the Lord.

[24]Prof. Blomberg, like many LDS, misinterprets 2 Nephi 25:23 (p. 177), which says, "We know that it is by grace that we are saved, after all we can do." In this passage, "all we *can* do" is to have faith in Christ. This is made clear in the following verses, particularly 25:26, "And we talk of Christ, we rejoice in Christ, we preach of Christ, we prophesy of Christ, and we write according to our prophecies, that our children may know to what source they may look for a remission of their sins." Moreover, the Book of Mormon explicitly states elsewhere that "all *we* can do" is to repent and turn to Christ (Alma 24:10-11).

[25]Compare John 15:10. I won't haggle about what Jesus' commandments may be, but I would argue that they include *at least* the injunctions of the Sermon on the Mount, and to "love one another" (Jn 15:12), and probably much more (like "Beware of the leaven of the Pharisees and the Sadducees" [Mt 16:6] or "He that is without sin among you, let him first cast a stone at her" [Jn 8:7]).

[26]In my parable of the bicycle, "sixty-one cents" is symbolic of our inability to earn

our own salvation and also of the commitment *in principle* required of the saved. The believer who has only forty-one cents, or twenty-one or eleven—or none—is still justified if he or she holds nothing back. It is not the quantity, but the *commitment* that matters. Without a commitment that translates into behavior, we are not saved. With such a commitment, be it ever so small at first, we are.

[27]Provided Evangelicals studied the *real* Mormon faith and not that obscene caricature invented by anticultists.

[28]However, several Evangelicals (including Prof. Blomberg, p. 40 and in private conversation) have insisted to me that such a procedure would be wrong, since the Bible (interpreted evangelically) already provides the answers—which seems to me to beg the question—and since personal communion with the Spirit is subjective and therefore not a reliable guide for Christian doctrine (Jas 1:5 notwithstanding).

[29]See my article, "1 Nephi 13-14 and Early Christianity," in *First Nephi: The Doctrinal Foundation,* ed. Monte Nyman (Provo, Utah: Religious Studies Center, 1988), pp. 177-91; reprinted as "Warring Against the Saints of God," *Ensign,* January 1988, pp. 34-39, esp. 37-38.

[30]See p. 61 and n. 11.

[31]See pp. 54, 127, 181-82.

[32]On the one hand "orthodox" Christians are certainly justified in seeking to clarify that Mormons are not "orthodox," while on the other hand calling us "non-Christian" implies falsely that we do not worship Christ or accept the New Testament witness to him. Perhaps Evangelicals should refer to us as "LDS Christians" or something similar to distinguish us from historical "orthodoxy," a distinction we do not resist, while at the same time granting the genuine focus of LDS worship on Christ.

[33]C. S. Lewis, *The Silver Chair* (New York: Macmillan, 1970), pp. 142-46.

Chapter 4: Salvation/Blomberg

[1]The seriousness of Paul's proposition is underscored by his earlier words: "But even if we or an angel from heaven should preach a gospel other than the one we preached to you, let him be eternally condemned" (Gal 1:8). Given that the problem triggering such concern in Galatia was a form of legalism, Evangelicals have been particularly sensitive to religions or denominations that have seemed to practice a similar legalism, and have often noted the striking coincidence between Paul's reference to an angel preaching a message and the LDS story of the ministry of Moroni.

[2]Apparently both physical and spiritual healing is involved in at least three of these passages, so that the NIV at times renders the Greek for "save" as "heal" or "make well." See further Craig L. Blomberg, " 'Your Faith Has Made You Whole': The Evangelical Liberation Theology of Jesus," in *Jesus of Nazareth: Lord and Christ,* ed. Joel B. Green and Max Turner (Grand Rapids: Eerdmans, 1994), pp. 75-93.

[3]The apparent contradiction between James and Paul has been a classic example used by

liberal scholars to undermine the trustworthiness of Scripture. But an examination of Paul's and James's use of the key terms *faith* and *works* in context demonstrates that Paul is describing Christian faith and Jewish works, while James addresses Jewish faith and Christian works. Both agree that true commitment to Christ will result in a transformed lifestyle of increasing obedience to his commands. See, programmatically, Joachim Jeremias, "Paul and James," *Expository Times* 66 (1955): 368-71.

[4]For an excellent contemporary articulation of evangelical Calvinism, see Anthony A. Hoekema, *Saved by Grace* (Grand Rapids: Eerdmans, 1989).

[5]Technically, Arminius redefined (1) and (2), had considerable doubts about (5), and rejected (3) and (4) out of hand. But "Arminianism" over the subsequent centuries has frequently jettisoned the whole lot. I am grateful to Prof. Timothy P. Weber for this clarification.

[6]For an excellent contemporary articulation of Evangelical Arminianism, see Clark H. Pinnock, ed., *The Grace of God, the Will of Man: A Case for Arminianism* (Grand Rapids: Zondervan, 1989).

[7]For examples of well-known writers moving toward the middle of the theological spectrum on these matters, see respectively Millard Erickson, *Christian Theology,* vol. 3 (Grand Rapids: Baker, 1985), a "soft" Calvinist; and William L. Craig, *The Only Wise God* (Grand Rapids: Baker, 1987), a "soft" Arminian.

[8]Two excellent popular-level expositions of these themes and their numerous practical consequences are Charles R. Swindoll, *Grace Awakening* (Dallas: Word, 1990), and Chap Clark, *The Performance Illusion* (Colorado Springs, Colo.: NavPress, 1993).

[9]For an example of these perspectives among recent writers, see, respectively, Charles C. Ryrie, *So Great Salvation* (Wheaton, Ill.: Victor, 1989); John F. Mac-Arthur Jr., *The Gospel According to Jesus* (Grand Rapids: Zondervan, 1988).

[10]See further Darrell L. Bock, "A Review of *The Gospel According to Jesus,*" *Bibliotheca Sacra* 146 (1989): 21-40. This appears also to be Robinson's position.

[11]The classic modern study of the topic, by an internationally known Baptist New Testament scholar, is G. R. Beasley-Murray, *Baptism in the New Testament* (London: Macmillan, 1962). For a briefer treatment of comparable quality by an Evangelical proponent of infant baptism, see Geoffrey W. Bromiley, *Children of Promise* (Grand Rapids: Eerdmans, 1979).

[12]Critics dispute whether or not the Book of Mormon demonstrates actual literary dependence on any of these sources, but it is clear that other writings of the day bore at least an interesting resemblance to its basic plot line. See, for example, Wayne L. Cowdrey, Howard A. Davis and Donald R. Scales, *Who Really Wrote the Book of Mormon?* (Santa Ana, Calif.: Vision House, 1977).

[13]Norman Anderson, "A Christian Approach to Comparative Religion," in *The World's Religions,* ed. Norman Anderson (Grand Rapids: Eerdmans, 1976), p. 234.

[14]For a good survey of the main proponents throughout church history of each of these

(and other) positions, and the biblical passages they rely on, see John Sanders, *No Other Name: An Investigation into the Destiny of the Unevangelized* (Grand Rapids: Eerdmans, 1992). See also John Sanders, ed., *What About Those Who Have Never Heard? Three Views on the Destiny of the Unevangelized* (Downers Grove, Ill.: InterVarsity Press, 1995). Interestingly, one of these three views, presented by an otherwise moderately conservative Christian theologian, defends the opportunity for salvation after death (Gabriel Fackre, "Divine Perseverance," pp. 71-95). I doubt that this perspective will receive noticeable acceptance as a legitimate Evangelical option, however.

[15]See Peter T. O'Brien, *The Epistle to the Philippians* (Grand Rapids: Eerdmans, 1991), p. 243: "One ought to understand the bowing of the knee as an act of submission to one whose power they cannot resist."

[16]For a complete history of the interpretation of this passage and for a defense of the position adopted here, generally agreed on by most modern biblical scholars, see W. J. Dalton, *Christ's Proclamation to the Spirits: A Study of 1 Peter 3:18—4:6* (Rome: Pontifical Biblical Institute, 1965).

[17]See, for example, Peter H. Davids, *The First Epistle of Peter* (Grand Rapids: Eerdmans, 1990), p. 154. One other text often brought into this debate is 1 Corinthians 15:29. This passage speaks of those in the church of Corinth who practiced baptism for the dead, a practice early church fathers also describe as found among certain Gnostic sects. But Paul hardly condones the practice; much less does he command it. Instead he argues from the fact that some Corinthians are practicing it to the logical conclusion that they must really believe in the resurrection of the dead. He makes the same kind of ad hoc argument in the next three verses, without condoning or commanding the premises there either—his daily suffering persecution and having fought wild beasts in Ephesus (vv. 30-32). See further Craig Blomberg, *1 Corinthians* (Grand Rapids: Zondervan, 1994), pp. 299, 304-5.

[18]Craig L. Blomberg, "Degrees of Reward in the Kingdom of Heaven?" *Journal of the Evangelical Theological Society* 35 (1992): 159-72.

[19]From "The Sum of the Christian Life," preached in Wörlitz, Germany, November 24, 1532. In *Luther's Works* (Philadelphia: Muhlenberg, 1959), 51:282-83.

[20]For additional Evangelical debates on the nature of hell, see William Crockett, ed., *Four Views on Hell* (Grand Rapids: Zondervan, 1992).

[21]For a Greek word study, see A. J. Dewey, "The Synoptic Use of ΠΙΣΤΙΣ: An Appeal for a Context-Sensitive Translation," *Forum* 5 (1989): 83-86.

[22]Tracing its roots in large measure to the Plymouth Brethren sect of nineteenth-century England, transplanted to the United States through an interpretive tradition known as "dispensationalism" and made famous through the ministries of the "Bible church" and "Bible college" movements.

[23]A classic modern example is Charles C. Ryrie, *Balancing the Christian Life*

(Chicago: Moody Press, 1969).

[24]See also Stephen E. Robinson, *Believing Christ* (Salt Lake City: Deseret, 1992), pp. 91-92. Here Robinson interprets *after* to mean "apart from" or "regardless of." An acceptable paraphrase of the entire sentence might read, "We are still saved by grace, after all is said and done." It must be admitted, however, that this is by no means the most natural or straightforward reading of the text. Contrast Bruce C. Hafen, "Grace," in *Encyclopedia of Mormonism,* 2:502, where "after all we can do" is defined as "in addition to our best efforts."

[25]See especially George B. Arbaugh, *Revelation in Mormonism* (Chicago: University of Chicago Press, 1932), for details of Smith's pilgrimage from the theology of the Campbellite restorationist sect of Sidney Rigdon's earlier years to full-fledged heterodoxy.

[26]Bruce R. McConkie, *A New Witness for the Articles of Faith* (Salt Lake City: Deseret, 1985), pp. 152, 192.

[27]Ibid., pp. 217, 214.

[28]Ibid., p. 217.

[29]Sterling M. McMurrin, *The Theological Foundations of the Mormon Religion* (Salt Lake City: University of Utah Press, 1965), p. 72.

[30]Stephen E. Robinson, *Are Mormons Christians?* (Salt Lake City: Bookcraft, 1991), p. 105.

[31]Ibid., pp. 105-6.

[32]Robinson, *Believing Christ,* pp. 32, 33.

[33]Ibid., p. 33.

[34]Ibid., p. 73.

[35]Ibid., p. 70.

[36]My friend and former student Thom Wood, until recently a pastor in a strongly Mormon part of the United States, has told me that Robinson's "bicycle parable" is well known in his region and has proved a very effective conversation starter for him in Evangelical-Mormon dialogue. Wood suggests that the Evangelical version of this parable would have the father telling his daughter, "Never mind about the sixty-one cents. I'll buy the bike. But you use your money to buy me an ice-cream cone on the way home." Our good works, in other words, are done out of thanksgiving for Christ's purchasing our pardon *entirely* through his merits.

[37]The term comes from Richard Mouw, president of a leading Evangelical graduate school, Fuller Theological Seminary in Pasadena, California, who discerns a trend among at least a handful of leading Mormon scholars and writers moving noticeably closer to historic Christian orthodoxy. See "Evangelical Mormonism?" *Christianity Today* 35 (November 1991): 30.

[38]Robinson, *Are Mormons Christians?* p. 108.

[39]Robinson, *Believing Christ,* p. 45.

[40]JST reads, "Also celestial bodies, and bodies terrestrial, *and bodies telestial;* but the glory of the celestial, one; and the terrestrial, another; *and the telestial, another.*" The italicized words reflect Joseph Smith's additions to the text. If Joseph did not think that Doctrine and Covenants 76 was based on 1 Corinthians 15:40, why did he make the two texts match each other this way?

[41]So the vast majority of commentators. See especially Gordon D. Fee, *The First Epistle to the Corinthians* (Grand Rapids: Eerdmans, 1987), pp. 782-84. A few scholars argue that the heavenly bodies are those of angels, similar to the resurrection bodies believers will one day enjoy, in contrast to the earthly bodies we now have. Either way, there is no basis for understanding Paul to be speaking about more than one kind of body in the life to come.

[42]See Joseph F. Smith, *Doctrines of Salvation* (Salt Lake City: Bookcraft, 1954), 3:283: "For hundreds of years the world was wrapped in a veil of spiritual darkness, until there was not one fundamental truth belonging to the plan of salvation that was not, in the year 1820, so obscured by false tradition and ceremonies, borrowed from paganism, as to make it unrecognizable, or else it was entirely denied." Richard R. Hopkins's intriguing *Biblical Mormonism: Responding to Evangelical Criticism of LDS Theology* (Bountiful, Utah: Horizon, 1994) consistently censures Evangelical thought (at times misrepresented) as worthy of the damnation Paul threatens in Galatians 1:6-8, demonstrating that Smith's attitudes are alive and well in at least some contemporary LDS circles.

[43]For example, Sir Norman Anderson, *Christianity and World Religions* (Downers Grove, Ill.: InterVarsity Press, 1984); Stephen Neill, *Christian Faiths and Other Faiths* (Downers Grove, Ill.: InterVarsity Press, 1984).

[44]Polls consistently reflect the deeply embedded belief in American religion that "goodness" is what gets us into heaven. At times even the pollsters do not know how to phrase the question accurately. An influential survey by George Gallup Jr. and Sarah Jones, *100 Questions and Answers: Religion in America* (Princeton, N.J.: Princeton Religion Research Center, 1989), p. 14, asks, "Do you think there is a heaven where people who had led good lives are eternally rewarded?" Seventy-one percent of Americans said yes. Presumably most thought they were saying simply that they believed in heaven, but strictly speaking Evangelicals should answer the question no because we believe that no one leads a good enough life to deserve heaven.

[45]Known as Pascal's Wager. For the state of the art in philosophical discussion, see Douglas Groothuis, "Wagering Belief: Examining Two Objections to Pascal's Wager," *Religious Studies* 30 (1994): 479-86.

[46]In Stephen E. Robinson, *Following Christ* (Salt Lake City: Deseret, 1995), a book I acquired too late to interact with in the body of this work, I think Robinson's discussion of salvation by faith through grace followed by a life of (hopefully) increasing obedience to Christ as the fruit of that faith more closely approximates

classic Protestant (albeit Arminian) formulation than in any of his previous works. He also repeatedly notes how various LDS have not caught on. One example must suffice, but it is representative: "Too many of the saints see their mortal lives in the Church as a kind of porch or anteroom outside the kingdom doors. If they work hard enough in this life, they feel, the doors will eventually open up and admit them at some future time. *Horse feathers! . . .* Those members who think their place in the kingdom is not yet established either did not enter the Church in good faith in the first place or else came to Christ honestly but did not understand what happened when they believed, repented, were baptized, and received the gift of the Holy Ghost" (p. 8). Robinson of course understands this as a return to LDS basics. Be that as it may, it is a position to be welcomed.

Chapter 4: Joint Conclusion

[1]Although most Mormons would never use the term "salvation by grace," and they would probably deny believing in it if asked. This is because "salvation" in LDS terminology is usually the equivalent of "sanctification" in Evangelical terminology, and sanctification requires personal *obedience* as well as God's grace.

Conclusion/Robinson & Blomberg

[1]Stephen E. Robinson, *Are Mormons Christians?* (Salt Lake City: Bookcraft, 1991), pp. 25-29, citing Walter Martin, *The New Cults* (Ventura, Calif.: Regal, 1980), pp. 17-21.

[2]See David G. Bromley and Anson D. Shupe Jr., *Strange Gods: The Great American Cult Scare* (Boston: Beacon, 1981), p. 23: "The most consistent use of the term [cult] by modern scholars, in particular sociologists, is organizational. Sociologically, a cult is the starting point of every religion. Its organization is extremely simple. There is no bureaucracy or priesthood. In fact, there is barely any structure at all except for the single charismatic leader and his or her small band of devoted followers. . . . The cult is thus nonconformist for two reasons. First, it struggles to start a radically new religious tradition, and, second, it exists in tension and conflict with what it regards as a corrupt, troubled world. Most cults are short-lived. They either take seed, thrive, and go on to become what we know as larger religious traditions, such as Islam, Buddhism, or Christianity, or they disintegrate and fade away."